Language & Writing Portfolio

Course C

Copyright © by HMH Education Company

All rights reserved. No part of this work may be reproduced or transmitted in any form or by any means, electronic or mechanical, including photocopying or recording, or by any information storage or retrieval system, without the prior written permission of the copyright owner unless such copying is expressly permitted by federal copyright law. As an EdTech company, HMH uses a myriad of innovation tools to create content. This includes use of technology by our Subject Matter Experts and may include use of Generative AI technologies and other similar automations. Requests for permission to make copies of any part of the work should be submitted through our Permissions website at https://customercare.hmhco.com/contactus/Permissions.html or mailed to HMH Education Company, Attn: Compliance, 9400 Southpark Center Loop, Orlando, Florida 32819-8647.

Printed in the U.S.A.

ISBN 978-0-358-60948-3

8 2025

4500910368   r3.25

If you have received these materials as examination copies free of charge, HMH retains title to the materials and they may not be resold. Resale of examination copies is strictly prohibited.

Possession of this publication in print format does not entitle users to convert this publication, or any portion of it, into electronic format.

TABLE OF CONTENTS

GETTING STARTED 4

ISSUE 1

Teen Sleep

Building Concepts and Language/Analyzing and Discussing Text 18

Academic Writing: Formal Summary 32

Building Concepts and Language/Analyzing and Discussing Text 38

Presenting Ideas: Debate 42

Academic Writing: Justification 44

ISSUE 2

Learning Languages

Building Concepts and Language/Analyzing and Discussing Text 50

Academic Writing: Formal Summary 64

Analyzing and Discussing Text 70

Presenting Ideas: Debate 74

Academic Writing: Justification 76

Presenting Ideas: 60-Second Speech 82

ISSUE 3

Behind the Wheel

Building Concepts and Language/Analyzing and Discussing Text 84

Academic Writing: Formal Summary 98

Building Concepts and Language/Analyzing and Discussing Text 102

Presenting Ideas: Debate 106

Academic Writing: Justification Essay 108

ISSUE 4

Money Matters

Building Concepts and Language/Analyzing and Discussing Text 116

Academic Writing: Formal Summary 130

Building Concepts and Language/Analyzing and Discussing Text 134

Presenting Ideas: Debate 138

Academic Writing: Justification Essay 140

Presenting Ideas: 60-Second Speech 148

2 Table of Contents

ISSUE 5

Virtual vs. Reality

Building Concepts and Language/Analyzing and Discussing Text 150

Academic Writing: Formal Summary 164

Analyzing and Discussing Text 168

Presenting Ideas: Debate 172

Academic Writing: Argument Research Paper 174

ISSUE 6

Ready to Work

Building Concepts and Language/Analyzing and Discussing Text 182

Academic Writing: Formal Summary 196

Building Concepts and Language/Analyzing and Discussing Text 200

Presenting Ideas: Debate 204

Academic Writing: Argument Research Paper 206

Presenting Ideas: Two-Minute Speech 214

ISSUE 7

Your Vote, Your Voice

Building Concepts and Language/Analyzing and Discussing Text 216

Academic Writing: Formal Summary 230

Analyzing and Discussing Text 234

Presenting Ideas: Debate 238

Academic Writing: Argument Research Paper 240

ISSUE 8

Future Focus

Building Concepts and Language/Analyzing and Discussing Text 248

Academic Writing: Formal Summary 262

Analyzing and Discussing Text 266

Presenting Ideas: Debate 270

Academic Writing: Argument Research Paper 272

Presenting Ideas: Two-Minute Speech 280

DAILY DO NOW 282

Welcome to English 3D

Preview the English 3D Issues by taking this survey. After you complete each Issue, check back to see if your ideas or perspectives have changed.

1 Teen Sleep

Are you getting enough sleep? Check the box for how many hours you sleep most nights.

- [ ] less than 6 hours
- [ ] 6–7 hours
- [ ] 7–8 hours
- [ ] 8–9 hours
- [ ] more than 9 hours

How many hours of sleep do you think your body needs? _____

2 Learning Languages

Are you taking the classes you need to graduate? Check any of the statements that apply.

- [ ] I don't need to take a world language.
- [ ] I need to take a certain number of credits of a world language.
- [ ] I can earn credits in a world language or another class.
- [ ] I can take a test in my first language instead of taking a world language.
- [ ] I need to take a world language to graduate.

3 Behind the Wheel

Your friend is driving you home from school and starts texting while driving. What would you do? Circle your most likely response.

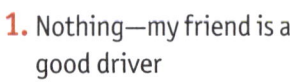

1. Nothing—my friend is a good driver
2. Refuse a ride from my friend next time
3. Ask if I can send the message for my friend
4. Tell my friend to stop texting
5. Ask my friend to pull over so I can get out

4 Money Matters

What are your priorities when it comes to money? Number these from most important (1) to least important (5).

____ Buying clothes, apps, or video games

____ Buying food or snacks

____ Saving for larger purchases like a car or computer

____ Helping pay family bills

____ Saving for college

5 Virtual vs. Reality

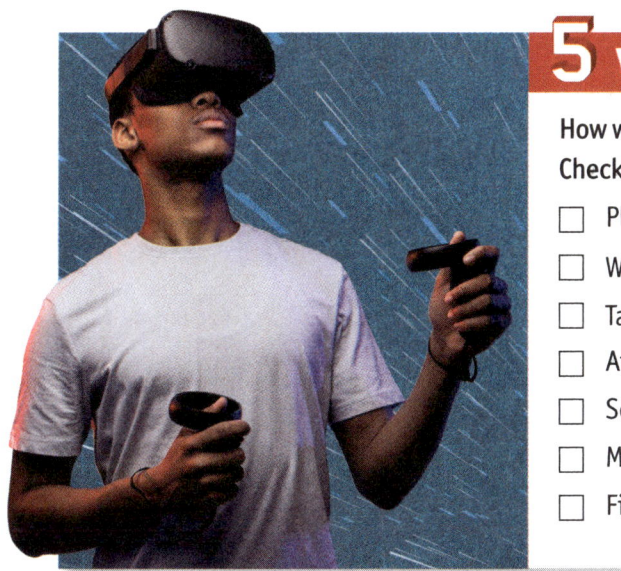

How would you like to use virtual reality technology? Check any of the following actions that apply.

- ☐ Play games
- ☐ Watch VR movies
- ☐ Take virtual classes
- ☐ Attend virtual concerts or live events
- ☐ Socialize with friends
- ☐ Meditate or relax
- ☐ Fitness or exercize

6 Ready to Work

List three careers you would like to learn more about.

1. _____
2. _____
3. _____

7 Your Vote, Your Voice

What do you know about voting in the United States? Write T for true and F for false.

_____ People age 17 and older can vote.
_____ Only citizens can vote.
_____ You can choose not to vote.
_____ If you don't vote, you must pay a fine.

8 Future Focus

How important is it to you to think about the future? Write A if you agree. Write D if you disagree.

_____ Leaving a positive legacy is important to me.
_____ What is meant to be will be.
_____ People today shouldn't be forced to solve problems for future generations.
_____ We are responsible for the well-being of those who come after us.
_____ Today's problems matter more than future concerns.

Building Concepts and Language

SPEAKING AND LISTENING

Academic Discussion

What are the characteristics of an effective lesson partner?

Language to REPORT
We would like to suggest the precise adjective _____.

💡 BRAINSTORM IDEAS
Write precise words to discuss and write about the topic.

Everyday	Precise
• smart *(adjective)*	• creative, clever,
• good *(adjective)*	• organized, focused,
• nice *(adjective)*	• respectful, patient,
• fun *(adjective)*	• amusing, witty,

✏️ MAKE A CLAIM
Rewrite two ideas using the frame and precise words.

Frame: In my opinion, an effective lesson partner is _____ (**adjective:** prepared, organized) and _____ (**adjective:** respectful, creative)

Response: _____

_____

💬 COLLABORATE
Listen attentively, restate, and record your partner's ideas.

Classmate's Name	Ideas

Language to RESTATE
So your opinion is that _____.

Yes, that's correct.

No, not exactly. What I meant was _____.

🎤 PRESENT IDEAS
Listen attentively, compare ideas, and take notes. Then indicate whether you agree (+) or disagree (–).

Language to COMPARE IDEAS
My idea is similar to _____'s.

Classmate's Name	Idea	+/–

Preparing to Read Informational Text
ACADEMIC VOCABULARY

Words to Go

BUILD WORD KNOWLEDGE
Complete the meanings and examples for this high-utility academic word.

Word to Go	Meanings	Examples
advantage ad•van•tage *noun*	something that helps you to be better or more _____; something that is good or _____ about a place, thing, or situation	In today's multicultural workplace, _____ _____ _____ is an **advantage**. An **advantage** of having a pet is _____

DISCUSS AND WRITE EXAMPLES
Discuss your response with a partner. Then complete the sentence in writing.

One **advantage** of owning a smartphone is that it allows you to _____
_____

Write your response and read it aloud to a partner.

Having a part-time job is a definite _____ for high school students who want to _____

BUILD WORD KNOWLEDGE
Complete the meaning and examples for this high-utility academic word.

Word to Go	Meaning	Examples
collaborative col•lab•o•ra•tive *adjective*	able to work closely with others to _____ something	Movie awards for _____ _____ are usually won by a **collaborative** team of artists. _____ classes often require more **collaborative** projects than traditional _____ classes.

DISCUSS AND WRITE EXAMPLES
Discuss your response with a partner. Then complete the sentence in writing.

One advantage of a **collaborative** project is that classmates have the opportunity to _____
_____

Write your response and read it aloud to a partner.

At home, one _____ chore that we all pitch in on is _____
_____

Getting Started 7

Analyzing and Discussing Text
SUMMARIZING TEXT

Language to Summarize

BUILD FLUENCY
Read the text and prepare to state the key idea.

The Collaborative Advantage

Today, most jobs are too complex to be done by just one person. In the twenty-first century, a person who knows how to **collaborate**—to work effectively with other people—has a career **advantage**. **Collaboration** is necessary in jobs from construction to retail to medicine.

A medical trauma team is an excellent example of a **collaborative** group. Each team member has a special set of skills and responsibilities. When an accident victim arrives at a hospital, the trauma team has about one hour, known as the golden hour, to save the patient.

A team leader directs about 10 doctors, nurses, and support staff. One nurse cuts off the patient's clothes. A trauma doctor examines the patient and makes a diagnosis. The radiologist **contributes** by taking X-rays. An anesthesiologist makes sure the patient is breathing and is free from pain. Another nurse calls out the patient's vital signs every five minutes.

The team interacts constantly and works with competence and confidence. No one person could save the patient alone; it takes **collaborative** teamwork.

Not all jobs are a matter of life and death. However, most jobs do require **collaboration**. If you want to succeed in a career, join the team.

IDENTIFY KEY IDEAS AND DETAILS
Take turns asking and answering questions with a partner. Then write brief notes.

Discussion Frames	Text Notes
Q: What is this text **mainly about**? **A:** This text is **mainly about** _____.	• jobs in which people _____
Q: What are two **important details** in this text? **A:** One **important detail** in this text is _____. **A:** Another **important detail** in this text is _____.	• a medical trauma _____ has about an hour to save a _____ • about 10 medical _____ collaborate and each team _____ has a job

8 Getting Started

Building Concepts and Language

SPEAKING AND LISTENING

Academic Discussion

What are the advantages and disadvantages of collaborative assignments?

BRAINSTORM IDEAS
Briefly record at least two ideas in each column using everyday English.

Advantages	Disadvantages
• many ideas to think about	• more ideas to listen to
• could finish faster	• could take longer to finish
•	•
•	•

ANALYZE WORDS
Complete the chart with precise verbs to discuss and write about the topic.

Language to REPORT
We would like to suggest the precise verb _____.

Everyday	Precise
get *(verb)*	experience, consider,
finish *(verb)*	accomplish, attain,
deal with *(verb phrase)*	tolerate, endure,

MAKE A CLAIM
Rewrite two ideas using the frames and precise words.

1. **Frame:** In my opinion, one potential advantage of working collaboratively is being able to _____ (**base verb:** complete, brainstorm, divide)

   Response: _____
   _____
   _____

2. **Frame:** In my experience, one serious disadvantage of working in some groups is having to _____ (**base verb:** tolerate, consider, handle)

   Response: _____
   _____
   _____

Getting Started 9

SPEAKING AND LISTENING

Academic Discussion (continued)

💬 COLLABORATE
Listen attentively, restate, and record your partner's ideas.

Classmate's Name	Ideas
	1.
	2.

Language to RESTATE

So your (opinion/experience) is that _____.

Yes, that's correct.

No, not exactly. What I meant was _____.

🎤 PRESENT IDEAS
Listen attentively, compare ideas, and take notes. Then indicate whether you agree (+) or disagree (–).

Language to COMPARE IDEAS

My (opinion/experience) is similar to _____'s.

Classmate's Name	Idea	+/–

10 Getting Started

Preparing to Read Informational Text

ACADEMIC VOCABULARY

Words to Go

BUILD WORD KNOWLEDGE
Complete the meanings and examples for this high-utility academic word.

Word to Go	Meanings	Examples
consider con•si•der *verb*	to think about something _____ ; to have an _____ about someone or something	Due to rising gas prices, many commuters are **considering** _____ . _____ In my community, many business owners **consider** _____ to be a major problem.

DISCUSS AND WRITE EXAMPLES
Discuss your response with a partner. Then complete the sentence in writing.

When assigning a final grade, I think teachers should **consider** their students'

_____ as well as scores on assignments and tests.

Write your response and read it aloud to a partner.

When I purchase a gift for friends or siblings, two factors I _____

are _____ and _____.

BUILD WORD KNOWLEDGE
Complete the meaning and examples for this high-utility academic word.

Word to Go	Meaning	Examples
productive pro•duc•tive *adjective*	_____ a lot	When students have a substitute teacher, they are typically more **productive** if their usual teacher _____ _____ A room with _____ _____ makes studying more **productive** for me.

DISCUSS AND WRITE EXAMPLES
Discuss your response with a partner. Then complete the sentence in writing.

When I have an important assignment, I am usually most **productive** working in

_____ because _____

Write your response and read it aloud to a partner.

To have a _____ planning meeting for a school event, classmates need

to _____

Getting Started 11

Analyzing and Discussing Text
SUMMARIZING TEXT

Language to Summarize

 TAKE A SURVEY
Complete the Classroom Collaboration Survey.

 BUILD FLUENCY
Read the article and prepare to state the key idea.

Being a Team Player

Are you a natural team player who enjoys working with others? Or are you a lone wolf who prefers to work independently? No matter what kind of person you are, everyone can strive to be a more effective team member.

A construction crew is a group of people all working for the same goal: to construct a solid building that satisfies a client. However, problems often come up. For example, a construction crew might have to work around a beautiful, old tree that the client wants to save. The backhoe driver cannot move his machine easily around the tree. He wants to bulldoze it down. How can the crew solve this problem?

Productive team members have to express their own ideas clearly and listen attentively to the **perspectives** of others. They have to **consider** other approaches to the problem and be willing to compromise. They have to put the project ahead of their own personal feelings.

In the case of the construction crew, the backhoe driver and the architect compromise to come up with a new solution that saves the tree. No one loses. The team wins.

How was the problem resolved? It took skilled communication and **collaboration**.

 IDENTIFY KEY IDEAS AND DETAILS
Take turns asking and answering questions with a partner. Then write brief notes.

Discussion Frames	Text Notes
Q: What is this text **mainly about**? **A:** This text is **mainly about** _____.	• team members who are _____
Q: What are the **most important details** in this text? **A:** One **important detail** in this text is _____. **A:** Another **important detail** in this text is _____.	• productive team members have to _____ effectively • working collaboratively also requires being able to _____

12 Getting Started

Preparing to Read Informational Text

ACADEMIC VOCABULARY

Words to Go

 BUILD WORD KNOWLEDGE

Complete the meaning and examples for this high-utility academic word.

Word to Go	Meaning	Examples
competent com·pe·tent *adjective*	having enough _____ or knowledge to do something well	Becoming a **competent** soccer player requires _____ Employers often look for job applicants who are **competent** users of _____

DISCUSS AND WRITE EXAMPLES

Discuss your response with a partner. Then complete the sentence in writing.

The most reliable way for teens to become **competent** drivers is to _____

_____

because _____

Write your response and read it aloud to a partner.

One of the most noticeable characteristics of a _____ leader is the ability to _____

 BUILD WORD KNOWLEDGE

Complete the meaning and examples for this high-utility academic word.

Word to Go	Meaning	Examples
complex com·plex *adjective*	having many parts or details and often _____ to understand	The rules of some video games are too **complex** for most _____ Science textbooks tend to be more **complex** than other books because they include a lot of _____

DISCUSS AND WRITE EXAMPLES

Discuss your response with a partner. Then complete the sentence in writing.

Adults often have to ask children for assistance with using _____

_____ because they can be quite **complex**.

Write your response and read it aloud to a partner.

From my perspective, _____ is a musician who sings interesting and **complex** lyrics, such as those in the song _____

Getting Started 13

Analyzing and Discussing Text
SUMMARIZING TEXT

Language to Summarize

 BUILD FLUENCY
Read the article and prepare to state the key idea.

The Importance of Face-to-Face Communication

You can probably text, email, and video chat without a problem. But are you equally comfortable with face-to-face communication? Working with a team requires a great deal of face time with other team members. **Collaboration** is challenging if you are not sure how to communicate.

How do **competent** communicators behave? Here is an example. A school club wants to sell snacks at a weekend event. Some members of the club want to sell candy because kids like it. Others want to try healthier alternatives. Each group presents its side of the issue at a meeting.

When the first side speaks, the team members present facts as well as feelings. They give reasons and evidence for their **perspectives**. Their body language is calm and confident. As the second side listens, its members take notes and look for ideas that they agree with as well as disagree with. They respond with questions and their own opinions. They do not react with feelings and criticism. They do not explode, shut down, or ridicule.

The communication leads to a compromise that satisfies both sides. The club members avoid conflict. Communication helps the team work **productively** and find the best solution.

Use these tips for successful teamwork:
- Present your ideas effectively.
- Listen attentively to others' ideas.
- Prepare to compromise to solve **complex** problems.
- Remember your team's goal—and make it a success.

 ASK AND ANSWER QUESTIONS
Take turns asking and answering questions with a partner. Then write brief notes.

Discussion Frames	Text Notes
Q: What is this text **mainly about**? **A:** This text is **mainly about** _____ .	• in-person _____
Q: What are the **most important details** in this text? **A:** (One/Another) **important detail** in this text is _____ .	• competent communicators remain _____ and don't insult people who _____ • compromising can _____ • complex _____

14 Getting Started

Building Concepts and Language
SPEAKING AND LISTENING

Academic Discussion

Is technology negatively affecting teen communication?

BRAINSTORM IDEAS
Briefly record at least two ideas in each column using everyday English.

Agree	Disagree
• use short sentences when texting • •	• gets teens chatting with people they wouldn't have the chance to normally • •

ANALYZE WORDS
Complete the chart with precise adjectives to discuss and write about the issue.

Language to REPORT
We would like to suggest the precise adjective ____.

Everyday	Precise
quick *(adjective)*	efficient, immediate,
boring *(adjective)*	inefficient, tedious,
casual *(adjective)*	informal, common,
fancy *(adjective)*	formal, appropriate,

MAKE A CLAIM
Rewrite one idea using the frame and a precise adjective.

Frame: In my opinion, _____ (**form of technology:** texting, social networking, email) has made teen communication _____ (**more/less**) (**adjective:** impressive, precise, informal)

Response: _____
_____
_____

Getting Started 15

Building Concepts and Language

SPEAKING AND LISTENING

Academic Discussion (continued)

💬 COLLABORATE
Listen attentively, restate, and record your partner's idea.

Classmate's Name	Idea

Language to RESTATE

So your perspective is that _____.

Yes, that's correct.

No, not exactly. What I meant was _____.

🎤 PRESENT IDEAS
Listen attentively, compare ideas, and take notes. Then indicate whether you agree (+) or disagree (–).

Language to AGREE/DISAGREE

I (agree/disagree) with _____'s perspective that _____.

Classmate's Name	Idea	+/–

16 Getting Started

Building Concepts and Language
SPEAKING AND WRITING

Ten-Minute Response

A **ten-minute response** begins with a well-stated **claim**, followed by **two detail sentences** that elaborate with relevant examples and precise words.

> **Language to COLLABORATE**
> What should we write?
> We could put _____. What do you think makes sense?
> We could also write _____.

✏️ **ELABORATE IN WRITING**
Read and analyze the teacher's ten-minute response. Circle three precise adjectives.

In my opinion, email has made teen communication more efficient. For example, if absent students have questions about a major assignment, they can quickly send a message to a responsible classmate instead of interrupting their studies with a phone call. As a result, the classmate can simply reply with a brief message explaining the homework instructions rather than taking the time to go into extensive detail in a phone conversation.

Work with the teacher to write a ten-minute response. Include two precise adjectives.

In my opinion, texting has made teen communication less precise. For example, texting requires use of _____ vocabulary that everyone will understand and abbreviations for _____ expressions, such as _____ for _____.
As a result, English teachers have noticed an increase in inappropriate _____, spelling _____, and texting expressions in their students' formal _____.

Work with a partner to write a ten-minute response. Include two precise adjectives.

In my opinion, _____ has made teen communication
(less/more) _____ (adjective) _____
For example, _____
_____
_____
As a result, _____
_____
_____

Getting Started 17

Issue 1 Teen Sleep

DO TEENS NEED A WAKE-UP CALL WHEN IT COMES TO SLEEP?

📖 BUILD KNOWLEDGE
Read and respond to the Data File (*Issues*, p. 4).

💡 BRAINSTORM IDEAS
Write a brief list of reasons why teens stay up late.

- doing household chores
- _____
- _____
- _____

🎤 PRESENT IDEAS
Use the frames to discuss ideas with your group. Listen attentively and record the strongest ideas to complete the concept web.

> **Language to FACILITATE DISCUSSION**
> So _____, what's your experience?
> _____, what reason did you come up with?

1. Some teens stay up late because they are _____ (**verb + –ing**: completing)
2. Teens might also stay up late _____ (**verb + –ing**: worrying about)
3. Sometimes I (have to/decide to) stay up late _____ (**verb + –ing**: reading)
4. I occasionally have to stay up late _____ (**verb + –ing**: studying for)

Concept web — **REASONS TEENS STAY UP LATE**
- writing essays

18 Issue 1

Building Concepts and Language

ACADEMIC VOCABULARY

Words to Know

 BUILD WORD KNOWLEDGE
Rate your word knowledge. Then discuss word meanings and examples with your group.

① Don't Know   ② Recognize   ③ Familiar   ④ Know

Word to Know	Meaning	Example
1 adolescent noun ① ② ③ ④	a young person who is becoming an adult; _____	Many **adolescents** like to _____ _____ _____ after school.
2 stage noun ① ② ③ ④	a particular _____ _____ that something reaches as it grows or develops	My 16-month-old sister has reached the **stage** of life where she is _____ _____
3 sleep-deprived adjective ① ② ③ ④	lacking the _____ needed over a period of time	When my baby brother was born, my parents were so **sleep-deprived** that they _____ _____ _____
4 puberty noun ① ② ③ ④	the time when a person's body changes _____ _____ _____	During **puberty**, teens often have to start _____ _____ _____
1 deficit noun ① ② ③ ④	the difference between how much _____ and how much _____	Our team needed to overcome a **deficit** of _____ _____ to win the championship game.
2 hormone noun ① ② ③ ④	chemicals _____ _____ that affect how it grows and develops	Sometimes **hormones** can make teens _____ _____ _____
3 metabolism noun ① ② ③ ④	the process in the body that _____ _____ for working and growing	When you _____ _____ your **metabolism** is higher because your body needs more energy.
4 symptom noun ① ② ③ ④	something wrong with your _____ that shows you are ill	**Symptoms** of the flu include _____ _____ _____

Teen Sleep 19

Building Concepts and Language

SPEAKING AND LISTENING

Academic Discussion

What are some reasons why adolescents fail to get sufficient sleep?

BRAINSTORM IDEAS
Briefly record at least two ideas in each column using everyday English.

Personal Reasons	Environmental Reasons
• dealing with social problems • •	• noisy traffic outside • •

ANALYZE WORDS
Complete the chart with precise words to discuss and write about the topic.

Everyday	Precise
problems *(plural noun)*	worries,
work *(noun)*	assignments,
finish *(verb)*	revise,

MAKE A CLAIM
Rewrite two ideas using the frames and precise words. Then prepare to elaborate verbally.

1. **Frame:** I know from experience that many adolescents fail to get adequate sleep during the school week because they stay up late _____ (**verb + -ing**: revising essays for English class, reading novels)

   Response: _____

   _____

2. **Frame:** Based on my experience, adolescents fail to get sufficient sleep on school nights because of _____ (**noun phrase:** social issues, lengthy homework assignments)

   Response: _____

   _____

Language to ELABORATE

For example, _____.

I know this firsthand because _____.

COLLABORATE
Listen attentively, restate, and record your partner's ideas.

Classmate's Name	Ideas
	1.
	2.

Language to RESTATE

So you believe that _____.

Yes, that's correct.

No, not exactly. What I (pointed out/stated) was _____.

20 Issue 1

Ten-Minute Response

A **ten-minute response** begins with a well-stated **claim**, followed by **two detail sentences** that elaborate with relevant examples and precise words.

Language to AGREE/DISAGREE
I agree with _____'s idea.
I don't quite agree with _____'s idea.

🎤 PRESENT IDEAS

Listen attentively and take notes. Then indicate whether you agree (+) or disagree (−).

Classmate's Name	Idea	+/−

✏️ ELABORATE IN WRITING

Work with the teacher to write a ten-minute response.

Language to COLLABORATE
What should we write?
We could put _____. What do you think makes sense?
We could also write _____.

I know from experience that many adolescents fail to get adequate sleep during the school week because they stay up late completing various homework assignments. For example, I recently studied well past midnight because I had to read an entire history _____ and take notes, prepare for an exam in _____ and finish editing a _____ As a result, I only got _____ hours of sleep and I felt _____ and _____ during my morning classes.

Work with a partner to write a ten-minute response.

I know from experience that many adolescents fail to get adequate sleep during the school week because they stay up late _____ _____ For example, I regularly fall asleep no earlier than _____ because I spend several hours _____ As a result, I have a great deal of trouble staying awake and _____ _____ the next school day, especially in challenging classes such as _____

Analyzing and Discussing Text
ACADEMIC VOCABULARY

Words to Go

BUILD WORD KNOWLEDGE
Complete the meanings and examples for these high-utility academic words.

Word to Go	Meaning	Example
tend to tend to *verb*	to be likely to _____ a certain way	If I am nervous about making a presentation in class, I **tend to** _____ _____
tendency ten•den•cy *noun*	part of your character that makes you likely to act or think _____	Students have a **tendency** to _____ _____ _____ when there is a substitute teacher.

DISCUSS AND WRITE EXAMPLES
Discuss your response with a partner. Then complete the sentence in writing.

My English teacher **tends to** reward students who have completed their assignments well with _____

Write your response and read it aloud to a partner.

The coach's _____ to _____

during games made him unpopular with many athletes and parents.

BUILD WORD KNOWLEDGE
Complete the meaning and examples for this high-utility academic word.

Word to Go	Meaning	Examples
consequence con•se•quence *noun*	something that happens because of an _____	The **consequence** of not doing my homework was _____ _____ He _____ _____ so now he must face the **consequences**.

DISCUSS AND WRITE EXAMPLES
Discuss your response with a partner. Then complete the sentence in writing.

When I ate a large snack after school, the **consequence** was _____

Write your response and read it aloud to a partner.

The _____ of preparing my presentation in advance and practicing it several times in front of _____ was that I _____

Text ❶ • Magazine Article
RESPONDING TO TEXT

Close Reading

BUILD FLUENCY
Read the text "Who Needs Sleep?" (*Issues*, pp. 5–8).

IDENTIFY KEY IDEAS AND DETAILS
Take turns asking and answering questions with a partner. Then write brief notes.

Discussion Frames	Text Notes
Q: What is the **key idea** of this text? **A:** The **key idea** of this text is ____. **Q:** What are the **most important details** in this text? **A:** (One/Another) **important detail** in this text is ____.	• sleep is _____ to adolescent health, but teens don't get enough • 4 sleep stages: need sleeping/dreaming to _____ • teens need an average of _____ hours of sleep a night • teen body's _____ is pushed back; doesn't feel _____ until _____ • chronic _____ causes serious health issues: depressed mood, weakened _____ weight gain

RESPOND WITH EVIDENCE

Use the frame and evidence from the text to construct a formal written response.

1. According to the author, what are some physical consequences of inadequate sleep?

   According to the author, _____
   are physical consequences of inadequate sleep. In addition, accumulating a sleep deficit can lead to _____

Use the frame to analyze the author's word choice.

2. What is the effect of describing teenagers as "walking zombies" on page 7?

   One effect of describing teenagers as "walking zombies" is to compare _____

   Zombies are _____

   Describing sleep-deprived adolescents as "walking zombies" suggests that teens _____

IDENTIFY PRECISE WORDS
Review Text 1 and your *Portfolio* (pp. 18–23) to identify words for your writing.

Topic Words	High-Utility Academic Words
• sleep-debt • •	• adequate • •

Teen Sleep **23**

Building Concepts and Language

SPEAKING AND LISTENING

Academic Discussion

What are the consequences of sleep deprivation?

BRAINSTORM IDEAS
Briefly record at least two ideas in each column using everyday English.

Physical Consequences	Mental Consequences
• getting out of shape • •	• less interest in friends • •

ANALYZE WORDS
Complete the chart with precise words to discuss and write about the issue.

Everyday	Precise
often *(adverb)*	regularly,
tired *(adjective)*	fatigued,
moody *(adjective)*	antisocial,

MAKE A CLAIM
Rewrite two ideas using the frames and precise words. Then prepare to elaborate verbally.

1. **Frame:** One physical (consequence/impact/outcome) of sleep deprivation for adolescents is _____ (**verb + –ing:** having, getting, gaining)

    Response: _____

    _____

2. **Frame:** A mental (consequence/impact/outcome) of chronic fatigue is that adolescents can become _____ (**adjective:** distracted, alienated, antisocial)

    Response: _____

    _____

Language to ELABORATE
For example, _____.
I know this firsthand because _____.

COLLABORATE
Listen attentively, restate, and record your partner's ideas.

Classmate's Name	Ideas
	1. 2.

Language to RESTATE
So you believe that _____.
Yes, that's correct.
No, not exactly. What I (pointed out/stated) was _____.

SPEAKING AND WRITING

Ten-Minute Response

A **ten-minute response** begins with a well-stated **claim**, followed by **two detail sentences** that elaborate with relevant examples and precise words.

Language to AGREE/DISAGREE
I agree with _____'s idea.
I don't quite agree with _____'s idea.

🎙️ PRESENT IDEAS
Listen attentively and take notes. Then indicate whether you agree (+) or disagree (–).

Classmate's Name	Idea	+/–

✏️ ELABORATE IN WRITING
Work with the teacher to write a ten-minute response.

Language to COLLABORATE
What should we write?
We could put _____. What do you think makes sense?
We could also write _____.

One _____ consequence of sleep deprivation for adolescents is getting sick _____
For example, not getting _____
sleep throughout the week weakens an individual's immune system. As a result, _____
teens commonly develop illnesses such as _____
and _____ and have to miss _____
days of school.

Work with your partner to write a ten-minute response.

A _____ impact of chronic fatigue is that adolescents can become forgetful. For example, insufficient sleep can cause _____ with short-term memory and _____ As a result, teens who _____ come to school feeling _____
have considerable difficulty _____
_____

Teen Sleep 25

Analyzing and Discussing Text
ACADEMIC VOCABULARY

Words to Go

📖 BUILD WORD KNOWLEDGE
Complete the meaning and examples for this high-utility academic word.

Word to Go	Meaning	Examples
affect af•fect *verb*	to _____ someone or something	_____ _____ _____ would positively **affect** my grades. _____ _____ **affects** what I decide to wear in the morning.

💬 DISCUSS AND WRITE EXAMPLES
Discuss your response with a partner. Then complete the sentence in writing.

When buying a new cell phone, _____

is likely to **affect** an adolescent customer's decision.

Write your response and read it aloud to a partner.

_____

will _____ my success after high school.

📖 BUILD WORD KNOWLEDGE
Complete the meaning and examples for this high-utility academic word.

Word to Go	Meaning	Examples
factor fac•tor *noun*	one of the things that _____ _____	A **factor** in the family's decision to move was _____ _____ Eating a healthy breakfast is a **factor** in _____ _____

💬 DISCUSS AND WRITE EXAMPLES
Discuss your response with a partner. Then complete the sentence in writing.

_____ is

a **factor** that contributes to the problem of teen drug use.

Write your response and read it aloud to a partner.

Two _____ that I consider when choosing a book to read are

_____ and _____

Text ❷ • Section ❶ • News Article

SUMMARIZING TEXT

Section Shrink

 BUILD FLUENCY
Read the introduction and Section 1 of "Sleep Is One Thing Missing in Busy Teenage Lives" (*Issues*, pp. 9–12).

 IDENTIFY KEY IDEAS AND DETAILS
Take turns asking and answering questions with a partner. Then write brief notes.

Discussion Frames	Text Notes
Q: What is the **key idea** of this section? **A:** The **key idea** of this section is _____. **Q:** What are the **most important details** in this section? **A:** (One/Another) **important detail** in this section is _____. **A:** Perhaps the **most important detail** in this section is _____.	• teens are often _____ on school days • internal clock _____ so teens fall asleep later and wake up early feeling _____ • physical consequences: _____ impaired immune system, risk of _____ and _____ • mental consequences: memory lapses, trouble _____ moodiness, _____

✏️ **SUMMARIZE**

"Shrink" Section 1 of the text by writing a summary in 40 or fewer words.

CLASS SUMMARY   **WORD COUNT:** _____

Many adolescents are _____ at school because their

_____ are off, making them regularly fall asleep late

and get less than _____ hours of sleep per night, resulting in a

number of _____ and emotional _____

PARTNER SUMMARY   **WORD COUNT:** _____

Many adolescents are typically _____ during the school

week because their internal clocks _____ making them feel

_____ instead of _____ and this can lead to

_____ with their _____ and _____

 IDENTIFY PRECISE WORDS
Review Section 1 and your *Portfolio* (pp. 24–27) to identify words for your writing.

Topic Words	High-Utility Academic Words
• sleep-deprived • •	• consequence • •

Teen Sleep **27**

Analyzing and Discussing Text
ACADEMIC VOCABULARY

Words to Go

BUILD WORD KNOWLEDGE
Complete the meanings and examples for these high-utility academic words.

Word to Go	Meaning	Example
respond re•spond *verb*	to _____ to something that has been said or done	After seeing destruction caused by the hurricane, people **responded** by _____
response re•sponse *noun*	a _____ to something that has been said or done	The principal's decision to allow _____ elicited an enthusiastic student **response**.

DISCUSS AND WRITE EXAMPLES
Discuss your response with a partner. Then complete the sentence in writing.

If I found out that I had won the state lottery and become a multimillionaire, I would **respond**

by _____

Write your response and read it aloud to a partner.

When some high school students have a major writing assignment, a common _____

is to _____

_____

BUILD WORD KNOWLEDGE
Complete the meaning and examples for this high-utility academic word.

Word to Go	Meaning	Examples
survey sur•vey *verb*	to _____ many people the same questions to find out their opinions	I would enjoy **surveying** my classmates about _____ A new business might want to **survey** people who _____

DISCUSS AND WRITE EXAMPLES
Discuss your response with a partner. Then complete the sentence in writing.

If our school **surveyed** students about changes they want at our school, it would probably find that

many want _____

Write your response and read it aloud to a partner.

Before organizing an end-of-the-year party, I would _____ classmates to

find out _____

_____

28 Issue 1

Text ❷ • Section ❷ • News Article

SUMMARIZING TEXT

Section Shrink

BUILD FLUENCY
Read Section 2 of "Sleep Is One Thing Missing in Busy Teenage Lives" (*Issues*, pp. 12–13).

IDENTIFY KEY IDEAS AND DETAILS
Take turns asking and answering questions with a partner. Then write brief notes.

Discussion Frames	Text Notes
Q: What is the **key idea** of this section? A: The **key idea** of this section is _____. Q: What are the **most important details** in this section? A: (One/Another) **important detail** in this section is _____. A: Perhaps the **most important detail** in this section is _____.	• changing school _____ • The Sleep Foundation says schools should start at _____ • schools that changed times have better _____ and _____ • reasons against changing times: _____ • after-school _____

✏️ SUMMARIZE
"Shrink" Section 2 of the text by writing a summary in 40 or fewer words.

CLASS SUMMARY   **WORD COUNT:** _____

High schools have found that making the school day start _____

can _____ attendance and _____

but some people want to keep _____ start times because of bus

_____ and _____ activities.

PARTNER SUMMARY   **WORD COUNT:** _____

While _____ high school start times has improved

_____ and graduation rates, _____

want to keep earlier start times due to _____

with bus schedules and student participation in _____

_____

IDENTIFY PRECISE WORDS
Review Section 2 and your *Portfolio* (pp. 28–29) to identify words for your writing.

Topic Words	High-Utility Academic Words
• attendance • •	• survey • •

Teen Sleep 29

Analyzing and Discussing Text
ACADEMIC VOCABULARY

Words to Go

BUILD WORD KNOWLEDGE
Complete the meaning and examples for this high-utility academic word.

Word to Go	Meaning	Examples
approach ap•proach *noun*	a _____ of doing something	My **approach** to preparing for a test is to _____ During a job interview, _____ is definitely the wrong **approach**.

DISCUSS AND WRITE EXAMPLES
Discuss your response with a partner. Then complete the sentence in writing.

One **approach** for dealing with an argument with a friend is _____

_____

Write your response and read it aloud to a partner.

An effective _____ to getting a curfew extension might be

_____

BUILD WORD KNOWLEDGE
Complete the meaning and examples for this high-utility academic word.

Word to Go	Meaning	Examples
data da•ta *noun*	information or _____	A research paper about teen driving habits might include **data** about _____ Before purchasing a car for an adolescent driver, a parent should gather **data** on _____

DISCUSS AND WRITE EXAMPLES
Discuss your response with a partner. Then complete the sentence in writing.

Useful **data** for choosing a place to take a vacation might include _____

_____

Write your response and read it aloud to a partner.

Before applying to a particular college or trade school, I would review

_____ on _____

Text ❷ • Section ❸ • News Article

SUMMARIZING TEXT

Section Shrink

 BUILD FLUENCY
Read Section 3 of "Sleep Is One Thing Missing in Busy Teenage Lives" (*Issues*, pp. 14–15).

 IDENTIFY KEY IDEAS AND DETAILS
Take turns asking and answering questions with a partner. Then write brief notes.

Discussion Frames	Text Notes
Q: What is the **key idea** of this section? **A:** The **key idea** of this section is _____.	• Navy _____ _____
Q: What are the **most important details** in this section? **A:** (One/Another) **important detail** in this section is _____. **A:** Perhaps the **most important detail** in this section is _____.	• changed "rack time" to _____ but recruits couldn't _____ that early • new "rack time" is _____ • Navy studying whether it improves test _____ • mental consequences: memory lapses, moodiness, trouble _____

SUMMARIZE
"Shrink" Section 3 of the text by writing a summary in 40 or fewer words.

CLASS SUMMARY   **WORD COUNT:** _____

The Navy changed its "rack time" to _____ so _____ can get _____ hours of sleep per night, and it is _____ whether it improves behavior and _____

PARTNER SUMMARY   **WORD COUNT:** _____

The new Navy _____ is 10 p.m. to 6 a.m., which allows sailors to _____ eight hours per night, and the Navy is collecting _____ about whether the sleep schedule _____ test scores and _____

IDENTIFY PRECISE WORDS
Review Section 3 and your *Portfolio* (pp. 30–31) to identify words for your writing.

Topic Words	High-Utility Academic Words
• psychologists • •	• data • •

Teen Sleep **31**

Academic Writing

ANALYZING TEXT ELEMENTS

Student Writing Model

Academic Writing Type

A **formal written summary** provides an objective overview of the topic and important details from an informational text. The writer credits the author: but writes in primarily their own words, without including personal opinions.

- **A.** The **topic sentence** includes the text type, title, author, and topic.
- **B.** **Detail sentences** include the important details from the summarized text.
- **C.** The **concluding sentence** restates the author's conclusion in the writer's own words.

ANALYZE TEXT
Read this student model to analyze the elements of a formal summary.

A

In the magazine article titled "Who Needs Sleep?," Kristen Weir investigates why sleep is so crucial for teens. First, Weir reports that 60 percent of middle and high school students say that they experience chronic fatigue at school. The author also explains that teens should average nine or more hours of sleep a night, but most tend to get about seven. In addition, she clarifies that this adolescent sleep deficit is due to numerous factors, such as busy schedules and a shift during puberty in the body's internal clock. Furthermore, the author describes multiple consequences of being sleep-deprived, such as issues with digestion and memory.

B

Finally, Weir concludes that teens should make sure they regularly get sufficient sleep to stay healthy and happy.

C

MARK AND DISCUSS ELEMENTS
Mark the summary elements and use the frames to discuss them with your partner.

1. **Number (1–4) the four elements of the topic sentence.**
   The topic sentence includes the _____.

2. **Draw a box around four transition words or phrases.**
   One transition (word/phrase) is _____.

3. **Underline four important details.** One important detail in this summary is _____.

4. **Circle four citation verbs.** One citation verb that the writer uses is _____.

5. **Star four precise topic words and check four high-utility academic words.**
   An example of a (precise topic word/high-utility academic word) is _____.

Paraphrasing Text

Guidelines for Paraphrasing a Sentence
Paraphrase one sentence from a source text by keeping important topic words and replacing key words and phrases with synonyms.

Source Text	Key Words and Phrases ➔	Synonyms	Paraphrasing
"Most are lucky to get six, seven, or eight hours of sleep a night, even though studies have shown repeatedly that people in their teens and possibly even early 20's need nine to 10 hours" (Grady 9).	most [teens] ➔	adolescents	Adolescents tend to only sleep eight or fewer hours per night although research often demonstrates they actually need nine to 10 hours.
	are lucky to get ➔	tend to only sleep	
	six, seven, or eight hours ➔	eight or fewer hours	
	even though studies have shown ➔	although research demonstrates	
	repeatedly ➔	often	

IDENTIFY PRECISE SYNONYMS
Read these statements and replace the words in parentheses with synonyms.

1. Tired students have (a hard time) _____ paying attention, and even if they do somehow manage to focus, they may (forget) _____ _____ what they were taught because memory formation takes place partly during sleep.

2. Some school districts have already (changed) _____ their schedules so that high school classes (start) _____ later, between 8 and 9, instead of before 8.

3. Navy researchers are (studying) _____ the (sailors) _____ to see if the extra sleep makes a difference.

PARAPHRASE IDEAS
Paraphrase the three statements from above using primarily your own words.

1. Grady reports that _____
   _____
   _____

2. The author explains that _____
   _____
   _____

3. She describes how _____
   _____
   _____

Formal Summary — FRONTLOADING LANGUAGE

Teen Sleep

Academic Writing
FRONTLOADING CONVENTIONS

Nouns and Pronouns to Credit an Author

Guidelines to Credit an Author
Topic Sentence: State the author's full name.
1st Important Detail: State the author's last name.
2nd Important Detail: Use the term *author, writer,* or *researcher.*
3rd Important Detail: Use the pronoun *he, she,* or *they.*
4th Important Detail: Use the term *author, writer,* or *researcher.*
Concluding Sentence: Use the author's last name.

IDENTIFY NOUNS AND PRONOUNS
Read the summary and circle the nouns and pronouns that credit the author.

> In the news story titled "Falling Asleep in Class? Blame Biology," Madison Park discusses why adolescents have difficulty getting adequate sleep. First, Park points out that teens' body clocks conflict with high school schedules. The writer also reports that a Kentucky district altered its high school start time to 8:30 a.m., and half of students surveyed said they were sleeping eight hours per night. In addition, she explains that later start times can reduce car accidents and improve attendance. Furthermore, the writer points out that the glow of technological devices such as cell phones and computer screens can make falling asleep more difficult. Finally, Park concludes that schools should also consider parents' and employers' points of view before changing schedules.

TAKE NOTES
Write nouns and pronouns to credit the author in your formal summary of Text 2.

Summary Sentence	Noun/Pronoun to Credit the Author
Topic Sentence	
1st Detail	
2nd Detail	
3rd Detail	
4th Detail	
Concluding Sentence	

Formal Summary
PLANNING TO WRITE

Organize a Formal Summary

Prompt Write a formal summary of "Sleep Is One Thing Missing in Busy Teenage Lives."

Guidelines for Paraphrasing Multiple Sentences
Paraphrase related details from a source text by combining key information into one sentence. Replace key words and phrases with synonyms and keep important topic words.

Text Detail 1	Text Detail 2	Text Detail 3
". . . tired students have a hard time paying attention, and even if they do somehow manage to focus, they may forget what they were taught" (Grady 10).	"Dr. Carskadon said studies had repeatedly linked sleep deprivation to depressed mood—a temporary case of the blues" (Grady 11).	"Lack of sleep also increases teenage drivers' already elevated risk of car accidents" (Grady 12).

✏️ PARAPHRASE IDEAS
Combine key information from the three text details above into one detail sentence.

There are physical and mental impacts of sleep deprivation, including

(text detail 1) _____

(text detail 2) _____ and

(text detail 3) _____

📋 PLAN KEY IDEAS AND DETAILS
State the text information to write a topic sentence.

In the news article titled (Title) _____
_____

(Author's Full Name) _____ (citation verb: explores, examines, discusses)

_____ (topic) _____

List four important details from the article using primarily your own words.

1. _____
_____

2. _____
_____

3. _____
_____

4. _____
_____

Restate the author's conclusion in your own words.

_____
_____

Academic Writing
WRITING A DRAFT

Write a Formal Summary

Prompt | Write a formal summary of "Sleep Is One Thing Missing in Busy Teenage Lives."

✎ WRITE A PARAGRAPH
Use the frame to write your topic sentence, detail sentences, and concluding sentence.

A

In the magazine article titled _____
                                       (Title)
_____

_____   _____
(Author's Full name)   (citation verb)

_____
(topic)

B

First, _____ explains _____
       (Author's Last Name)   (1st important detail)
_____
_____
_____

The (author/writer/researcher) _____ also reports
_____
(2nd important detail)
_____
_____

In addition, _____ describe _____
              (pronoun)   (3rd important detail)
_____
_____
_____

Furthermore, the (author/writer/researcher) _____ points out
(4th important detail)
_____
_____

C

Finally, _____ concludes that _____
         (Author's Last Name)   (restate author's conclusion)
_____

36 Issue 1

Formal Summary
ASSESSING AND REVISING

Rate Your Summary

Scoring Guide	
1	Insufficient
2	Developing
3	Sufficient
4	Exemplary

ASSESS YOUR DRAFT
Rate your formal summary. Then have a partner rate it.

1. Does the topic sentence state the title, author, and topic?	Self	1	2	3	4
	Partner	1	2	3	4
2. Did you paraphrase the most important details from the text?	Self	1	2	3	4
	Partner	1	2	3	4
3. Did you include precise topic words and high-utility academic words?	Self	1	2	3	4
	Partner	1	2	3	4
4. Did you restate the author's conclusion using your own words?	Self	1	2	3	4
	Partner	1	2	3	4

REFLECT AND REVISE
Record specific priorities and suggestions to help you and your partner revise.

(Partner) Positive Feedback: I appreciate how you (used/included) _____
_____
_____

(Partner) Suggestion: As you revise your summary, focus on _____
_____
_____

(Self) Priority 1: My summary paragraph needs _____
_____
_____

(Self) Priority 2: I plan to improve my summary by _____
_____
_____

CHECK AND EDIT
Use this checklist to proofread and edit your formal summary.

☐ Did you capitalize the title of the article and proper nouns?

☐ Did you put quotation marks around the title of the article?

☐ Is each sentence complete?

☐ Are all words spelled correctly?

Teen Sleep 37

Building Concepts and Language

SPEAKING AND LISTENING

Academic Discussion

How can adolescents ensure they get adequate sleep?

BRAINSTORM IDEAS
Briefly record at least two ideas in each column using everyday English.

Healthy Habits	Activities
• don't drink caffeine after noon • •	• go to sleep by 11:00 • •

ANALYZE WORDS
Complete the chart with precise words to discuss and write about the topic.

Everyday	Precise
try to (verb)	attempt to,
stop (verb)	refrain from,
change (verb)	alter,

MAKE A CLAIM
Rewrite two ideas using the frames and precise words. Then prepare to elaborate verbally.

Language to ELABORATE
For example, _____.
I know this firsthand because _____.

1. **Frame:** In order to ensure adequate sleep on school nights, adolescents should _____ (base verb: avoid, exercise, attempt to)

   Response: _____
   _____

2. **Frame:** Based on my experience, one way adolescents can ensure adequate sleep during the school week is by _____ (verb + –ing: altering, completing, improving)

   Response: _____
   _____

COLLABORATE
Listen attentively, restate, and record your partner's ideas.

Language to RESTATE
So you believe that _____.
Yes, that's correct.
No, not exactly. What I (pointed out/stated) was _____.

Classmate's Name	Ideas
	1.
	2.

SPEAKING AND WRITING

Ten-Minute Response

A **ten-minute response** begins with a **claim**, followed by **two detail sentences** that elaborate with relevant examples and precise words.

Language to AGREE/DISAGREE
I agree with _____'s idea.
I don't quite agree with _____'s idea.

🎙 PRESENT IDEAS
Listen attentively and take notes. Then indicate whether you agree (+) or disagree (−).

Classmate's Name	Idea	+/−

✏ ELABORATE IN WRITING
Work with the teacher to write a ten-minute response.

Language to COLLABORATE
What should we write?
We could put _____. What do you think makes sense?
We could also write _____.

    In order to ensure adequate sleep on school nights, adolescents should strive to maintain a regular sleep schedule. For example, teens can start winding down at _____ p.m., turn off the lights by _____ p.m., and refrain from responding to _____ As a result, their internal clock will adjust to the new _____ and they will have an easier time _____
_____

Work with your partner to write a ten-minute response.

    Based on my experience, one way adolescents can ensure adequate sleep during the school week is by avoiding using bright technology before bedtime. For example, teens need to stop using their _____ and _____ before going to sleep and make sure their _____ are turned off. As a result, they will not be tempted to _____ and will instead wind down and improve their _____
_____

Teen Sleep 39

Analyzing and Discussing Text
ACADEMIC VOCABULARY

Words to Go

BUILD WORD KNOWLEDGE
Complete the meaning and examples for this high-utility academic word.

Word to Go	Meaning	Examples
trend trend *noun*	a general direction in which things are _____	A growing workplace **trend** is to _____ instead of making phone calls. A popular **trend** in 21st century learning is offering _____

DISCUSS AND WRITE EXAMPLES
Discuss your response with a partner. Then complete the sentence in writing.

A recent **trend** in teen fashion is wearing _____

_____

Write your response and read it aloud to a partner.

There is an increasing _____ in the number of car accidents due to people who _____ at the wheel.

BUILD WORD KNOWLEDGE
Complete the meaning and examples for this high-utility academic word.

Word to Go	Meaning	Examples
regulate reg•u•late *verb*	to manage or _____ especially by rules	Teens with demanding schedules need to **regulate** the amount of time spent _____ because it takes too long. The government **regulates** the speed limits near schools to _____

DISCUSS AND WRITE EXAMPLES
Discuss your response with a partner. Then complete the sentence in writing.

High schools **regulate** the _____ and _____ you need to graduate.

Write your response and read it aloud to a partner.

Dentists recommend that parents _____ the amount of _____ and _____ that children consume to reduce cavities.

40 Issue 1

Text ❸ • News Article
RESPONDING TO TEXT

Close Reading

BUILD FLUENCY
Read the text "Understanding the Zombie Teen's Body Clock" (*Issues*, pp. 16–19).

IDENTIFY KEY IDEAS AND DETAILS
Take turns asking and answering questions with a partner. Then write brief notes.

Discussion Frames	Text Notes
Q: What is the **key idea** of this text? **A:** The **key idea** of this text is _____.	• sleep loss helps explain teenage _____
Q: What are the **most important details** in this text? **A:** (One/Another) **important detail** in this text is _____.	• exhausted adolescents act _____ or make _____ decisions • sleep loss contributes to _____ and _____ problems in school • being sleep-deprived can also make teens feel _____ and more likely to think about committing _____

RESPOND WITH EVIDENCE
Use the frames and evidence from the text to construct a formal written response.

1. What are some trends that are causing adolescents to get inadequate sleep?

   According to the text, one trend that is causing adolescents to get inadequate sleep is
   _____

   This causes teens to get inadequate sleep because _____
   _____

   Another trend that is causing adolescents to get inadequate sleep is _____
   _____

Use the frame to analyze the author's word choice.

2. Use context clues to determine the meaning of *volatile* on page 17.

   Volatile means _____

   One context clue that helped me determine the meaning was when Jeremy said his emotions were _____

IDENTIFY PRECISE WORDS
Review Text 3 and your *Portfolio* (pp. 38–41) to identify words for your writing.

Topic Words	High-Utility Academic Words
• sleep-deprived	• trend
•	•
•	•

Teen Sleep 41

Presenting Ideas

Take a Stand

Debate | Should school start later to accommodate adolescent sleep needs?

🗨 COLLABORATE
Read the debate question about teen sleep. Then take turns using a frame to respond with your initial reaction.

Language to RESPOND

So _____, what's your initial reaction?

My initial reaction is _____.

My initial reaction is (similar to/different from) _____'s.

🔍 ANALYZE SOURCES
Read a quote that either supports or opposes the debate question. Then paraphrase.

Quote	Paraphrase
Model: "A study by the National Sleep Foundation (NSF) found that 60 percent of middle and high school students felt tired during the day, and over 15 percent of students report falling asleep at school" (Weir 5).	To put it another way, a sleep research organization found that a majority of _____ feel _____ at school, and some claimed to have actually _____ in class.
1. "Lack of sleep can interfere with learning: tired students have a hard time paying attention, and even if they do somehow manage to focus, they may forget what they are taught because memory formation takes place partly during sleep" (Grady 10).	This quote clarifies that sleep-deprived students may have difficulty _____ in class, and may not remember recent lesson _____ because you make _____ when _____.
2. "Suburban schools say students behave better, and in the city schools, attendance and graduation rates have gone up and tardiness has decreased" (Grady 13).	This quote clarifies that secondary schools report benefits of _____ including improvements in _____ and _____.
3. "The drawback is that some students, especially in city schools, are unable to take part in after-school activities, and some say they are earning less at their after-school jobs" (Grady 13).	This quote clarifies that delaying school start times has _____ on teens' participation in _____ _____ and their wages earned at _____.
4. "Many schools, however, have rejected parental pressure to delay school starts, citing bus-cost savings, or the need to keep afternoons open for teens' sports or other activities" (Shellenbarger 18).	To put it another way, a lot of schools simply refuse to shift to a later schedule due to _____ and _____ _____.

42 Issue 1

Debate Ideas

SYNTHESIZE IDEAS

Write a response to the debate question, including a paraphrase of a text quote and elaboration on the quote.

Claim: My position is that schools (should/should not) _____
start later to accommodate adolescent sleep needs.

Transitional Statement: I have (one key reason/a compelling reason) _____
_____ for taking this stance.

Quote Paraphrase: (According to _____,/The author points out _____.)
_____
_____
_____

Quote Elaboration: (As a result, _____./Consequently, _____.)
_____
_____
_____

PRESENT EVIDENCE

Connecting With Your Audience

When presenting ideas during class or in a meeting, **connect** with your audience. Look at your audience when you speak and make sure to look up from your notes every few seconds so that you look confident and engage your listeners.

LISTEN AND TAKE NOTES

Listen attentively and take notes. Then indicate whether you agree (+) or disagree (−).

> **Language to AFFIRM AND CLARIFY**
> That's an interesting opinion.
> Will you explain _____ again?

Classmate's Name	Idea	+/−

Teen Sleep 43

Academic Writing
ANALYZING TEXT ELEMENTS

Student Writing Model

Academic Writing Type

A **justification** states a claim and supports it with logical reasons and relevant evidence from texts.

A. The **topic sentence** clearly states the writer's claim about the issue.

B. **Detail sentences** support the claim with reasons and evidence from texts.

C. The **concluding sentence** restates the writer's claim about the issue.

ANALYZE TEXT
Read this student model to analyze the elements of a justification.

A Evidence from the texts supports the idea that schools should alter start times to accommodate adolescents' sleep needs. **B** One reason is that adolescents would be more alert in school with a later start time. Denise Grady points out in "Sleep Is One Thing Missing in Busy Teenage Lives" that teachers in Minnesota reported that students were less likely to fall asleep in morning classes when they had a one-hour delay in school start time (13). This evidence makes it quite clear that being able to sleep adequately and eat breakfast enables teens to focus instead of nap during early morning classes. An additional reason is that many teens cannot help how sleep-deprived they are in the early morning. In "Understanding the Zombie Teen's Body Clock," Sue Shellenbarger explains how hormones and puberty cause teens' internal clocks to change during adolescence so that they want to stay up later and sleep later (17). This is significant because while younger siblings and parents are becoming tired and preparing to sleep, teens feel wide awake and have trouble settling down. **C** For these reasons, high schools should start later to match teens' sleep patterns.

MARK AND DISCUSS ELEMENTS
Mark the justification elements and use the frames to discuss them with your partner.

1. **Circle the writer's claim within the topic sentence.** *The writer's claim is _____.*

2. **Draw a box around four transition words or phrases.**
   One transition (word/phrase) is _____.

3. **Underline and label two reasons that support the writer's claim with the letter R.**
   One reason that supports the writer's claim is _____.

4. **Underline and label two pieces of evidence that support the writer's claim with the letter E.**
   One piece of evidence that supports the writer's claim is _____.

5. **Star four precise topic words and check four high-utility academic words.**
   An example of a (precise topic word/high-utility academic word) is _____.

Justification
FRONTLOADING LANGUAGE

Transitions to Introduce Evidence

Transitions	Examples
For example, ____. For instance, ____. To illustrate, ____. As an illustration, ____. According to (source), ____. The text points out ____. In addition, the text states ____. In the text, (author's name) explains ____. (Author's name) emphasizes ____.	**For example,** some students in Minnesota say they are more likely to eat breakfast now that they wake up later for school. **According to the National Sleep Foundation,** drowsy drivers cause more than half of the 6,400 traffic deaths a year. **The text points out** that 15 percent of students say they have fallen asleep in school during the last year. **In the text, Weir explains** that we cycle through the four stages of sleep four to five times a night.

IDENTIFY TRANSITIONS
Review the transitions that writers use to introduce evidence that supports a claim. Then complete each sentence below with an appropriate transition.

1. _____
   that teenagers who are sleep-deprived are more likely to feel depressed.

2. _____
   it is true that many teens are not tired at 9 or 10 p.m.

3. _____
   that many teenagers are resistant to setting bedtimes.

WRITE SUPPORTING EVIDENCE
Write four sentences using transitions to introduce evidence that supports your claim.

1. _____
   _____
   _____

2. _____
   _____
   _____

3. _____
   _____
   _____

4. _____
   _____
   _____

Academic Writing

FRONTLOADING CONVENTIONS

Modal Verbs

Guidelines for Using Modal Verbs

Use **modal verbs** in your justification to describe what is possible or preferable.

The modal verb *should* tells about **something you believe needs to happen**.

*In my opinion, students **should** finish high school if they want to be successful.*

The modal verb *would* tells about **something you believe is possible in the future**.

*Higher ticket prices **would** help the drama club raise money.*

The modal verb *could* tells about **something that might be possible in the future.**

*Students **could** earn more money if the government raised the minimum wage.*

IDENTIFY MODAL VERBS

Read the justification and circle the modal verbs.

> Evidence from the texts supports the idea that schools should not start later to accommodate teen sleep needs. One reason is that adolescents should be trying to keep the same sleep schedule during the week and on weekends. Grady points out in "Sleep Is One Thing Missing in Busy Teenage Lives" that many teens "binge sleep" on the weekends, which leads to more irregular sleep schedules (9). This evidence makes it quite clear that teens could have more regular sleep schedules if they didn't "binge sleep." An additional reason is that many adolescents could take steps to regulate their internal clocks. In "Who Needs Sleep?," Weir explains that viewing bright screens before bedtime can push teens' internal clocks back even further (7). This is significant because if teens stop using bright phones and watching bright TVs in the hour before bed, they would sleep better. For these reasons, schools should not have to change to accommodate adolescents' sleep schedules.

WRITE MODAL VERBS

Write modal verbs to complete the sentences.

1. Evidence from the texts supports the idea that schools _____ start after 9 a.m.

2. Many students _____ feel less irritable if they were able to sleep longer in the mornings.

3. Delaying school start times _____ also reduce the number of teen car accidents due to drowsiness.

4. In addition, many students' grades _____ improve.

5. This option _____ also benefit teachers because students _____ be more alert and focused in class.

Organize a Justification

Prompt Should schools start later to accommodate adolescent sleep needs? Write a justification that states and supports your claim.

IDENTIFY TEXT EVIDENCE
Review the texts to identify evidence that supports each reason.

Reason	Text Evidence
Adolescents who don't get enough sleep might get sick more often.	
Schools are concerned that changing start times will affect bus schedules.	

PLAN REASONS AND EVIDENCE
Use academic language to clearly state your claim as a topic sentence.

Evidence from the texts supports the idea that _____

_____

List two reasons that support your claim and give text evidence for each reason.

Reason 1: _____

_____

Text Evidence: _____

_____

Reason 2: _____

_____

Text Evidence: _____

_____

Restate your claim as a concluding sentence.

For these reasons, _____

_____

Teen Sleep 47

Academic Writing
WRITING A DRAFT

Write a Justification

Prompt Should schools start later to accommodate adolescent sleep needs? Write a justification that states and supports your claim.

✏️ WRITE A PARAGRAPH
Use the frame to write your topic sentence, detail sentences, and concluding sentence.

A

Evidence from the texts supports the idea that _____
(claim)
_____
_____
_____
_____

B

One reason is that _____
(1st reason that supports the claim)
_____
_____
_____

_____ points out in _____
(author's name)   (title of source)
that _____
(text evidence)
_____
_____

This evidence makes it quite clear that _____
(elaborate on the evidence)
_____
_____

An additional reason is that _____
(2nd reason that supports the claim)
_____

In _____, _____
(title of source)   (author's name)
explains that _____
(text evidence)
_____

This is significant because _____
(elaborate on the evidence)
_____
_____

C

For these reasons, _____
(restate your claim)
_____
_____

48 Issue 1

Justification
ASSESSING AND REVISING

Rate Your Justification

Scoring Guide
1	Insufficient
2	Developing
3	Sufficient
4	Exemplary

ASSESS YOUR DRAFT
Rate your justification. Then have a partner rate it.

1. Does the topic sentence clearly state your claim?	Self	1	2	3	4
	Partner	1	2	3	4
2. Did you include strong reasons to support your claim?	Self	1	2	3	4
	Partner	1	2	3	4
3. Did you provide strong text evidence to support your claim?	Self	1	2	3	4
	Partner	1	2	3	4
4. Did you use transitions to introduce reasons and evidence?	Self	1	2	3	4
	Partner	1	2	3	4
5. Did you include precise topic words and high-utility academic words?	Self	1	2	3	4
	Partner	1	2	3	4
6. Does the concluding sentence restate your claim using new wording?	Self	1	2	3	4
	Partner	1	2	3	4

REFLECT AND REVISE
Record specific priorities and suggestions to help you and your partner revise.

(Partner) Positive Feedback: You did an effective job of (organizing/including/stating) _____
_____

(Partner) Suggestion: Your justification would be stronger if you _____
_____

(Self) Priority 1: I will revise my justification so that it _____
_____

(Self) Priority 2: I also need to _____
_____

CHECK AND EDIT
Use this checklist to proofread and edit your justification.

☐ Did you capitalize proper nouns, such as authors' last names?

☐ Did you cite sources using parentheses?

☐ Is each sentence complete?

☐ Are all words spelled correctly?

Issue 2 Learning Languages

SHOULD NOT KNOWING ANOTHER LANGUAGE KEEP A DIPLOMA OUT OF REACH?

📖 BUILD KNOWLEDGE
Read and respond to the Data File (*Issues*, p. 20).

💡 BRAINSTORM IDEAS
Write a brief list of reasons why students should learn a new language.

- to learn about other countries
- _____
- _____
- _____

🎤 PRESENT IDEAS
Use the frames to discuss ideas with your group. Listen attentively and record the strongest ideas to complete the concept web.

Language to FACILITATE DISCUSSION
So _____, what's your perspective?
_____, what reason did you come up with?

1. Learning another language helps students to _____ (**base verb:** learn)
2. Another reason to learn a new language is to _____ (**base verb:** complete)
3. Students who know multiple languages may be able to _____ (**base verb:** work)
4. I would like to learn another language so I could _____ (**base verb:** speak)

- travel to other countries

REASONS STUDENTS LEARN A NEW LANGUAGE

50 Issue 2

Words to Know

BUILD WORD KNOWLEDGE
Rate your word knowledge. Then discuss word meaning and examples with your group.

① Don't Know ② Recognize ③ Familiar ④ Know

Word to Know	Meaning	Example
1 admit *verb* ① ② ③ ④	to let someone _____ a club, school, or group	The honor society only **admits** students who _____
2 valuable *adjective* ① ② ③ ④	of great _____	Knowing how to _____ is a **valuable** skill if you want to find a good after-school job.
3 bilingual *adjective* ① ② ③ ④	speaking two _____ equally well	The **bilingual** students in our school _____
4 competitive *adjective* ① ② ③ ④	as good as or _____ than others at a job, task, or contest	Our school's _____ is **competitive** with those at other schools because we have _____
1 culture *noun* ① ② ③ ④	the way of _____ shared by people in a particular place or society	_____ can be very different from one **culture** to another.
2 communicate *verb* ① ② ③ ④	to _____ information or ideas with others	Most teens **communicate** with their friends _____
3 cognitive *adjective* ① ② ③ ④	relating to activities of the mind, such as _____ and _____	I use my **cognitive** skills when I _____
4 linguistic *adjective* ① ② ③ ④	relating to _____ and _____	The many _____ in our city show its **linguistic** variety.

Learning Languages 51

Building Concepts and Language

SPEAKING AND LISTENING

Academic Discussion

What are some reasons why students participate in world language classes?

BRAINSTORM IDEAS
Briefly record at least two ideas in each column using everyday English.

Academic/Career Reasons	Personal Reasons
• graduating from high school • •	• learning about new cultures • •

ANALYZE WORDS
Complete the chart with precise words to discuss and write about the topic.

Everyday	Precise
job *(noun)*	employment,
talk *(verb)*	communicate,
get *(verb)*	receive,

MAKE A CLAIM
Rewrite two ideas using the frames and precise words. Then prepare to elaborate verbally.

1. **Frame:** One reason why students participate in world language classes is to _____ (**base verb:** learn, fulfill, communicate)

   Response: _____

   _____

2. **Frame:** Based on my experience, students study new languages to _____ (**verb phrase:** graduate from high school, travel to another country, apply to college)

   Response: _____

   _____

Language to ELABORATE

For instance, _____.

I have found that _____.

COLLABORATE
Listen attentively, restate, and record your partner's ideas.

Classmate's Name	Ideas
	1. 2.

Language to RESTATE

So your opinion is that _____.

Yes, that's correct.

No, not exactly. What I (stated/reported) was _____.

SPEAKING AND WRITING

Ten-Minute Response

A **ten-minute response** begins with a well-stated **claim**, followed by **two detail sentences** that elaborate with relevant examples and precise words.

Language to AGREE/DISAGREE
I (agree/disagree) with _____'s opinion.

🎤 PRESENT IDEAS
Listen attentively and take notes. Then indicate whether you agree (+) or disagree (−).

Classmate's Name	Idea	+/−

✏️ ELABORATE IN WRITING
Work with the teacher to write a ten-minute response.

Language to COLLABORATE
What should we write?
We could put _____. What do you think works well?
We could also write _____.

One reason why students participate in world language classes is to become more competitive candidates for employment. For example, many companies with international offices need _____ employees to _____ with both English and non-English speakers. As a result, an increasing number of English speakers are taking courses that develop their _____ _____ abilities.

Work with a partner to write a ten-minute response.

Based on my experience, students study new languages to _____ _____

For example, some of my friends wanted to _____ _____

As a result, they felt it was critical that they be able to _____ _____ in their native language.

Learning Languages 53

Analyzing and Discussing Text
ACADEMIC VOCABULARY

Words to Go

BUILD WORD KNOWLEDGE
Complete the meanings and examples for these high-utility academic words.

Word to Go	Meaning	Example
benefit ben•e•fit *noun*	something that is _____ or good for you	Being able to _____ is a **benefit** of getting older.
beneficial ben•e•fi•cial *adjective*	having a _____ or _____ effect	_____ can be **beneficial** to a teen's social life.

DISCUSS AND WRITE EXAMPLES
Discuss your response with a partner. Then complete the sentence in writing.

_____ and _____ have **benefits** for football players.

Write your response and read it aloud to a partner.

In my opinion, _____

would be highly _____ for teens' health.

BUILD WORD KNOWLEDGE
Complete the meanings and examples for these high-utility academic words.

Word to Go	Meaning	Example
require re•quire *verb*	to _____ something by law or rule	The state **requires** that people _____ to get a driver's license.
requirement re•quire•ment *noun*	something that must be _____ by law or rule	At the restaurant where I work, _____ is a **requirement** for keeping your job.

DISCUSS AND WRITE EXAMPLES
Discuss your response with a partner. Then complete the sentence in writing.

The new school policy **requires** all students to _____

Write your response and read it aloud to a partner.

Maintaining a good attendance record should be a _____ for teens to _____

54 Issue 2

Text 1 • News Article
RESPONDING TO TEXT

Close Reading

📖 BUILD FLUENCY
Read the text "Many Benefits Come With Learning a World Language" (*Issues*, pp. 21–24).

💬 IDENTIFY KEY IDEAS AND DETAILS
Take turns asking and answering questions with a partner. Then write brief notes.

Discussion Frames	Text Notes
Q: What is the **key idea** of this text? **A:** The **key idea** of this text is _____.	• learning a world language has many _____
Q: What are the **most important details** in this text? **A:** (One/Another) **important detail** in this text is _____.	• helps for _____ and _____ • develops other _____ skills • teaches about other _____

✏️ RESPOND WITH EVIDENCE
Use the frames and evidence from the text to construct a formal written response.

1. Based on the text, how is learning a world language beneficial?

According to the author, learning a world language is beneficial for a student's _____

_____

In addition, participation in world language classes can open up opportunities for _____

Use the frame to analyze the author's word choice.

2. Use context clues to determine the meaning of the word *stringent* in the first paragraph on page 22.

Stringent means _____ One context clue that helped me determine the meaning was comparing Stanford's requirement of _____ _____ with most colleges' requirement of _____

🔍 IDENTIFY PRECISE WORDS
Review Text 1 and your *Portfolio* (pp. 50–55) to identify words for your writing.

Topic Words	High-Utility Academic Words
• world language	• improve
•	•
•	•

Learning Languages **55**

Building Concepts and Language

SPEAKING AND LISTENING

Academic Discussion

What are the cognitive and cultural benefits of studying a second language?

BRAINSTORM IDEAS
Briefly record at least two ideas in each column using everyday English.

Cognitive Benefits	Cultural Benefits
• increase vocabulary skills • •	• reading books in another language • •

ANALYZE WORDS
Complete the chart with precise words to discuss and write about the issue.

Everyday	Precise
grow (verb)	cultivate,
need (verb)	entail,
plus (noun)	advantage,

MAKE A CLAIM
Rewrite two ideas using the frames and precise words. Then prepare to elaborate verbally.

Language to ELABORATE
For instance, _____.
I have found that _____.

1. **Frame:** One (cognitive/cultural) benefit of studying a new language is _____ (**verb + –ing:** developing skills, scoring well on tests, appreciating others)

   Response: _____

2. **Frame:** Studying a new language is (cognitively/culturally) beneficial because it _____ (**present-tense verb:** enables, allows, requires, increases)

   Response: _____

COLLABORATE
Listen attentively, restate, and record your partner's ideas.

Language to RESTATE
So your opinion is that _____.
Yes, that's correct.
No, not exactly. What I (stated/reported) was _____.

Classmate's Name	Ideas
	1.
	2.

56 Issue 2

SPEAKING AND WRITING

Ten-Minute Response

A **ten-minute response** begins with a well-stated **claim**, followed by **two detail sentences** that elaborate with relevant examples and precise words.

Language to AGREE/DISAGREE

I (agree/disagree) with _____'s opinion.

🎤 PRESENT IDEAS

Listen attentively and take notes. Then write whether you agree (+) or disagree (–).

Classmate's Name	Idea	+/–

✏️ ELABORATE IN WRITING

Work with the teacher to write a ten-minute response.

Language to COLLABORATE

What should we write?

We could put _____. What do you think works well?

We could also write _____.

One _____ benefit of studying a new language is developing memorization skills that can be an asset in other academic areas. For example, studying English requires that I _____ a great number of _____ One result of this _____ _____ is that when I had to take _____ _____ I found the material _____ to remember.

Work with a partner to write a ten-minute response.

Studying a new language is _____ beneficial because it cultivates relationships with _____ who live in other countries. For example, studying _____ can help someone _____ cousins in _____ One result of _____ _____ is that by the time I left, _____ _____

Learning Languages 57

Analyzing and Discussing Text

ACADEMIC VOCABULARY

Words to Go

📚 BUILD WORD KNOWLEDGE

Complete the meanings and examples for these high-utility academic words.

Word to Go	Meaning	Example
global glo•bal *adjective*	affecting or involving the whole _____	A *global* ban on _____ would make _____
globalization glo•bal•i•za•tion *noun*	the process of something becoming present all over the _____	American _____ have _____ become more popular in other countries with the spread of *globalization*.

💬 DISCUSS AND WRITE EXAMPLES

Discuss your response with a partner. Then complete the sentence in writing.

Scientists have studied the effects of **global** warming on _____

_____

Write your response and read it aloud to a partner.

Being able to _____ with a friend on the other

side of the world is one benefit of the _____ of the internet.

📚 BUILD WORD KNOWLEDGE

Complete the meaning and examples for this high-utility academic word.

Word to Go	Meaning	Example
capacity ca•pac•i•ty *noun*	the mental or physical _____ to do or learn something	My brother's *capacity* for _____ is legendary in our family. Having limited *capacity* for _____ I often need _____

💬 DISCUSS AND WRITE EXAMPLES

Discuss your response with a partner. Then complete the sentence in writing.

I firmly believe that everyone has the **capacity** to _____

_____

Write your response and read it aloud to a partner.

The fact that teens can _____

proves that their brains have the _____ to do two things at once.

Text ❷ • Section ❶ • Blog Post

SUMMARIZING TEXT

Section Shrink

📖 BUILD FLUENCY
Read Section 1 of "The Effects of a Second Language on the Brain" (*Issues*, pp. 25–26).

💬 IDENTIFY KEY IDEAS AND DETAILS
Take turns asking and answering questions with a partner. Then write brief notes.

Discussion Frames	Text Notes
Q: What is the **key idea** of this section? **A:** The **key idea** of this section is _____.	• bilingualism no longer thought to be harmful
Q: What are the **most important details** in this section? **A:** (One/Another) **important detail** in this section is _____. **A:** Perhaps the **most important detail** in this section is _____.	• today, being bilingual is a _____ skill, and some countries require world language study for _____ • many years ago, believed that bilingualism caused _____ _____ or "split personality" • thought the brain had limited _____ to learn _____

✏️ SUMMARIZE
"Shrink" Section 1 of the text by writing a summary in 40 or fewer words.

CLASS SUMMARY   **WORD COUNT:** _____

Today, becoming _____ is very popular because people value

and often _____ it as an academic and professional

skill, but a century ago, people viewed bilingualism as _____

and _____ for people's brains.

PARTNER SUMMARY   **WORD COUNT:** _____

Today, people consider _____ _____

because it is a _____ for many colleges

and employers, but long ago, people thought it was _____

and beyond the brain's _____

🔍 IDENTIFY PRECISE WORDS
Review Section 1 and your *Portfolio* (pp. 56–59) to identify words for your writing.

Topic Words	High-Utility Academic Words
• interconnectivity • •	• ability • •

Learning Languages **59**

Analyzing and Discussing Text
ACADEMIC VOCABULARY

Words to Go

📖 BUILD WORD KNOWLEDGE
Complete the meanings and examples for these high-utility academic words.

Word to Go	Meaning	Example
invariable in•var•i•a•ble *adjective*	never _____	The **invariable** result of my cooking is _____
invariably in•var•i•a•bly *adverb*	in _____ case; always	Science class is **invariably** so _____ that I _____ every day.

💬 DISCUSS AND WRITE EXAMPLES
Discuss your response with a partner. Then complete the sentence in writing.

Every year, a student requests that _____
_____ but the principal's **invariable** response is "No."

Write your response and read it aloud to a partner.

Vandals _____ paint graffiti _____
_____

📖 BUILD WORD KNOWLEDGE
Complete the meanings and examples for these high-utility academic words.

Word to Go	Meaning	Example
retain re•tain *verb*	to _____ something or continue to have something; to remember	**retains** its _____ if properly cared for.
retention re•ten•tion *noun*	the _____ to keep something in your memory	My mother has a problem with **retention** of _____

💬 DISCUSS AND WRITE EXAMPLES
Discuss your response with a partner. Then complete the sentence in writing.

After _____, I **retained** the information that I needed to _____

Write your response and read it aloud to a partner.

My _____ of facts helps me do well _____

60 Issue 2

Text ❷ • Section ❷ • Blog Post

SUMMARIZING TEXT

Section Shrink

📖 BUILD FLUENCY
Read Section 2 of "The Effects of a Second Language on the Brain" (*Issues*, pp. 27–28).

💬 IDENTIFY KEY IDEAS AND DETAILS
Take turns asking and answering questions with a partner.

Discussion Frames	Text Notes
Q: What is the **key idea** of this section? **A:** The **key idea** of this section is _____.	• learning a _____ has cognitive advantages
Q: What are the **most important details** in this section? **A:** (One/Another) **important detail** in this section is _____. **A:** Perhaps the **most important detail** in this section is _____.	• students who _____ a second language had improved English _____ • _____ studying world languages had higher verbal and math _____ • _____ children have improved language development

✏️ SUMMARIZE
"Shrink" Section 2 of the text by writing a summary in 40 or fewer words.

CLASS SUMMARY   **WORD COUNT:** _____

Numerous _____ have discovered that learning a second

language is _____

in that it has been shown to _____ students' test

scores in other academic areas and gives children _____

_____ over their peers.

PARTNER SUMMARY   **WORD COUNT:** _____

_____ has proven that world-language study provides many

_____ such as _____

_____ students' scores on math and English tests and

_____ linguistic abilities.

🔍 IDENTIFY PRECISE WORDS
Review Section 2 and your *Portfolio* (pp. 60–61) to identify words for your writing.

Topic Words	High-Utility Academic Words
• monolingual • •	• distinguish between • •

Learning Languages **61**

Analyzing and Discussing Text

ACADEMIC VOCABULARY

Words to Go

📖 BUILD WORD KNOWLEDGE
Complete the meanings and examples for these high-utility academic words.

Word to Go	Meaning	Example
acquire ac•quire *verb*	to _____ or learn something	I need to practice every day to **acquire** _____
acquisition ac•qui•si•tion *noun*	the process by which someone gains or _____ something	My sister's recent **acquisition** of _____ has caused me to avoid her.

💬 DISCUSS AND WRITE EXAMPLES
Discuss your response with a partner. Then complete the sentence in writing.

When I read an article about _____ I **acquired** some unsettling

knowledge about _____

Write your response and read it aloud to a partner.

The _____ of _____

is crucial if you want to get a job that _____

📖 BUILD WORD KNOWLEDGE
Complete the meanings and examples for these high-utility academic words.

Word to Go	Meaning	Example
impact im•pact *noun*	the _____ of one thing on another	_____ has had a major **impact** on how well I sleep.
impact im•pact *verb*	to have an _____ on someone or something	Other people's opinions will **impact** my decision about which _____

💬 DISCUSS AND WRITE EXAMPLES
Discuss your response with a partner. Then complete the sentence in writing.

If schools want to have an **impact** on the problem of _____

they need to _____

Write your response and read it aloud to a partner.

The overuse of plastic bags has greatly _____ the _____

Text ❷ • Section ❸ • Blog Post

SUMMARIZING TEXT

Section Shrink

📖 BUILD FLUENCY
Read Section 3 of "The Effects of a Second Language on the Brain" (*Issues*, pp. 28–31).

💬 IDENTIFY KEY IDEAS AND DETAILS
Take turns asking and answering questions with a partner.

Discussion Frames	Text Notes
Q: What is the **key idea** of this section? **A:** The **key idea** of this section is _____.	• second languages impact brain _____
Q: What are the **most important details** in this section? **A:** (One/Another) **important detail** in this section is _____. **A:** Perhaps the **most important detail** in this section is _____.	• _____ children and teens have denser _____ _____ • learning a second language at _____ _____ can alter brain _____ • can _____ the onset of Alzheimer's and _____

✏️ SUMMARIZE
"Shrink" Section 3 of the text by writing a summary in 40 or fewer words.

CLASS SUMMARY　　　　　　　　　　　　　　　　　　　　　**WORD COUNT:** _____

Brain _____ have shown that learning a second language impacts the _____ of brain tissue in young people, _____ the brain's structure if learned at _____ _____ and helps _____ avoid early onset of Alzheimer's and dementia.

PARTNER SUMMARY　　　　　　　　　　　　　　　　　　　　**WORD COUNT:** _____

Scientists have found that _____ a world language _____ the brains of children and teens with _____ _____ gray matter, alters the brain's _____ if learned early enough, and aids in _____ Alzheimer's and dementia.

🔍 IDENTIFY PRECISE WORDS
Review Section 3 and your *Portfolio* (pp. 62–63) to identify words for your writing.

Topic Words	High-Utility Academic Words
• hemisphere • •	• correlation • •

Learning Languages **63**

Academic Writing
ANALYZING TEXT ELEMENTS

Student Writing Model

Academic Writing Type

A **formal written summary** provides an objective overview of the topic and important details from an informational text. The writer credits the author but writes in primarily their own words, without including personal opinions.

A. The **topic sentence** includes the text type, title, author, and topic.
B. **Detail sentences** include the important details from the summarized text.
C. The **concluding sentence** restates the author's conclusion in the writer's own words.

ANALYZE TEXT
Read this student model to analyze the elements of a formal summary.

> **A** In the news article titled "Many Benefits Come With Learning a World Language," Kalli Damschen examines the advantages of studying a new language in school.
>
> **B** First, Damschen explains that learning a new language can improve students' chances of being admitted to certain colleges. The author also discusses how knowing a world language is essential for certain international jobs and may give a competitive edge for other positions. In addition, she reports that learning another language can improve students' memorization skills. Furthermore, the author describes the cultural benefits, such as learning about other cultures and traveling abroad.
>
> **C** Finally, Damschen concludes that bilingualism presents opportunities for students to be connected to the international community.

MARK AND DISCUSS ELEMENTS
Mark the summary elements and use the frames to discuss them with your partner.

1. **Number (1–4) the four elements of the topic sentence.**
   The topic sentence includes the _____.

2. **Draw a box around four transition words or phrases.**
   One transition (word/phrase) is _____.

3. **Underline four important details.** One important detail in this summary is _____.

4. **Circle four citation verbs.** One citation verb that the writer uses is _____.

5. **Star four precise topic words and check four high-utility academic words.**
   An example of a (precise topic word/high-utility academic word) is _____.

Formal Summary

FRONTLOADING CONVENTIONS

Simple Present-Tense Verbs

Guidelines for Using Simple Present-Tense Verbs

Writers use **simple present-tense verbs** in formal summaries to cite an author or text. For singular nouns *(author* or *writer)* and third-person singular pronouns *(he, she,* or *they)*, **simple-present tense verbs** end in *–s* or *–es*.

Topic Sentence: State the topic.
 Andrianes Pinantoan explores . . .   *The author discusses . . .*   *The article investigates . . .*

Important Details: Summarize details.
 He reports . . .   *The writer describes . . .*   *The article explains . . .*

Concluding Sentence: Restate the conclusion.
 Pinantoan concludes . . .   *The author sums up . . .*   *Harris ends by . . .*

IDENTIFY PRESENT-TENSE VERBS
Read the summary below and circle the present-tense verbs that cite the author.

> In the news article titled "Language Immersion Schools Make Strides in St. Louis Area," Jessica Bock explores language immersion schools. First, Bock explains that the latest school to open is a Chinese immersion program. The author also reports that the school teaches all subjects in Chinese and begins teaching English in the middle of second grade. In addition, she points out that the administrators expect students to score below the state average on standardized tests until they reach fifth grade. Furthermore, the author discusses how students learn a third language in middle school. Finally, Bock concludes that the global business advantages of multilingualism is attracting parents.

WRITE PRESENT-TENSE VERBS
Complete each sentence with a present-tense citation verb.

1. Kalli Damschen _____ the benefits of studying a world language.
2. Damschen _____ that many colleges require world language study.
3. The author _____ that better job opportunities may arise for bilingual people.
4. Finally, Damschen _____ that knowing a world language is quite valuable.

Learning Languages 65

Academic Writing

FRONTLOADING LANGUAGE

Transitions to Organize Details

Organization	Transitions		Examples
first detail	First,	To begin with,	**To begin with,** the author reports that second-language courses are on the rise.
additional details	The article also	The author also	**The author also** points out that bilingual applicants often impress employers.
	In addition,	Additionally,	
	Moreover,	Furthermore,	**In addition,** she explains that a second language is often a requirement for getting into college.
last detail	Finally,	Lastly,	**Finally,** the author concludes that a second language can offer many opportunities.

🔍 IDENTIFY TRANSITIONS

Review the transitions that writers use to organize details in a formal summary. Then complete the model summary with appropriate transitions.

_____ the author explains that many world language immersion programs are available. _____ discusses how American students live with host families in countries abroad. _____ he describes how the teens are surrounded by people who only speak the different language. _____ the author clarifies that the teens also take language courses. _____ the author concludes that immersion programs are highly successful at helping teens become bilingual.

✏️ WRITE IMPORTANT DETAILS

Write three sentences about "The Effects of a Second Language on the Brain" using transitions.

1. _____ _____
   (Transition)   (noun/pronoun)
   _____ that _____
   (citation verb)   (important detail)
   _____
   _____

2. _____ _____
   (Transition)   (noun/pronoun)
   _____ that _____
   (citation verb)   (important detail)
   _____
   _____

3. _____ _____
   (Transition)   (noun/pronoun)
   _____ that _____
   (citation verb)   (important detail)
   _____

Formal Summary
PLANNING TO WRITE

Organize a Formal Summary

Prompt Write a formal summary of "The Effects of a Second Language on the Brain."

Guidelines for Paraphrasing Multiple Sentences
Paraphrase related details from a source text by combining key information into one sentence. Replace key words and phrases with synonyms and keep important topic words.

Text Detail 1	Text Detail 2	Text Detail 3
"... babies from bilingual homes were able to distinguish between different languages, while those from monolingual homes could not" (Pinantoan 27).	"... students who studied a world language invariably did better on the English portion of the Louisiana Basic Skill tests than those who did not" (Pinantoan 23).	"While those who did not study world language had a mean of 366 on the verbal SAT and 409 on the math SAT, those with ... five years of world language scored dramatically higher (504 and 535)" (Pinantoan 27).

✏️ PARAPHRASE IDEAS
Combine key information from the three text details above into one detail sentence.

Bilingual babies, children, and teens have outperformed their monolingual peers with

(text detail 1) _____

(text detail 2) _____ and

(text detail 3) _____

📋 PLAN KEY IDEAS AND DETAILS
State the text information to write a topic sentence.

In the blog post titled (title) _____

(author's full name) _____

(citation verb: explores, examines, discusses) _____

(topic) _____

List four important details from the article primarily using your own words.

1. _____
   _____

2. _____
   _____

3. _____
   _____

4. _____
   _____

Restate the author's conclusion in your own words.

_____
_____

Learning Languages

Academic Writing

WRITING A DRAFT

Write a Formal Summary

Prompt Write a formal summary of "The Effects of a Second Language on the Brain."

✏️ WRITE A PARAGRAPH
Use the frame to write your topic sentence, detail sentences, and concluding sentence.

A

In the blog post titled _____
             (Title)

_____

_____ _____
(Author's Full Name)   (citation verb)

_____
(topic)

B

_____ _____ _____
(Transition)   (Author's Last Name) (citation verb)

_____
(1st important detail)

_____

The (author/writer) _____ also _____
                                        (citation verb)

_____
(2nd important detail)

_____

_____ _____ _____
(Transition)   pronoun   (citation verb)

_____
(3rd important detail)

_____

_____ the (author/writer) _____
(Transition)

_____ _____
(citation verb)   (4th important detail)

_____

C

_____ _____ _____ concludes that
(Transition)   (Author's Last Name)

_____
(restate author's conclusion)

_____

68 Issue 2

Formal Summary
ASSESSING AND REVISING

Rate Your Summary

Scoring Guide	
1	Insufficient
2	Developing
3	Sufficient
4	Exemplary

ASSESS YOUR DRAFT
Rate your formal summary. Then have a partner rate it.

1. Does the topic sentence state the title, author, and topic?	Self	1	2	3	4
	Partner	1	2	3	4
2. Did you paraphrase the most important details from the text?	Self	1	2	3	4
	Partner	1	2	3	4
3. Did you use citation verbs to credit the author?	Self	1	2	3	4
	Partner	1	2	3	4
4. Did you use transitions to introduce and sequence details?	Self	1	2	3	4
	Partner	1	2	3	4
5. Did you include precise topic words and high-utility academic words?	Self	1	2	3	4
	Partner	1	2	3	4
6. Did you restate the author's conclusion using your own words?	Self	1	2	3	4
	Partner	1	2	3	4

REFLECT AND REVISE
Record specific priorities and suggestions to help you and your partner revise.

(Partner) Positive Feedback: I appreciate how you (used/included)

_____

_____

(Partner) Suggestion: As you revise your summary, focus on

_____

_____

(Self) Priority 1: My summary paragraph needs

_____

_____

(Self) Priority 2: I plan to improve my summary by

_____

_____

CHECK AND EDIT
Use this checklist to proofread and edit your formal summary.

☐ Did you capitalize the title of the article and proper nouns?

☐ Did you put quotation marks around the title of the article?

☐ Do simple present-tense verbs end in –s?

☐ Is each sentence complete?

☐ Are all words spelled correctly?

Analyzing and Discussing Text

ACADEMIC VOCABULARY

Words to Know

📖 BUILD WORD KNOWLEDGE

Rate your word knowledge. Then discuss word meanings and examples with your group.

① Don't Know ② Recognize ③ Familiar ④ Know

Word to Know	Meaning	Example
1 **conflict** noun ① ② ③ ④	a situation in which people do not _____	_____ _____ can cause **conflicts** between friends. I had a **conflict** with my parents about _____ _____ _____
2 **generation** noun ① ② ③ ④	all the people who are about the same _____	My **generation** is known for communicating by _____ _____ _____ Families often pass down _____ _____ _____ from **generation** to **generation**.
3 **identity** noun ① ② ③ ④	a sense of _____ ; a feeling of _____ to a particular group or race	An important part of my **identity** is my _____ _____ _____ Teens sometimes shape their **identities** by _____ _____
4 **primary language** noun ① ② ③ ④	the language that someone uses most _____	My family's **primary language** is _____ _____ While learning a new language, it is important to maintain fluency in your **primary language** by _____ _____ _____ _____

Text ❸ • Poem

RESPONDING TO TEXT

Close Reading

📖 READ THE TEXT
Read the poem "Bilingual/Bilingüe" (*Issues*, pp. 32–33).

🔍 IDENTIFY STRUCTURE

> **Poetry's Structure**
> The **structure** of a poem is how it is organized. A **couplet** is two lines of poetry that usually rhyme. A poem's **rhyme scheme** is the pattern it uses for words that rhyme. To identify a rhyme scheme, write *A* at the end of the first line and then write *A* at the end of any lines that end with a rhyming word. Write *B* at the end of the next line that does not rhyme, and so on.

Use the frames to analyze the poem's structure.

1. What is the structure of the poem "Bilingual/Bilingüe"?

    The poem "Bilingual/Bilingüe" contains _____ couplets, each of

    which consists of _____

2. What is the rhyme scheme of the poem "Bilingual/Bilingüe"?

    The rhyme scheme of the poem "Bilingual/Bilingüe" is that _____

    _____

    For example, the words _____ and _____ rhyme.

✏️ ANALYZE CRAFT AND STRUCTURE
Use the frames to analyze the author's use of language.

3. What is the effect of including Spanish words in the poem?

    One effect of including Spanish words in the poem is to show _____

    _____

    _____

    Most of the Spanish words are surrounded by _____

    which separate them from the English words. However, in the last couplet, the author says

    _____

    which shows that _____

    _____

✏️ ANALYZE THEME
Use the frames to analyze the poem's theme.

4. How does "and still the heart was one" contribute to the poem's theme, or overall message?

    The phrase "and still the heart was one" means that Espaillat remained _____

    _____

    She wants the reader to understand that _____

    _____

Learning Languages **71**

Analyzing and Discussing Text

SPEAKING AND LISTENING

Academic Discussion

How does language influence our identity?

BRAINSTORM IDEAS
Briefly record at least two ideas in each column using everyday English.

Individual Effects	Community Effects
• what someone is able to read • •	• references to music, TV shows, and movies • •

ANALYZE WORDS
Complete the chart with precise words to discuss and write about the topic.

Everyday	Precise
decide *(verb)*	determine,
difference of opinion *(noun)*	disagreement,
group of people *(noun)*	peers,

MAKE A CLAIM
Rewrite two ideas using the frames and precise words. Then prepare to elaborate verbally.

Language to ELABORATE
For instance, _____.
I have found that _____.

1. **Frame:** Language influences our identity because it _____
   (**present-tense verb:** allows, affects, determines)

   Response: _____
   _____

2. **Frame:** Rhina P. Espaillat shows that language influences her identity by _____
   (**verb + –ing:** saying, writing, showing)

   Response: _____
   _____

COLLABORATE
Listen attentively, restate, and record your partner's ideas.

Language to RESTATE
So your opinion is that _____.

Yes, that's correct.

No, not exactly. What I (stated/reported) was _____.

Classmate's Name	Ideas
	1.
	2.

Text 3 • Poem

SPEAKING AND WRITING

Ten-Minute Response

A **ten-minute response** begins with a well-stated **claim**, followed by **two detail sentences** that elaborate with relevant examples and precise words.

Language to AGREE/DISAGREE

I (agree/disagree) with _____'s opinion.

🎤 PRESENT IDEAS

Listen attentively and take notes. Then write whether you agree (+) or disagree (–).

Classmate's Name	Idea	+/–

✏️ ELABORATE IN WRITING

Work with the teacher to write a ten-minute response.

Language to COLLABORATE

What should we write?

We could put _____. What do you think works well?

We could also write _____.

Language influences our identity because it determines which people are in our social circle. For example, Spanish speakers often shop at stores where _____ _____ speak the same _____. As a result, people who speak the same language often live _____ _____ and form _____. Rhina P. Espaillat explores this in her poem "Bilingual/Bilingüe" when she writes that keeping English and Spanish separate could _____ _____.

Work with a partner to write a ten-minute response.

Language influences our identity because it influences _____ _____ For example, when families immigrate to a new country, the children often _____. As a result, different language abilities in a family can cause _____ _____. Rhina P. Espaillat explores this in her poem "Bilingual/Bilingüe" when she discusses _____ _____.

Learning Languages **73**

Presenting Ideas

Take a Stand

Debate | Should studying a new language be a graduation requirement?

COLLABORATE
Read the debate question about new languages. Then take turns using a frame to respond with your initial reaction.

Language to RESPOND

So _____, what's your initial reaction?

My initial reaction is _____.

My initial reaction is (similar to/different from) _____'s.

ANALYZE SOURCES
Read a quote that either supports or opposes the debate topic. Then paraphrase.

Quote	Paraphrase
Model: "World language classes foster abilities such as memorization and critical thinking that can improve academic performance in other subjects" (Damschen 23).	In other words, _____ a new language can benefit students in other classes because it helps them _____ and _____
1. "A study of 1,100 U.S. colleges and universities found that only 12% require intermediate-level language proficiency in a language other than English" (Center for Language Teaching Advancement 20).	In other words, a _____ of _____ do not require language study for _____
2. "Prestigious schools often have more stringent requirements. Stanford, for example, requires three or more years of a world language. Princeton expects four, while only requiring two years of both history and science" (Damschen 22).	This quote clarifies that the best universities _____ students to _____ while in _____
3. "Bryan Andrews, a senior studying French at Northridge, says, 'It's really hard because there are so many different verbs you have to learn. You have to have a lot of memorization skills and learn a lot of new concepts'" (Damschen 23).	In other words, to _____ a new language, students must be able to _____ a lot of material, which may be very _____
4 "Bilingualism can very well translate to better job opportunities and better pay. In some career paths, fluency in more than one language is an absolute requirement" (Pinantoan 25).	This quote clarifies that becoming _____ in a new language can _____ students by helping them obtain _____

Debate Ideas

SYNTHESIZE IDEAS

Write a response to the debate question, including a paraphrase of a text quote and elaboration on the quote.

Claim: My position is that a new language (should/should not) _____ be a graduation requirement.

Transitional Statement: I have (one key reason/a compelling reason) _____ _____ for taking this stance.

Quote Paraphrase: (According to _____,/The author points out _____.)

_____
_____
_____

Quote Elaboration: (As a result, _____./Consequently, _____.)

_____
_____
_____

PRESENT EVIDENCE

Using a Public Voice

When presenting ideas during class or in a meeting, use your **public voice**. Speak two times slower and three times louder than when you interact socially to make sure your audience grasps your key points.

LISTEN AND TAKE NOTES

Listen attentively and take notes. Then indicate whether you agree (+) or disagree (–).

Language to AFFIRM AND CLARIFY
That's an interesting claim.
I have a question about _____.

Classmate's Name	Idea	+/–

Learning Languages 75

Academic Writing
ANALYZING TEXT ELEMENTS

Student Writing Model

Academic Writing Type

A **justification** states a claim and supports it with logical reasons and relevant evidence from texts.

A. The **topic sentence** clearly states the writer's claim about the issue.
B. **Detail sentences** support the claim with reasons and evidence from texts.
C. The **concluding sentence** restates the writer's claim about the issue.

ANALYZE TEXT
Read this student model to analyze the elements of a justification.

A
Evidence from the texts supports the position that a second language should not be a requirement for graduation. One reason is that retaining the information necessary to learn a second language is difficult for some students. Kalli Damschen points out in "Many Benefits Come With Learning a World Language" that Bryan Andrews struggled to learn French verbs (23). This evidence makes it quite clear

B
that students with less developed linguistic skills may risk losing valuable points from their GPAs. An additional reason is that such a strict requirement is unnecessary. According to the Center for Language Teaching Advancement, only 12% of colleges require language proficiency in a second language. This is significant because most universities do not require language study and pursuing other interests can make applicants competitive. For these reasons, schools should not require students to

C
study a world language to earn a diploma.

MARK AND DISCUSS ELEMENTS
Mark the justification elements and use the frames to discuss them with your partner.

1. **Circle the writer's claim within the topic sentence.** *The writer's claim is* _____.

2. **Draw a box around four transition words or phrases.**
   One transition (word/phrase) is _____.

3. **Underline and label two reasons that support the writer's claim with the letter *R*.**
   One reason that supports the writer's claim is _____.

4. **Underline and label two pieces of evidence that support the writer's claim with the letter *E*.**
   One piece of evidence that supports the writer's claim is _____.

5. **Star four precise topic words and check four high-utility academic words.**
   An example of a (precise topic word/high-utility academic word) is _____.

76 Issue 2

Justification
FRONTLOADING LANGUAGE

Paraphrasing Text

Guidelines for Paraphrasing a Sentence
Paraphrase one sentence from a source text by keeping important topic words and replacing key words and phrases with synonyms.

Source Text	Key Words and Phrases	→	Synonyms	Paraphrasing
"There are hundreds of thousands of people who don't know English, making the ability to speak and write a different language a valuable commodity in many careers" (Damschen 22).	hundreds of thousands	→	countless	Countless people cannot communicate in English, so being bilingual is a highly beneficial skill to have in numerous careers.
	don't know	→	cannot communicate in	
	ability to speak and and write a different language	→	being bilingual	
	valuable commodity	→	highly beneficial skill	
	many	→	numerous	

IDENTIFY PRECISE SYNONYMS
Read these statements and replace the words in parentheses with synonyms.

1. Studying a world language is (a requirement) _____ in some schools in the United States.

2. (The ability to speak two languages) _____ can be very helpful in any job that deals with people, particularly in careers that have (an international) _____ focus.

3. In fact, various (experiments) _____ since then have shown that the study of world languages is linked to various (cognitive advantages.) _____
_____

PARAPHRASE IDEAS
Paraphrase the three statements above using primarily your own words.

1. Pinantoan points out that _____
_____
_____

2. According to "Many Benefits Come With Learning a World Language," _____
_____
_____

3. Pinantoan also explains that _____
_____

Learning Languages 77

Academic Writing

FRONTLOADING CONVENTIONS

Regular Past-Tense Verbs

Guidelines for Using Regular Past-Tense Verbs

A **regular past-tense verb** tells about an action that already happened. Regular past-tense verbs end in *–ed*.

Use regular past-tense verbs in your justification to describe relevant evidence from your experience.

> I **watched** a documentary that **explained** the benefits of studying world languages.
>
> I **completed** the language course with a barely passing grade.
>
> My brother **studied** two languages in high school, and three colleges **admitted** him.

IDENTIFY PAST-TENSE VERBS

Read the justification and circle the regular past-tense verbs.

> Evidence from the texts supports the claim that schools should make learning a new language a requirement to graduate. One reason is that it would improve graduates' job opportunities. Andrianes Pinantoan points out in "The Effects of a Second Language on the Brain" that some careers require bilingualism (25). For example, my sister was not qualified for some positions because she never studied Spanish, so the employers hired other candidates. An additional reason is that speaking another language allows teens to fully engage with people from other parts of the world. According to Kalli Damschen's article "Many Benefits Come With Learning a World Language," knowing another language helps people understand other cultures (24). In my own experience, when I visited Mexico after learning Spanish, I experienced the culture and the people in a different way. For these reasons, world language study should be required for graduating from high school.

WRITE PAST-TENSE VERBS

Complete the sentences with the past tense of the regular verbs in parentheses.

1. Last year, I _____ to learn Arabic because I want to have an international job someday. (try)

2. At first, I found the classes extremely difficult, and I _____ that I would never learn the language. (believe)

3. However, soon I _____ almost everything. (comprehend)

4. By the end of the course, I _____ that I could even make jokes in Arabic. (realize)

5. Last week, I _____ to find out about an internship at a company with offices in Qatar. (call)

78 Issue 2

Organize a Justification

Prompt: Should studying a new language be a graduation requirement? Write a justification that states and supports your claim.

IDENTIFY TEXT EVIDENCE

Review the texts to identify evidence that supports each reason.

Reason	Text Evidence
Students should have time to pursue other subjects, such as technology and the arts.	
Learning a new language can make teens better equipped to work in a global economy.	

PLAN REASONS AND EVIDENCE

Use academic language to clearly state your claim as a topic sentence.

Evidence from the texts supports the idea that _____

_____

List two reasons that support your claim and give text evidence for each reason.

Reason 1: _____

_____

_____

Evidence: _____

_____

_____

Reason 2: _____

_____

_____

Evidence: _____

_____

_____

Restate your claim as a concluding sentence.

For these reasons, _____

_____

Academic Writing
WRITING A DRAFT

Write a Justification

Prompt: Should studying a new language be a graduation requirement? Write a justification that states and supports your claim.

✏️ WRITE A PARAGRAPH
Use the frame to write your topic sentence, detail sentences, and concluding sentence.

A
Evidence from the texts supports the (idea/position/premise)
_____ that _____
                                                            (claim)
_____
_____

B
One reason is that _____
                    (1st reason that supports the claim)
_____
_____
_____

_____ points out in _____
(Author's)   (Title of Source)
_____
that _____
    (text evidence)
_____

This (evidence/data) _____ makes it quite clear that _____
(elaborate on evidence)
_____
_____

An additional reason is that _____
                            (2nd reason that supports the claim)
_____
_____

According to _____
           (Source)
_____
_____
(text evidence)

This is significant because _____
                       (elaborate on the evidence)
_____
_____

C
For these reasons, _____
                (restate the claim)
_____
_____

Justification
ASSESSING AND REVISING

Rate Your Justification

Scoring Guide
1	Insufficient
2	Developing
3	Sufficient
4	Exemplary

ASSESS YOUR DRAFT
Rate your justification. Then have a partner rate it.

1. Does the topic sentence clearly state your claim?	Self	1	2	3	4
	Partner	1	2	3	4
2. Did you include strong reasons to support your claim?	Self	1	2	3	4
	Partner	1	2	3	4
3. Did you provide strong text evidence to support your claim?	Self	1	2	3	4
	Partner	1	2	3	4
4. Did you use transitions to introduce reasons and evidence?	Self	1	2	3	4
	Partner	1	2	3	4
5. Did you include precise topic words and high-utility academic words?	Self	1	2	3	4
	Partner	1	2	3	4
6. Does the concluding sentence restate your claim using new wording?	Self	1	2	3	4
	Partner	1	2	3	4

REFLECT AND REVISE
Record specific priorities and suggestions to help you and your partner revise.

(Partner) Positive Feedback: You did an effective job of (organizing/including/stating) _____

_____

(Partner) Suggestion: Your justification would be stronger if you _____

_____

(Self) Priority 1: I will revise my justification so that it _____

_____

(Self) Priority 2: I also need to _____

_____

CHECK AND EDIT
Use this checklist to proofread and edit your justification.

- ☐ Did you capitalize proper nouns, such as authors' names?
- ☐ Did you cite sources using parentheses?
- ☐ Is each sentence complete?
- ☐ Are all words spelled correctly?

Presenting Ideas

60-Second Speech

IDENTIFY TOPIC
Choose one of the questions below to address in a 60-second speech.

☐ Should our school change its start time?

☐ Should our school make any changes to its world language program?

BRAINSTORM IDEAS
Write your claim and two reasons that support it.

My Claim: _____

Reason 1: _____

Reason 2: _____

SYNTHESIZE IDEAS
Take notes on supporting evidence and a counterclaim.

Evidence 1: _____

_____

Evidence 2: _____

_____

Counterclaim: _____

_____

Response: _____

_____

WRITE A SPEECH
Write a 60-second speech that states your claim and includes reasons, evidence, and a counterclaim.

I believe that _____

_____

One reason I maintain this position is that _____

_____

Secondly, _____

_____

To illustrate, _____

_____

The opposition might claim that _____

_____

However, _____

_____

For these reasons, I _____ that _____

_____

Present and Rate Your Speech

Using a Public Voice
When presenting ideas during class or in a meeting, use your **public voice**. Speak two times slower and three times louder than when you interact socially to make sure your audience grasps your key points.

PRESENT YOUR SPEECH
Present your speech to the small group. Make sure to use a public voice.

LISTEN AND TAKE NOTES

Language to AFFIRM AND CLARIFY
That's an interesting claim.
I have a question about _____.

Listen attentively and take notes. Then indicate whether you agree (+) or disagree (–).

Classmate's Name	Idea	+/–

ASSESS YOUR SPEECH

Scoring Guide
| 1 | Insufficient | 3 | Sufficient |
| 2 | Developing | 4 | Exemplary |

Use the Scoring Guide to rate your speech.

1. Did your topic sentence clearly state your claim?	1	2	3	4
2. Did you include strong reasons and evidence to support your speech?	1	2	3	4
3. Did you include precise topic words?	1	2	3	4
4. Were you easy to understand?	1	2	3	4
5. Did you use a public voice?	1	2	3	4

REFLECT
Write two ways you can improve for your next speech.

Priority 1: I can improve my next speech by _____

_____

_____

Priority 2: When I present my next speech, I will focus on _____

_____

_____

Issue 3 Behind the Wheel

Are teens old enough to get behind the wheel?

📖 BUILD KNOWLEDGE
Read and respond to the Data File (*Issues*, p. 34).

💡 BRAINSTORM IDEAS
Write a brief list of the pros and cons of allowing teens to drive.

- pro: get around on their own
- _____
- _____
- _____

🎤 PRESENT IDEAS
Use the frames to discuss ideas with your group. Listen attentively and record the strongest ideas to complete the T-chart.

- I know teen drivers who _____ (**present-tense verb:** give)
- Allowing teens to drive means they (may/may not) _____ (**base verb:** help)
- Teen drivers might also _____ (**base verb:** enjoy)
- Additionally, some teen drivers like to _____ (**base verb:** talk)

Language to FACILITATE DISCUSSION
So _____, what's your perspective?
_____, what example did you come up with?

PROS	CONS
• get around on their own	• fill car with too many people
•	•
•	•
•	•

Words to Know

BUILD WORD KNOWLEDGE

Rate your word knowledge. Then discuss word meanings and examples with your group.

① Don't Know ② Recognize ③ Familiar ④ Know

Word to Know	Meaning	Example
1 distraction noun ① ② ③ ④	something that takes your _____ away from what you are doing	In order to avoid **distractions**, I usually do my homework _____
2 experienced adjective ① ② ③ ④	having _____ because you have done something for a long time	After years of _____ I have become an **experienced** _____
3 risk noun ① ② ③ ④	the chance that something _____ may happen; something likely to cause _____	I never _____ because the **risk** of _____ is too great.
4 ban verb ① ② ③ ④	to not _____ something to be done, seen, or used	Our principal wants to **ban** students from _____ because it leads to _____
1 impulsive adjective ① ② ③ ④	acting _____ thinking about the possible results or dangers	I have plans for my future, so I would never be so **impulsive** as to _____
2 supervision noun ① ② ③ ④	the act of watching over an activity or person to make sure things are done _____	My little brother needs a lot of **supervision**, so my parents often _____
3 impose verb ① ② ③ ④	to _____ people to accept a rule, punishment, or tax	After I _____ my parents **imposed** a rule that I had to _____
4 inconvenience noun ① ② ③ ④	a _____ caused by someone or something, which affects or annoys you	_____ may seem like an **inconvenience**, but it is a responsible thing to do.

Building Concepts and Language

SPEAKING AND LISTENING

Academic Discussion

What are some distractions that prevent drivers from being safe?

BRAINSTORM IDEAS
Briefly record at least two ideas in each column using everyday English.

Technologies	Activities
• checking GPS	• eating or snacking
•	•
•	•

ANALYZE WORDS
Complete the chart with precise words to discuss and write about the topic.

Everyday	Precise
answer *(verb)*	reply,
look *(verb)*	examine,
many *(adjective)*	abundance,

MAKE A CLAIM
Rewrite two ideas using the frames and precise words. Then prepare to elaborate verbally.

Language to ELABORATE
In particular, _____.
I have noticed that _____.

1. **Frame:** One distraction that prevents drivers from being safe is _____ (**verb + –ing**: texting friends, listening to music, putting on makeup).

   Response: _____

2. **Frame:** Based on my experience, _____ (**noun phrase:** incoming text messages, phone calls, loud passengers) may distract drivers and prevent them from being safe.

   Response: _____

COLLABORATE
Listen attentively, restate, and record your partner's ideas.

Language to RESTATE
So your perspective is that _____.
Yes, that's correct.
No, not quite. What I (reported/expressed) is that _____.

Classmate's Name	Ideas
	1.
	2.

SPEAKING AND WRITING

Ten-Minute Response

A **ten-minute response** begins with a well-stated **claim** followed by **two detail sentences** that elaborate with relevant examples and precise words.

Language to AGREE/DISAGREE

I completely (agree/disagree) with _____'s perspective.

🎤 **PRESENT IDEAS**

Listen attentively and take notes. Then indicate whether you agree (+) or disagree (−).

Classmate's Name	Idea	+/−

✏️ **ELABORATE IN WRITING**

Work with the teacher to write a ten-minute response.

Language to COLLABORATE

What should we write?

We could choose _____. What do you think fits well?

Another option is _____.

　　One distraction that prevents drivers from being safe is having a serious or intense discussion with a passenger. For example, at a particularly sensitive point in the conversation, the driver may have the _____ to glance at the passenger. As a result, the driver _____ not _____ what is happening on the _____.

Work with a partner to write a ten-minute response.

　　One distraction that prevents drivers from being safe is responding to _____ _____ For example, in order to _____ to a _____ the driver not only has to _____ but also has to _____

As a result, the driver's eyes are not _____

and has only one hand _____

_____

Behind the Wheel **87**

Analyzing and Discussing Text
ACADEMIC VOCABULARY

Words to Go

BUILD WORD KNOWLEDGE
Complete the meanings and examples for these high-utility academic words.

Word to Go	Meaning	Example
restriction re•stric•tion *noun*	a rule or law that _____ what you can do or what can happen	My parents put a **restriction** on _____ _____
restricted re•strict•ed *adjective*	limited or _____	Most students have **restricted** access to _____ at school.

DISCUSS AND WRITE EXAMPLES
Discuss your response with a partner. Then complete the sentence in writing.

Most amusement park rides have **restrictions**, limiting _____
_____ and requiring _____

Write your response and read it aloud to a partner.

The sidewalk outside our apartment has a _____ amount of space, so we go to the park when we want to _____

BUILD WORD KNOWLEDGE
Complete the meaning and examples for this high-utility academic word.

Word to Go	Meaning	Example
alternative al•ter•na•tive *noun*	something you can choose _____ _____ something else	As an **alternative** to _____ _____ I chose to _____ If you want to have a snack, a healthy **alternative** is _____ _____

DISCUSS AND WRITE EXAMPLES
Discuss your response with a partner. Then complete the sentence in writing.

As an **alternative** to watching TV, sometimes I _____
_____

Write your response and read it aloud to a partner.

Reusable and biodegradable bags are good _____ to using _____

88 Issue 3

Text ① • Magazine Article
RESPONDING TO TEXT

Close Reading

BUILD FLUENCY
Read the text "DN'T TXT N DRV" (*Issues*, pp. 35–38).

IDENTIFY KEY IDEAS AND DETAILS
Take turns asking and answering questions **with a partner. Then write brief notes.**

Discussion Frames	Text Notes
Q: What is the author's **main idea**? **A:** The author's **main idea** is _____.	• texting and driving _____ not worth the _____
Q: What are the **key details** in this text? **A:** (One/Another) **key detail** in this text is _____.	• distracted driving causes high _____ of crashes • many states _____ the use of phones while driving • teens _____ taking steps to _____ accidents

RESPOND WITH EVIDENCE
Use the frame and evidence from the **text to construct a formal written response.**

1. According to the author, how does texting **compare to other driver distractions**?

   According to the author, texting is _____

   than _____ because

   _____ while texting.

Use the frame to analyze the structure the **author uses to organize the text.**

2. What is the effect of the bulleted text in the section "Why Phones and Driving Don't Mix"?

   The bulleted text in the section "Why Phones **and Driving Don't Mix" has the effect of**

   _____

   _____

   The bulleted text accomplishes this effect **because it includes** _____

   _____

IDENTIFY PRECISE WORDS
Review Text 1 and your *Portfolio* (pp. 84–89) **to identify words for your writing.**

Topic Words	High-Utility Academic Words
• fatal accidents	• concentrate
•	•
•	•

Behind the Wheel **89**

Building Concepts and Language

SPEAKING AND LISTENING

Academic Discussion

What is an alternative to distracted driving?

BRAINSTORM IDEAS
Briefly record at least two ideas in each column using everyday English.

Drivers	Passengers
• use talking GPS	• don't argue with driver
•	•
•	•

ANALYZE WORDS
Complete the chart with precise words to discuss and write about the issue.

Everyday	Precise
pay attention (verb)	focus,
careless (adjective)	distracted,
ask (verb)	solicit,

MAKE A CLAIM
Rewrite two ideas using the frames and precise words. Then prepare to elaborate verbally.

Language to ELABORATE
In particular, _____.
I have noticed that _____.

1. **Frame:** An alternative to _____ (verb + –ing: texting, eating, arguing) while driving is _____ (verb + –ing: turning off your cell phone, eating before leaving home, waiting until you arrive)

   Response: _____

2. **Frame:** As an alternative to _____ (verb + –ing: texting, making calls, searching for), drivers can _____ (verb phrase: ask a passenger, pull over to the side)

   Response: _____

COLLABORATE
Listen attentively, restate, and record your partner's ideas.

Language to RESTATE
So your perspective is that _____.
Yes, that's correct.
No, not quite. What I (reported/expressed) was _____.

Classmate's Name	Ideas
	1.
	2.

SPEAKING AND WRITING

Ten-Minute Response

A **ten-minute response** begins with a well-stated **claim** followed by **two detail sentences** that elaborate with relevant examples and precise words.

> **Language to AGREE/DISAGREE**
>
> I completely (agree/disagree) with _____'s perspective.

🎙️ **PRESENT IDEAS**

Listen attentively and take notes. Then indicate whether you agree (+) or disagree (−).

Classmate's Name	Idea	+/−

✏️ **ELABORATE IN WRITING**

Work with the teacher to write a ten-minute response.

> **Language to COLLABORATE**
>
> What should we write?
>
> We could choose _____. What do you think fits well?
>
> Another option is _____.

An alternative to eating while driving is stopping at a restaurant to have a meal. For example, eating while driving _____ requires the driver to _____ on the food and not making a mess, instead of _____ on the road. As a result, the driver may be too _____ to notice potential _____.

Work with a partner to write a ten-minute response.

As an alternative to placing a phone call while driving, drivers can _____
_____

For example, if you need to call _____
to inform them _____
you can hand the phone to _____ and request that
_____

As a result, your important _____
will still be delivered, and you will have reduced the risk of _____
_____

Behind the Wheel 91

Analyzing and Discussing Text
ACADEMIC VOCABULARY

Words to Go

BUILD WORD KNOWLEDGE
Complete the meanings and examples for these high-utility academic words.

Word to Go	Meaning	Example
mature ma•ture *adjective*	fully _____ or _____; to act _____ than your age	My brother's body is **mature**, which puts him at an advantage when _____ _____
immature im•ma•ture *adjective*	_____ grown or developed; to act _____ than your age	I'm only a freshman, so my plans for _____ _____ are still **immature**.

DISCUSS AND WRITE EXAMPLES
Discuss your response with a partner. Then complete the sentence in writing.

My little cousin made a **mature** decision when she chose to save her money instead of

_____

Write your response and read it aloud to a partner.

Even though my older brother is intelligent, he often makes _____

jokes when _____

BUILD WORD KNOWLEDGE
Complete the meaning and examples for this high-utility academic word.

Word to Go	Meaning	Examples
conduct con•duct *verb*	to _____ an activity or process, especially to get _____ or prove facts	As a reporter for the school paper, I got to **conduct** an interview with _____ The student council **conducted** a survey on _____

DISCUSS AND WRITE EXAMPLES
Discuss your response with a partner. Then complete the sentence in writing.

I strongly contend that scientists should not **conduct** experiments that _____

_____

Write your response and read it aloud to a partner.

Last year, my friends and I _____ a poll to find out _____

_____

Text ❷ • Section ❶ • News Article

SUMMARIZING TEXT

Section Shrink

📖 BUILD FLUENCY
Read the introduction and Section 1 of "Is 16 Too Young to Drive a Car?" (*Issues*, pp. 39–42).

💬 IDENTIFY KEY IDEAS AND DETAILS
Take turns asking and answering questions with a partner. Then write brief notes.

Discussion Frames	Text Notes
Q: What is this section **mainly about**? **A:** This section is **mainly about** _____.	• 16-year-old drivers are considered _____
Q: What are the **key details** in this section? **A:** (One/Another) **key detail** in this section is _____. **A:** Perhaps the **most important key detail** in this section is _____.	• part of brain that weighs risks, makes judgments, and controls impulses is _____ in teens • most American adults favor raising the _____ ; so far only _____ imposed • 16-year-olds involved in five times more fatal _____

✏️ SUMMARIZE
"Shrink" Section 1 of the text by writing a summary in 40 or fewer words.

CLASS SUMMARY: **WORD COUNT:** _____

Studies show that a critical part of 16-year-olds' brains is _____

explaining why teens cause more fatal accidents than _____

_____ and justifying driving _____

and the majority opinion that _____

PARTNER SUMMARY: **WORD COUNT:** _____

Studies prove that the brains of 16-year-olds are _____

clarifying why teen drivers cause _____ than

older drivers, and warranting enforced _____ and the claim of most

Americans that teens should be older before they _____

🔍 IDENTIFY PRECISE WORDS
Review Section 1 and your *Portfolio* (pp. 90–93) to identify words for your writing.

Topic Words	High-Utility Academic Words
• impulsive behavior • •	• vital • •

Behind the Wheel **93**

Analyzing and Discussing Text
ACADEMIC VOCABULARY

Words to Go

BUILD WORD KNOWLEDGE
Complete the meanings and examples for this high-utility academic word.

Word to Go	Meanings	Examples
involve in•volve *verb*	to be a _____ or a result of an activity or situation; to _____ something	I was _____ when I learned that my science class **involved** _____ Preparing for our high school play **involved** _____

DISCUSS AND WRITE EXAMPLES
Discuss your response with a partner. Then complete the sentence in writing.

Our school's day of community service **involved** _____

_____

Write your response and read it aloud to a partner.

When my parents decided to get a dog, my sister and I were _____

in _____

BUILD WORD KNOWLEDGE
Complete the meaning and examples for this high-utility academic word.

Word to Go	Meaning	Examples
acknowledge ac•know•ledge *verb*	to _____ _____ the truth about something	After I lost my keys again, I had to **acknowledge** that _____ My competitive sister finally **acknowledged** that _____

DISCUSS AND WRITE EXAMPLES
Discuss your response with a partner. Then complete the sentence in writing.

School administrators were forced to **acknowledge** that _____

was a serious problem when some students _____

_____

Write your response and read it aloud to a partner.

Many teens are _____ that they need to _____

_____ if they want to go to college.

Text ❷ • Section ❷ • News Article

SUMMARIZING TEXT

Section Shrink

📖 BUILD FLUENCY
Read Section 2 of "Is 16 Too Young to Drive a Car?" (*Issues*, pp. 42–45).

💬 IDENTIFY KEY IDEAS AND DETAILS
Take turns asking and answering questions with a partner. Then write brief notes.

Discussion Frames	Text Notes
Q: What is this section **mainly about**? **A:** This section is **mainly about** _____.	• laws and brain _____ related to _____
Q: What are the **key details** in this section? **A:** (One/Another) **key detail** in this section is _____. **A:** Perhaps the **most important key detail** in this section is _____.	• lawmakers concerned with _____ • fatal crashes often caused by _____ not lack of _____ • critical part of _____ underdeveloped until _____

✏️ SUMMARIZE
"Shrink" Section 2 of the text by writing a summary in 40 or fewer words.

CLASS SUMMARY: **WORD COUNT:** _____

Lawmakers, who are more concerned with _____ parents

than with reducing _____ won't change driving-age laws

even though researchers acknowledge that _____

occur because the _____

that thinks about consequences doesn't mature until age 25.

PARTNER SUMMARY: **WORD COUNT:** _____

Lawmakers, who are more worried about troubling parents than the safety of _____

_____ refuse to raise the _____ despite

research proving that young drivers have a lack of _____

_____ in the part of the brain that _____

_____

🔍 IDENTIFY PRECISE WORDS
Review Section 2 and your *Portfolio* (pp. 94–95) to identify words for your writing.

Topic Words	High-Utility Academic Words
• legislators • •	• encounter • •

Behind the Wheel **95**

Analyzing and Discussing Text
ACADEMIC VOCABULARY

Words to Go

📖 BUILD WORD KNOWLEDGE
Complete the meanings and examples for these high-utility academic words.

Word to Go	Meaning	Example
enforce en•force *verb*	to make sure that a law or rule is _____	School security guards **enforce** the rules about _____
enforcement en•force•ment *noun*	the act of making people obey a _____	The strict **enforcement** of the school dress code means I _____

💬 DISCUSS AND WRITE EXAMPLES
Discuss your response with a partner. Then complete the sentence in writing.

Many schools are **enforcing** rules against _____

by conducting random _____

Write your response and read it aloud to a partner.

The _____ of laws against _____

has helped to _____

📖 BUILD WORD KNOWLEDGE
Complete the meanings and examples for these high-utility academic words.

Word to Go	Meaning	Example
advocate ad•vo•cate *noun*	a person who publicly _____ an idea or plan	Now that I know about _____ I plan to become an **advocate** for _____
advocate ad•vo•cate *verb*	to support or _____ an idea or plan	Why do you **advocate** _____

💬 DISCUSS AND WRITE EXAMPLES
Discuss your response with a partner. Then complete the sentence in writing.

This year, the school administration **has heard** from several **advocates** for

_____

Write your response and read it aloud to a partner.

A group of students is _____ for _____

_____ for all of the school sports teams.

Text ❷ • Section ❸ • News Article

SUMMARIZING TEXT

Section Shrink

📖 BUILD FLUENCY
Read Section 3 of "Is 16 Too Young to Drive a Car?" (*Issues*, pp. 45–47).

💬 IDENTIFY KEY IDEAS AND DETAILS
Take turns asking and answering questions with a partner. Then write brief notes.

Discussion Frames	Text Notes
Q: What is this section **mainly about**? **A:** This section is **mainly about** _____.	• efforts to understand the _____ and make _____
Q: What are the **key details** in this section? **A:** (One/Another) **key detail** in this section is _____. **A:** Perhaps the **most important key detail** in this section is _____.	• hormones can cause teens to make _____ decisions • "graduated licensing" rules restrict _____ _____ but parents may not _____ • safety _____ say more brain research and public support necessary to get _____ to change laws

✏️ SUMMARIZE
"Shrink" Section 3 of the text by writing a summary in 40 or fewer words.

CLASS SUMMARY: **WORD COUNT:** _____

Teen drivers have difficulty making _____ due to _____ and brain development, which has led to legal restrictions on how and when teens _____ and safety advocates calling for _____

PARTNER SUMMARY: **WORD COUNT:** _____

The struggle that teen drivers have controlling their _____ is fueled by hormones and _____ and has resulted in some _____ being placed on them; but safety experts want additional _____ conducted and support for _____

🔍 IDENTIFY PRECISE WORDS
Review Section 3 and your *Portfolio* (pp. 96–97) to identify words for your writing.

Topic Words	High-Utility Academic Words
• thrill-seeking • •	• in theory • •

Behind the Wheel **97**

Academic Writing
ANALYZING TEXT ELEMENTS

Student Writing Model

Academic Writing Type

A **formal written summary** provides an objective overview of the topic and important details from an informational text. The writer credits the author, but writes in primarily their own words, without including personal opinions.

A. The **topic sentence** includes the text type, title, author, and topic.

B. **Detail sentences** include the important details from the summarized text.

C. The **concluding sentence** restates the author's conclusion in the writer's own words.

ANALYZE TEXT

Read this student model to analyze the elements of a formal summary.

A In the magazine article titled "DN'T TXT N DRV," Nancy Mann Jackson explores facts about texting while driving and its potentially fatal consequences.

B To begin with, Jackson points out that 1.6 million vehicle crashes every year are due to texting or speaking on a phone, with high percentages of 16- and 17-year-old drivers admitting to both practices. The author also explains that texting is the most hazardous distraction drivers face because it requires them to take their focus off the road for longer than other distractions, such as eating or changing the radio station. In addition, she reports that lawmakers have responded to the increase in fatal accidents caused by teens by banning the use of smartphones while driving. Furthermore, the author describes how some teens are avoiding distractions by shutting off their phones or informing people of their unavailability before getting behind the wheel.

C Finally, Jackson concludes that teens can advocate for safety by speaking up when friends attempt to text and drive.

MARK AND DISCUSS ELEMENTS

Mark the summary elements and use the frames to discuss them with your partner.

1. **Number (1–4) the four elements of the topic sentence.**
   The topic sentence includes the _____.

2. **Draw a box around four transition words or phrases.**
   One transition (word/phrase) is _____.

3. **Underline four important details.** One important detail in this summary is _____.

4. **Circle four citation verbs.** One citation verb that the writer uses is _____.

5. **Star four precise topic words and check four high-utility academic words.**
   An example of a (precise topic word/high-utility academic word) is _____.

Formal Summary
PLANNING TO WRITE

Organize a Formal Summary

Prompt Write a formal summary of "Is 16 Too Young to Drive a Car?"

Guidelines for Paraphrasing Multiple Sentences
Paraphrase related details from a source text by combining key information into one sentence. Replace key words and phrases with synonyms and keep important topic words.

Text Detail 1	Text Detail 2	Text Detail 3
"A crucial part of the teen's brain—the area that peers ahead and considers consequences—remains undeveloped" (Davis 29).	"... careless attitudes and rash emotions often drive teen decisions, says Jay Giedd, chief of brain imaging in the child psychiatric unit ..." (Davis 29).	"... that part of the brain involved in decision-making and controlling impulses is among the latest to come on board" (Davis 30).

✏️ PARAPHRASE IDEAS
Combine key information from the three text details above into one detail sentence.

Teen driver errors are linked to underdevelopment in the part of the brain that

(text detail 1) _____

(text detail 2) _____ and

(text detail 3) _____

📄 PLAN KEY IDEAS AND DETAILS
State the text information to write a topic sentence.

In the news article titled (Title) _____

(Author's Full Name) _____ (citation verb: investigates, explains)

_____ (topic) _____

_____

List four important details from the article using primarily your own words.

1. _____
   _____

2. _____
   _____

3. _____
   _____

4. _____
   _____

Restate the author's conclusion in your own words.

_____
_____

Academic Writing

WRITING A DRAFT

Write a Formal Summary

Prompt Write a formal summary of "Is 16 Too Young to Drive a Car?"

✎ WRITE A PARAGRAPH
Use the frame to write your topic sentence, detail sentences, and concluding sentence.

A

In the news article titled _____
(Title)

_____ _____
(Author's Full Name)

_____
(topic)
_____

B

_____ _____ _____
(Transition)   (Author's Last Name)   (citation verb)

(1st important detail)
_____
_____
_____

The (author/writer) _____ also _____
                                                  (citation verb)

(2nd important detail)
_____
_____
_____

_____ (pronoun) _____ _____
(Transition)   (citation verb)

(3rd important detail)
_____
_____
_____

_____ the (author/writer) _____
(Transition)

_____ _____
(citation verb) (4th important detail)
_____
_____
_____

C

_____ _____ _____ concludes that
(Transition)   (Author's Last Name)

(restate author's conclusion)
_____
_____

100 Issue 3

Formal Summary
ASSESSING AND REVISING

Rate Your Summary

Scoring Guide	
1	Insufficient
2	Developing
3	Sufficient
4	Exemplary

ASSESS YOUR DRAFT
Rate your formal summary. Then have a partner rate it.

1. Does the topic sentence state the title, author, and topic?	Self	1	2	3	4
	Partner	1	2	3	4
2. Did you paraphrase the most important details from the text?	Self	1	2	3	4
	Partner	1	2	3	4
3. Did you use citation verbs to credit the author?	Self	1	2	3	4
	Partner	1	2	3	4
4. Did you use transitions to introduce and sequence details?	Self	1	2	3	4
	Partner	1	2	3	4
5. Did you include precise topic words and high-utility academic words?	Self	1	2	3	4
	Partner	1	2	3	4
6. Did you restate the author's conclusion using your own words?	Self	1	2	3	4
	Partner	1	2	3	4

REFLECT AND REVISE
Record specific priorities and suggestions to help you and your partner revise.

(Partner) Positive Feedback: I appreciate how you (used/included) _____

_____

(Partner) Suggestion: As you revise your summary, focus on _____

_____

(Self) Priority 1: My summary paragraph needs _____

_____

(Self) Priority 2: I plan to improve my summary by _____

_____

CHECK AND EDIT
Use this checklist to proofread and edit your summary.

- [ ] Did you capitalize the title of the article and proper nouns?
- [ ] Did you put quotation marks around the title of the article?
- [ ] Did you use commas appropriately after transitions?
- [ ] Do simple present-tense verbs end in –s?
- [ ] Is each sentence complete?
- [ ] Are all words spelled correctly?

Behind the Wheel

Building Concepts and Language

SPEAKING AND LISTENING

Academic Discussion

What are the reasons why adolescent drivers are at a higher risk for car accidents?

BRAINSTORM IDEAS
Briefly record at least two ideas in each column using everyday English.

Biological Reasons	Environmental Reasons
• brain development	• not enough practice
•	•
•	•

ANALYZE WORDS
Complete the chart with precise words to discuss and write about the topic.

Everyday	Precise
very *(adverb)*	exceptionally,
fast *(adjective)*	abruptly,
well *(adverb)*	adequately,

MAKE A CLAIM
Rewrite two ideas using the frames and precise words. Then prepare to elaborate verbally.

Language to ELABORATE
In particular, _____.
I have noticed that _____.

1. **Frame:** One (biological/environmental) reason why adolescent drivers are at higher risk for car accidents is that they _____ (**verb phrase:** don't have experience, are immature, lack driving skills)

   Response: _____
   _____

2. **Frame:** Due to _____ (**noun phrase:** brain development, distracted driving, impulsive behavior), adolescent drivers are at higher risk for car accidents.

   Response: _____
   _____

COLLABORATE
Listen attentively, restate, and record your partner's ideas.

Language to RESTATE
So your perspective is that _____.
Yes, that's correct.
No, not quite. What I (reported/expressed) was _____.

Classmate's Name	Ideas
	1.
	2.

102 Issue 3

Ten-Minute Response

A **ten-minute response** begins with a well-stated **claim** followed by **two detail sentences** that elaborate with relevant examples and precise words.

Language to AGREE/DISAGREE

I completely (agree/disagree) with _____'s perspective.

🎤 PRESENT IDEAS

Listen attentively and take notes. Then indicate whether you agree (+) or disagree (−).

Classmate's Name	Idea	+/−

✏️ ELABORATE IN WRITING

Work with the teacher to write a ten-minute response.

Language to COLLABORATE

What should we write?

We could choose _____. What do you think fits well?

Another option is _____.

    One biological reason why adolescent drivers are at higher risk for car accidents is that they have hormone levels that make it difficult to control their emotions. For example, when another driver cut off my 16-year-old cousin, he thought he could get revenge by _____
_____
As a result, when the other driver _____
my cousin _____
_____

Work with a partner to write a ten-minute response.

    Due to _____ adolescent drivers are at a remarkably higher risk for car accidents. For example, _____
_____
As a result, _____
_____

Analyzing and Discussing Text
ACADEMIC VOCABULARY

Words to Go

📘 BUILD WORD KNOWLEDGE
Complete the meaning and examples for this high-utility academic word.

Word to Go	Meaning	Examples
incidence in•ci•dence *noun*	the _____ _____ something unpleasant happens	Being able to access the internet on smartphones has increased the **incidence** of _____ at school. There's been an unusually high **incidence** of _____ in our community lately.

💬 DISCUSS AND WRITE EXAMPLES
Discuss your response with a partner. Then complete the sentence in writing.

The growing **incidence** of _____ in this country is most likely

linked to _____

Write your response and read it aloud to a partner.

What steps can schools take to decrease the _____ of teens

_____

📘 BUILD WORD KNOWLEDGE
Complete the meanings and examples for these high-utility academic words.

Word to Go	Meaning	Example
violate vi•o•late *verb*	to _____ or _____ a promise, rule, or law	If you _____ _____ you will **violate** my privacy.
violation vi•o•la•tion *noun*	an action that breaks or ignores _____ _____	When I _____ _____ it was a **violation** of my parents' trust.

💬 DISCUSS AND WRITE EXAMPLES
Discuss your response with a partner. Then complete the sentence in writing.

It is my opinion that _____

in schools **violates** students' _____

Write your response and read it aloud to a partner.

Some people think _____

is not a serious offense, but I believe it is a terrible _____ of a

person's _____

104 Issue 3

Text ❸ • Magazine Article
RESPONDING TO TEXT

Close Reading

BUILD FLUENCY
Read the text "Unsafe Behind the Wheel?" (*Issues*, pp. 48–51).

IDENTIFY KEY IDEAS AND DETAILS
Take turns asking and answering questions with a partner. Then write brief notes.

Discussion Frames	Text Notes
Q: What is the author's **main idea**? **A:** The author's **main idea** is _____.	• restrictions against _____
Q: What are the **key details** in this text? **A:** One **key detail** in this text is _____. **A:** Another **key detail** in this text is _____.	• teen driving restrictions reduce _____ • Congress trying to strengthen teen driving _____ and anti-texting laws • opponents say tagging teen cars violates _____; many think _____ is more important

RESPOND WITH EVIDENCE
Use the frames and evidence from the text to construct a formal written response.

1. Based on the text, what do some of the restrictions against adolescent drivers involve?

   Based on the text, one of the restrictions against adolescent drivers involves
   _____

   Another restriction involves _____

Use the frames to analyze the structure of the text.

2. In the first two paragraphs, the author contrasts the way teenagers once celebrated being able to drive with the dangers and limitations they face today. Why does the author establish this contrast at the beginning of the text?

   By establishing this contrast at the beginning of the text, the author lets readers know that
   _____
   _____

IDENTIFY PRECISE WORDS
Review Text 3 and your *Portfolio* (pp. 102–105) to identify words for your writing.

Topic Words	High-Utility Academic Words
• probationary period	• forbid
•	•
•	•

Behind the Wheel 105

Presenting Ideas

Take a Stand

Debate | Should your state increase the minimum driving age?

COLLABORATE
Read the debate question about increasing the driving age. Then take turns using a frame to respond with your initial reaction.

Language to RESPOND
So _____, what's your initial reaction?
My initial reaction is _____.
My initial reaction is (the same/somewhat different).

ANALYZE SOURCES
Read a quote that either supports or opposes the debate topic. Then paraphrase.

Quote	Paraphrase
Model: "Driving is a new skill for teens, so doing multiple things simultaneously takes more effort for them than for more experienced drivers" (Jackson 36).	In this quote, the author states that teen drivers are _____ so _____ is more challenging for them.
1. "'We have parents who are pretty much tired of chauffeuring their kids around, and they want their children to be able to drive'" (Davis 41).	In other words, some parents are _____ by driving their teens places and would prefer that they acquire _____
2. "Sixteen-year-old drivers are involved in fatal crashes at a rate nearly five times the rate of drivers 20 or older" (Davis 41).	In this quote, the author states that adult drivers cause far fewer _____ than _____
3. "A study in The Journal of the American Medical Association suggests that restrictions for young drivers may lead to a higher incidence of fatal accidents for 18-year-olds, possibly because they didn't get enough practical driving experience earlier" (Zernike 49).	In other words, a study found that _____ teens from getting a license until age 18 may increase the number of _____ for 18-year-olds since they haven't had _____
4. "'The reality is, when teen drivers crash, it's people in other cars or teen passengers who end up dying,' says Justin McNaull of the auto club AAA, which supports passenger limits to age 21 or even 25" (Zernike 50).	In other words, AAA is an advocate for _____ in cars driven by young people because the _____ are often their teen passengers or other motorists on the road.

Debate Ideas

SYNTHESIZE IDEAS
Write a response to the debate question, including a paraphrase of a text quote and elaboration on the quote.

Claim: My position is that our state (should/should not) _____ increase the minimum driving age.

Transitional Statement: I have (one key reason/a compelling reason) _____ for taking this stance.

Quote Paraphrase: (According to _____,/The author points out _____.)

_____
_____
_____

Quote Elaboration: (As a result, _____./Consequently, _____.)

_____
_____
_____

PRESENT EVIDENCE

Ensuring Clear Pronunciation
When presenting ideas during class or in a meeting, ensure **clear pronunciation**. When you speak, make sure that you don't mumble and that you pronounce sounds and words properly so that your audience understands you. For example, make sure you say "going to" instead of "gonna."

LISTEN AND TAKE NOTES
Listen attentively and take notes.
Then indicate whether you agree (+) or disagree (−).

Language to AFFIRM AND CLARIFY
I see what you mean.
One question I have is _____.

Classmate's Name	Idea	+/−

Behind the Wheel 107

Academic Writing

ANALYZING TEXT ELEMENTS

Student Writing Model

Academic Writing Type

A **justification essay** states a claim and supports it with logical reasons and relevant evidence from texts.

A. The **thesis statement** clearly states the writer's claim and tells what the writer will explain about the topic.

B. **Supporting paragraphs** support the claim with reasons and evidence from texts.

C. The **conclusion statement** restates the writer's claim about the issue.

ANALYZE TEXT
Read this student model to analyze the elements of a justification essay.

A) After analyzing research on teens and driving, I disagree entirely that states should increase the minimum driving age.

B) One reason I maintain this position is because increasing the driving age might also increase the number of 18-year-old drivers in fatal accidents. In "Unsafe Behind the Wheel," Kate Zernike presents compelling data regarding the serious consequences of raising the driving age to 18. The author points out a study that argues that raising the driving age to 18 will only increase the number of fatal accidents involving 18-year-old drivers because they will be inexperienced (Zernike 49). This is significant because one of the main reasons for increasing the driving age is to reduce the number of fatalities, but in reality, it might just change which age group has the most traffic-related deaths.

Another fundamental reason I hold this position is that taking away 16-year-olds' right to drive would inconvenience parents. According to Robert Davis, many legislators and parents have resisted increasing the minimum driving age because they are "tired of chauffeuring their kids around" (41). This evidence underscores the need for 16-year-olds to be able to drive themselves unsupervised.

In addition, my own relevant experience as a teen with an after-school job has made me critically aware that 16- and 17-year-olds should be permitted to drive. As an illustration, my after-school job is located far from my home and school. There is no public transportation, and my parents are unavailable to drive me to work. This is proof that 16- and 17-year-olds need to be allowed to drive so that they are able to get to their jobs and earn money.

C) For these reasons, I contend that the minimum driving age should not be raised above 16.

Justification Essay
ANALYZING TEXT ELEMENTS

💬 MARK AND DISCUSS ELEMENTS
Mark the justification elements and use the frames to discuss them with your partner.

1. **Circle the writer's claim within the thesis statement.**
   The writer's claim is _____.

2. **Draw a box around five transition words or phrases.**
   One transition (word/phrase) is _____.

3. **Underline and label three reasons that support the writer's claim with the letter R.**
   One reason that supports the writer's claim is _____.

4. **Underline and label three pieces of evidence that support the writer's claim with the letter E.**
   One piece of evidence that supports the writer's claim is _____.

5. **Star four precise topic words and check four high-utility academic words.**
   An example of a (precise topic word/high-utility academic word) is _____.

⭐ ASSESS A STUDENT SAMPLE
Read an additional student model and rate it.

Scoring Guide			
1	Insufficient	3	Sufficient
2	Developing	4	Exemplary

1. Does the thesis statement clearly state the claim?	1	2	3	4
2. Do supporting paragraphs begin with a topic sentence that specifies a reason?	1	2	3	4
3. Did the writer give evidence drawn primarily from sources to support the claim?	1	2	3	4
4. Did the writer explain why the evidence is relevant and significant?	1	2	3	4
5. Did the writer use strong verbs to state and restate the claim?	1	2	3	4
6. Did the writer use transitions to introduce reasons and evidence?	1	2	3	4
7. Did the writer include precise topic words and high-utility words?	1	2	3	4
8. Does the conclusion statement strongly restate the claim using new wording?	1	2	3	4

💬 REFLECT AND REVISE
Record specific priorities and suggestions to help the writer.

The writer did an effective job of (organizing/including/stating) _____

_____

_____

One way the writer could make the justification essay stronger is _____

_____

_____

I noticed that the writer (forgot to/included/used) _____

_____

_____

This will support me with writing a justification essay because I will remember to

_____

_____

Academic Writing
FRONTLOADING LANGUAGE

Language for Quantity and Frequency

Reason (Why?)	Quantity (How many?)	Frequency (How often?)	Examples
because since due to as a result of	few some several many nearly all most every	never rarely occasionally frequently regularly usually always	**Many** teens are pledging to drive phone-free **because** they **never** want to be distracted while driving. **Since** teens **regularly** get up early for school, **most** are sleep deprived. **As a result of** teens **frequently** having accidents at night, **nearly all** states have restrictions on nighttime driving.

✎ USE PRECISE LANGUAGE

Rewrite each simple sentence as a complex sentence, using the reason, quantity, and frequency words in parentheses.

Simple Sentence: Students have trouble getting to bed early.

Complex Sentence: **Many** students **regularly** have trouble getting to bed early **since** they do not feel sleepy until later in the night.

1. Teens don't get enough sleep. (*as a result of, few, regularly*)

___

2. Getting enough sleep is challenging for teens. (*because, most, frequently*)

___

3. Teens who are sleep deprived exhibit signs of depression. (*due to, some, regularly*)

___

Add reason, quantity, and frequency to each simple sentence using the chart above.

4. Texting while driving is dangerous.

___

5. Teen drivers are impulsive.

___

6. States have enacted Graduated Driver Licensing laws.

___

Justification Essay
FRONTLOADING CONVENTIONS

Citing Sources

Guidelines for Citing Sources
Citations give credit for other people's ideas. They also help readers find the original information if they want to learn more.

To **cite a source**, use quotation marks around direct quotes or paraphrase the author's ideas in your own words. Identify the source in parentheses and put the period after the citation.

Type of Citation	Guidelines	Examples
when a source has one author	Include the author's last name followed by the page number.	A study by the National Sleep Foundation found that 15 percent of students reported falling asleep in school over the past year (Weir 5). This is worrisome because sleep-deprived students may have "problems with learning and memory" (Weir 7).
when the author's name is in the sentence	Include the page number(s) only.	According to Denise Grady, adolescents' demanding schedules often conflict with their internal clocks (8–9).
when a source has two authors	Include the authors' last names in the same order as the source.	Many schools have cut world language classes due to tighter budgets (Altschuler and Skorton 21).

WRITE CITATIONS
Rewrite each sentence with a citation and proper punctuation.

1. Approximately 39 percent of high school students surveyed have "admitted to texting or emailing while driving."
   Text 1: "DN'T TXT N DRV" by Nancy Mann Jackson

   _____
   _____

2. Scientists have discovered that the part of the brain that is "involved in decision-making and controlling impulses" is the last to develop.
   Text 2: "Is 16 Too Young to Drive a Car?" by Robert Davis

   _____
   _____

3. According to Kate Zernike, teens have more trouble with multitasking when they are behind the wheel.
   Text 3: "Unsafe Behind the Wheel?" by Kate Zernike

   _____
   _____

Academic Writing
PLANNING TO WRITE

Organize a Justification Essay

Prompt Should your state increase the minimum driving age? Write a justification essay that states and supports your claim.

Thesis Starters	Examples
After analyzing the research on . . . After reviewing the (evidence, data) on . . . After examining the issues surrounding . . .	**After analyzing the research on** teen sleep, I agree wholeheartedly that schools should start later to accommodate teen sleep needs. **After reviewing the data on** adolescent sleep needs, I believe strongly that schools should not start later.
Conclusion Starters	**Examples**
For these reasons, In light of this evidence,	**For these reasons,** I conclude that foreign language class should not be a mandatory component of a high school's curriculum. **In light of this evidence,** I maintain that foreign language should be a required class in high school.

WRITE A THESIS STATEMENT
Describe your claim.

My claim: _____

_____

Use academic language to restate your claim as a thesis statement.

_____ adolescents and driving,
(Thesis starter)
I (agree/disagree) _____ (strongly, firmly) _____
that _____
     (your claim)

CHOOSE SUPPORTING TOPICS
List each topic you will write about to support your claim.

Supporting Paragraph 1

Topic: _____

_____

Supporting Paragraph 2

Topic: _____

_____

Supporting Paragraph 3

Topic: _____

_____

Justification Essay
PLANNING TO WRITE

📋 PLAN SUPPORTING PARAGRAPHS
List reasons and evidence that support your claim. You may draw from texts, your experience, or a classmate's experience.

Supporting Paragraph 1

Reason 1: _____

_____

Evidence: _____

_____

Source: _____

Author: _____

Elaboration on this evidence: _____

_____

_____

Supporting Paragraph 2

Reason 2: _____

_____

Evidence: _____

_____

Source: _____

Author: _____

Elaboration on this evidence: _____

_____

_____

Supporting Paragraph 3

Reason 3: _____

_____

Relevant personal experience: _____

_____

Relevant personal connection: _____

Elaboration on this evidence: _____

_____

✏️ WRITE A CONCLUSION
Plan a conclusion statement that restates your claim.

_____ I contend that

(Conclusion starter)

_____

_____

Academic Writing

WRITING A DRAFT

Write a Justification Essay

Prompt Should your state increase the minimum driving age? Write a justification essay that states and supports your claim.

✏️ **WRITE AN ESSAY**
Use the frame to write your thesis statement, supporting paragraphs, and conclusion statement.

A

_____
(Thesis starter)
adolescents and driving, I (agree/disagree) _____
(strongly, firmly) _____ that _____
                                                        (claim)
_____
_____

B1

One reason I maintain this position is _____
                                        (1st reason that supports your claim)
_____
_____

In _____
    (Title of Source)
_____ presents (strong, convincing, compelling)
(Author's Name)
_____ (data, statistics, evidence) _____
regarding the (positive, negative, serious) _____ consequences of
_____
(topic)
_____

The author points out that _____
                            (text evidence)
_____
_____
_____

This is significant because _____
                             (elaborate on text evidence)
_____
_____

114 Issue 3

Justification Essay
ASSESSING AND REVISING

B2

Another (important, fundamental, critical) _____ reason I hold this position is that _____
(2nd reason that supports your claim)
_____
_____
_____

According to _____
(Source or Author's Name)
_____
(text evidence)
_____
_____

This (data, evidence) _____ underscores (the need for, the impact of, the seriousness of) _____
_____
(elaborate on text evidence)
_____
_____

B3

In addition, my own relevant experience as _____
(relevant personal connection)
has made me critically aware that _____
(claim)
_____
_____
_____

As an illustration, _____
(relevant personal experience)
_____
_____
_____

This is (evidence, proof) _____ that _____
(elaborate on personal experience)
_____
_____

C

_____ I contend that
(Conclusion starter)
_____
(restate your claim)
_____
_____
_____

Behind the Wheel 115

Issue 4 — Money Matters

DO TEENS KNOW THEIR LIMIT WHEN IT COMES TO CREDIT?

📖 BUILD KNOWLEDGE
Read and respond to the Data File (*Issues*, p. 52).

💡 BRAINSTORM IDEAS
Write a brief list of similarities and differences between credit and cash.

- difference: credit must be paid back
- _____

- _____
- _____

🎤 PRESENT IDEAS
Use the frames to discuss ideas with your group. Listen attentively and record the strongest ideas to complete the diagram.

> **Language to FACILITATE DISCUSSION**
> So _____, what's your perspective?
> _____, what (similarity/difference) did you come up with?

1. Cash and credit are similar in that they both _____ (**present-tense verb:** allow)
2. One difference between them is that (cash/credit) _____ (**present-tense verb:** requires)
3. Another way they are different is that (cash/credit) _____ (**present-tense verb:** can be)
4. Teens might use (cash/credit) because it _____ (**present-tense verb:** buys)

CREDIT
- can result in interest changes

BOTH
- are available in limited amounts

CASH
- cannot lead to overspending

Building Concepts and Language

ACADEMIC VOCABULARY

Words to Know

BUILD WORD KNOWLEDGE

Rate your word knowledge. Then discuss word meanings and examples with your group.

① Don't Know   ② Recognize   ③ Familiar   ④ Know

Word to Know	Meaning	Example
1 **debt** *noun* ① ② ③ ④	_____ or something else that is _____ and should be paid back	My sister did me a huge favor, so I _____ _____ to repay the **debt**.
2 **financial** *adjective* ① ② ③ ④	relating to the management and use of _____	My _____ has brought me some **financial** security.
3 **interest** *noun* ① ② ③ ④	the extra money paid for _____ money	The loan I plan to take out for _____ has a low rate of **interest**.
4 **credit** *noun* ① ② ③ ④	an agreement that allows you to _____ something and pay for it _____	Many people use **credit** to make large purchases, such as _____
1 **balance** *noun* ① ② ③ ④	the remaining amount of money that is still _____	Once I pay off the **balance** on _____ I will be able to start saving again.
2 **income** *noun* ① ② ③ ④	money that a person _____ from a job or other source	_____ is a great way for teens to earn some extra **income** during the summer.
3 **fee** *noun* ① ② ③ ④	the amount of money _____ for a service	_____ often charge an extra **fee** for _____
4 **bankrupt** *adjective* ① ② ③ ④	without enough _____ to pay what is owed	When the company went **bankrupt**, it had to _____

Money Matters 117

Building Concepts and Language

SPEAKING AND LISTENING

Academic Discussion

What are some ways adolescents earn and spend income?

BRAINSTORM IDEAS
Briefly record at least two ideas in each column using everyday English.

Income	Expenses
• receiving birthday money • •	• gas or public transportation • •

ANALYZE WORDS
Complete the chart with precise words to discuss and write about the topic.

Everyday	Precise
cost (noun)	expense,
work (verb)	to be employed,
buy (verb)	procure,

MAKE A CLAIM
Rewrite two ideas using the frames and precise words. Then prepare to elaborate verbally.

Language to ELABORATE
As an illustration, _____.
I have discovered that _____.

1. **Frame:** In my experience, adolescents (earn/spend) income by _____ (**verb + –ing:** babysitting, doing chores, buying clothes)

   Response: _____
   _____

2. **Frame:** A common (source of income/expense) for adolescents is _____ (**noun:** allowance, a part-time job, bus fare)

   Response: _____
   _____

COLLABORATE
Listen attentively, restate, and record your partner's idea.

Language to RESTATE
So your point of view is that _____.

Yes, that's correct.

No, not quite. What I (expressed/suggested) is that _____.

Classmate's Name	Ideas
	1. 2.

118 Issue 4

SPEAKING AND WRITING

Ten-Minute Response

A **ten-minute response** begins with a **claim,** followed by **two detail sentences** that elaborate with relevant examples and precise words.

Language to AGREE/DISAGREE

I (agree/disagree) with _____'s point of view about _____.

🎤 **PRESENT IDEAS**

Listen, compare ideas, and take notes. Then indicate whether you agree (+) or disagree (−).

Classmate's Name	Idea	+/−

✏️ **ELABORATE IN WRITING**

Work with the teacher to write a ten-minute response.

Language to COLLABORATE

What should we write?

We could choose _____. What do you think fits logically?

Another possibility is _____.

 In my experience, adolescents spend income by keeping up with the latest fashions. For example, when a certain brand of _____ (is/are) extremely _____ teens may feel _____ to own them. As a result, teens may have to pay a high _____ to _____ them.

Work with a partner to write a ten-minute response.

 A common _____ for adolescents is _____

For example, when teens _____

they may _____

_____

As a result, teens may end up _____

in exchange for _____

Money Matters **119**

Analyzing and Discussing Text
ACADEMIC VOCABULARY

Words to Go

BUILD WORD KNOWLEDGE
Complete the meanings and examples for these high-utility words.

Word to Go	Meaning	Example
minimum min•i•mum *noun/adjective*	the _____ amount allowed or needed; describing the smallest _____ allowed or needed	I need a **minimum** of _____ to _____ I meet the **minimum** age for _____
minimize min•i•mize *verb*	to _____ something as much as possible	To **minimize** costs, I _____

DISCUSS AND WRITE EXAMPLES
Discuss your response with a partner. Then complete the sentence in writing.

I _____ to meet the **minimum**

requirement for admission to _____

Write your response and read it aloud to a partner.

Many schools are eliminating _____

_____ in an effort to _____ the negative impact

_____

BUILD WORD KNOWLEDGE
Complete the meaning and example for this high-utility word.

Word to Go	Meaning	Example
evaluate e•val•u•ate *verb*	to decide how _____ or _____ something is	In class, we **evaluate** _____ _____ with a rubric.

DISCUSS AND WRITE EXAMPLES
Discuss your response with a partner. Then complete the sentence in writing.

The city **evaluated** the mural we painted and decided that it was _____

_____

Write your response and read it aloud to a partner.

After _____ the student's online behavior, the principal came to the

conclusion that _____

Text 1 • Magazine Article
RESPONDING TO TEXT

Close Reading

📖 BUILD FLUENCY
Read the text "Buyer, Beware!" (*Issues*, pp. 53–57).

💬 IDENTIFY KEY IDEAS AND DETAILS
Take turns asking and answering questions with a partner. Then write brief notes.

Discussion Frames	Text Notes
Q: What is the author's **main idea**? **A:** The author's **main idea** is _____. **Q:** What are the **key details** in this text? **A:** (One/Another) **key detail** in this text is _____.	• _____ can be helpful but _____ • credit good for _____ or getting _____ • _____ or fees on credit not _____ or on time create more _____ • bad _____ could cost you a _____ or _____

✏️ RESPOND WITH EVIDENCE
Use the frames and evidence from the text to construct a formal written response.

1. According to the author, what are some dangers to avoid when using a credit card?

According to the author, dangers to avoid when using a credit card include _____

_____

In addition, users should avoid making only minimum payments because _____

_____

Use the frame to analyze the author's development of ideas.

2. Why does the author include the anecdote about Sanyika Galloway Boyce?

The author includes the anecdote about Boyce to help the reader understand _____

_____

It allows the reader to imagine _____

_____

🔍 IDENTIFY PRECISE WORDS
Review Text 1 and your *Portfolio* (pp. 116–121) to identify words for your writing.

Topic Words	High-Utility Academic Words
• interest rate • •	• unnecessary • •

Money Matters 121

Building Concepts and Language

SPEAKING AND LISTENING

Academic Discussion

What are the benefits and drawbacks of using a credit card?

BRAINSTORM IDEAS
Briefly record at least two ideas in each column using everyday English.

Benefits	Drawbacks
• earn cash back	• can go over budget
•	•
•	•

ANALYZE WORDS
Complete the chart with precise words to discuss and write about the issue.

Everyday	Precise
forget *(verb)*	neglect,
go over *(verb)*	exceed,
set up *(verb)*	establish,

MAKE A CLAIM
Rewrite two ideas using the frames and precise words. Then prepare to elaborate verbally.

Language to ELABORATE
As an illustration, _____.
I have discovered that _____.

1. **Frame:** One (benefit/drawback) of using a credit card is _____ (**verb + –ing:** establishing credit, paying interest, overspending)

   Response: _____

2. **Frame:** Using a credit card can be (beneficial/harmful) when you _____ (**verb phrase:** incur fees, build credit history, pay only the minimum)

   Response: _____

COLLABORATE
Listen attentively, restate, and record your partner's idea.

Language to RESTATE
So your point of view is that _____.
Yes, that's correct.
No, not quite. What I (expressed/suggested) is that _____.

Classmate's Name	Ideas
	1.
	2.

122 Issue 4

SPEAKING AND WRITING

Ten-Minute Response

A **ten-minute response** begins with a **claim**, followed by **two detail sentences** that elaborate with relevant examples and precise words.

Language to AGREE/DISAGREE

I (agree/disagree) with _____'s point of view about _____.

🎤 PRESENT IDEAS

Listen, compare ideas, and take notes. Then indicate whether you agree (+) or disagree (–).

Classmate's Name	Idea	+/–

✏️ ELABORATE IN WRITING

Work with the teacher to write a ten-minute response.

Language to COLLABORATE

What should we write?

We could choose _____. What do you think fits logically?

Another possibility is _____.

One _____ of using a credit card is _____ _____ a strong credit score. For example, paying the card's _____ in full every month and never _____ raises your credit score. As a result, future _____ and _____ are more likely to see you as a desirable job candidate or tenant.

Work with a partner to write a ten-minute response.

Using a credit card can be _____ when you _____
_____

For example, a credit card user might have to _____
_____

As a result, an initial purchase of _____ could end up costing _____

Money Matters 123

Analyzing and Discussing Text
ACADEMIC VOCABULARY

Words to Go

BUILD WORD KNOWLEDGE
Complete the meanings and examples for these high-utility academic words.

Word to Go	Meaning	Example
significant sig•nif•i•cant *adjective*	large or _____ enough to have an effect on something	_____ had a **significant** impact on my dream of becoming _____
significantly sig•nif•i•cant•ly *adverb*	in an _____ or _____ way	I knew I had to **significantly** improve my grades if I wanted _____

DISCUSS AND WRITE EXAMPLES
Discuss your response with a partner. Then complete the sentence in writing.

Some social networking websites have made **significant** changes to their _____ in response to _____

Write your response and read it aloud to a partner.

_____

could _____ reduce the number of vehicle crashes involving teens.

BUILD WORD KNOWLEDGE
Complete the meaning and examples for this high-utility academic word.

Word to Go	Meaning	Example
accurately ac•cu•rate•ly *adverb*	in a way that is _____ and in every detail	To **accurately** measure _____ you should use _____ The _____ was so bizarre that I had trouble **accurately** describing it to my friends.

DISCUSS AND WRITE EXAMPLES
Discuss your response with a partner. Then complete the sentence in writing.

Generally, fashion magazines do not **accurately** portray _____

Write your response and read it aloud to a partner.

The eyewitness tried to _____ describe the _____

Text ❷ • Section ❶ • Newsletter

SUMMARIZING TEXT

Section Shrink

📖 BUILD FLUENCY
Read the introduction and Section 1 of "If at First You Don't Succeed" (*Issues*, pp. 58–61).

💬 IDENTIFY KEY IDEAS AND DETAILS
Take turns asking and answering questions with a partner. Then write brief notes.

Discussion Frames	Text Notes
Q: What is this section **mainly about**? **A:** This section is **mainly about** _____.	• young adults should _____ financial mistakes involving _____
Q: What are the **key details** in this section? **A:** (One/Another) **key detail** in this section is _____. **A:** Perhaps the **most important key detail** in this section is _____.	• fully repay purchases made with _____ credit cards, or risk increased charges • beware of _____ and correct it _____ • protect your _____ by _____ and _____

✏️ SUMMARIZE
"Shrink" Section 1 of the text by writing a summary in 40 or fewer words.

CLASS SUMMARY   **WORD COUNT:** _____

Manage your _____ and protect _____

by avoiding _____ seeking help for

_____ and paying

credit card bills _____

PARTNER SUMMARY   **WORD COUNT:** _____

Young adults should _____

by _____ not borrowing more money

to _____ and paying _____

_____ on _____

🔍 IDENTIFY PRECISE WORDS
Review Section 1 and your *Portfolio* (pp. 122–125) to identify words for your writing.

Topic Words	High-Utility Academic Words
• major purchases • •	• accomplish • •

Money Matters **125**

Analyzing and Discussing Text

ACADEMIC VOCABULARY

Words to Go

📖 BUILD WORD KNOWLEDGE
Complete the meanings and examples for these high-utility academic words.

Word to Go	Meaning	Example
potential po•ten•tial *adjective/noun*	possible, but not _____ actual or real; the _____ that something will develop in a certain way	The guidance counselor talked to me about **potential** _____ I worry about dating because of the **potential** for _____
potentially po•ten•tial•ly *adverb*	having the possibility of _____ in a certain way	Sleep deprivation is **potentially** harmful to teens' _____

💬 DISCUSS AND WRITE EXAMPLES
Discuss your response with a partner. Then complete the sentence in writing.

Some video games have the **potential** to help teens _____

_____

Write your response and read it aloud to a partner.

_____

is _____ risky for teen drivers.

📖 BUILD WORD KNOWLEDGE
Complete the meaning and examples for this high-utility academic word.

Word to Go	Meaning	Example
priority pri•or•i•ty *noun*	something that is more _____ than other things	_____ is a **priority** for me. Doing _____ _____ should be my **priority** when I get home from school.

💬 DISCUSS AND WRITE EXAMPLES
Discuss your response with a partner. Then complete the sentence in writing.

The top **priorities** for many teens are _____

and _____

Write your response and read it aloud to a partner.

One of the student council's _____ is _____

_____

Text ❷ • Section ❷ • Newsletter
SUMMARIZING TEXT

Section Shrink

📖 BUILD FLUENCY
Read Section 2 of "If at First You Don't Succeed" (*Issues*, pp. 61–64).

💬 IDENTIFY KEY IDEAS AND DETAILS
Take turns asking and answering questions with a partner.

Discussion Frames	Text Notes
Q: What is this section **mainly about**? **A:** This section is **mainly about** _____.	• budgeting and long-term _____ _____
Q: What are the **key details** in this section? **A:** (One/Another) **key detail** in this section is _____. **A:** Perhaps the **most important key detail** in this section is _____.	• avoid having too many _____ _____ so you don't hurt your chances of getting a good loan • a _____ helps you avoid _____ • saving money for the _____ and making _____ are two ways to _____

✏️ SUMMARIZE
"Shrink" Section 2 of the text by writing a summary in 40 or fewer words.

CLASS SUMMARY   **WORD COUNT:** _____

Limit the _____

you have so banks won't view you as _____

and prioritize your _____ with a _____ that

allows you to _____

PARTNER SUMMARY   **WORD COUNT:** _____

Protect _____

by having _____ credit cards,

creating _____ and depositing money

into _____

🔍 IDENTIFY PRECISE WORDS
Review Section 2 and your *Portfolio* (pp. 126–127) to identify words for your writing.

Topic Words	High-Utility Academic Words
• investment	• inclined
•	•
•	•

Money Matters **127**

Analyzing and Discussing Text

ACADEMIC VOCABULARY

Words to Go

📖 BUILD WORD KNOWLEDGE
Complete the meaning and examples for this high-utility academic word.

Word to Go	Meaning	Example
periodically pe•ri•od•i•cal•ly *adverb*	at _____ times	When I'm working at my computer, I **periodically** _____ _____ I **periodically** _____ my cell phone's _____

💬 DISCUSS AND WRITE EXAMPLES
Discuss your response with a partner. Then complete the sentence in writing.

Many students are unhappy that the school district will **periodically** _____

_____

Write your response and read it aloud to a partner.

Family is very important to me, so I _____ visit _____

_____

📖 BUILD WORD KNOWLEDGE
Complete the meanings and examples for these high-utility academic words.

Word to Go	Meaning	Example
indication in•di•ca•tion *noun*	a _____ or piece of _____ that points something out	Because her expression gave me no **indication** of her feelings, I couldn't tell whether or not _____ _____
indicate in•di•cate *verb*	to _____ or _____ something	The _____ coming from the cafeteria **indicate** that _____ _____

💬 DISCUSS AND WRITE EXAMPLES
Discuss your response with a partner. Then complete the sentence in writing.

All the **indications** suggest a strong connection between _____

_____ and teenagers' eating habits.

Write your response and read it aloud to a partner.

Yesterday, my inability to concentrate in class _____ that I _____

_____

128 Issue 4

Text 2 • Section 3 • Newsletter
SUMMARIZING TEXT

Section Shrink

BUILD FLUENCY
Read Section 3 of "If at First You Don't Succeed" (*Issues*, pp. 64–66).

IDENTIFY KEY IDEAS AND DETAILS
Take turns asking and answering questions with a partner. Then write brief notes.

Discussion Frames	Text Notes
Q: What is this section **mainly about**? **A:** This section is **mainly about** _____.	• taking _____ for your _____ independence
Q: What are the **key details** in this section? **A:** (One/Another) **key detail** in this section is _____. **A:** Perhaps the **most important key detail** in this section is _____.	• use own bank's _____ to minimize _____; don't _____ • periodically review _____; contact bank to _____ • take charge by paying _____ on credit card bills, _____ more, cutting _____

SUMMARIZE
"Shrink" Section 3 of the text by writing a summary in 40 or fewer words.

CLASS SUMMARY WORD COUNT: _____

Gain _____ by avoiding ATM

and _____ fees, reviewing your

accounts for _____

paying down _____ and spending _____

PARTNER SUMMARY WORD COUNT: _____

Be financially responsible by using _____

not _____ saving _____ and

periodically _____

IDENTIFY PRECISE WORDS
Review Section 3 and your *Portfolio* (pp. 128–129) to identify words for your writing.

Topic Words	High-Utility Words
• financial institution • •	• precaution • •

Money Matters 129

Academic Writing

ANALYZING TEXT ELEMENTS

Student Writing Model

Academic Writing Type

A **formal written summary** provides an objective overview of the topic and important details from an informational text. The writer credits the author, but writes in primarily their own words, without including personal opinions.

    A. The **topic sentence** includes the text type, title, author, and topic.

    B. **Detail sentences** include the important details from the summarized text.

    C. The **concluding sentence** restates the author's conclusion in the writer's own words.

ANALYZE TEXT
Read this student model to analyze the elements of a formal summary.

A
In the magazine article titled "Buyer, Beware!," Brooke Stephens discusses the important information teens should know about using credit cards.

B
To begin with, Stephens presents an anecdote about a college student whose reckless credit card use led to significant debt. The author also explains that using credit to make major purchases is smart, but using it to buy small items is not the best use of credit cards. Additionally, she emphasizes the importance of paying balances in full each month and not missing any payments so that users avoid interest and late fees. Moreover, the author describes how credit cards influence scores and how bad credit can potentially impact someone's ability to get a job or an apartment.

C
Lastly, Stephens concludes that having one major, universally accepted credit card with a low interest rate is better than having multiple high-interest department store cards.

MARK AND DISCUSS ELEMENTS
Mark the summary elements and use the frames to discuss them with your partner.

1. **Number (1–4) the four elements of the topic sentence.** *The topic sentence includes the _____.*

2. **Draw a box around four transition words or phrases.** *One transition (word/phrase) is _____.*

3. **Underline four important details.** *One important detail in this summary is _____.*

4. **Circle four citation verbs.** *One citation verb that the writer uses is _____.*

5. **Star four precise topic words and check four high-utility academic words.** *An example of a (precise topic word/high-utility academic word) is _____.*

Formal Summary
PLANNING TO WRITE

Organize a Formal Summary

Prompt Write a formal summary of "If at First You Don't Succeed."

Guidelines for Paraphrasing Multiple Sentences
Paraphrase related details from a source text by combining key information into one sentence. Replace key words and phrases with synonyms and keep important topic words.

Text Detail 1	Text Detail 2	Text Detail 3
"[Signs of a serious debt problem] may include borrowing money to make payments on loans you already have, deliberately paying bills late, and putting off doctor visits . . ." ("If at First" 59).	". . . try to pay off your highest interest-rate loans (usually your credit cards) as soon as possible, even if you have higher balances on other loans" ("If at First" 59).	"Companies called credit bureaus prepare credit reports for use by lenders, employers, insurance companies, landlords, and others who need to know someone's financial reliability . . ." ("If at First" 60).

PARAPHRASE IDEAS
Combine key information from the three text details above into one detail sentence.

Consumers should watch out for

(text detail 1) _____ and focus on

(text detail 2) _____ to protect their

(text detail 3) _____

PLAN KEY IDEAS AND DETAILS
State the text information to write a topic sentence.

In the newsletter titled (Title) _____

the author (citation verb: presents, investigates, discusses) _____

(topic) _____

_____

List four important details from the article primarily using your own words.

1. _____
   _____

2. _____
   _____

3. _____
   _____

4. _____
   _____

Restate the author's conclusion in your own words.

_____

_____

Money Matters

Academic Writing
WRITING A DRAFT

Write a Formal Summary

Prompt | Write a formal summary of "If at First You Don't Succeed."

✏️ WRITE A PARAGRAPH
Use the frame to write your topic sentence, detail sentences, and concluding sentence.

A

In the newsletter titled _____
(Title)

_____

the (author/writer) _____ _____
                        (citation verb)

_____
(topic)

_____

B

_____ the (author/writer) _____
(Transition)

_____ _____
(citation verb)   (1st important detail)

_____

_____

The (author/writer) _____ also _____
                                                  (citation verb)

_____
(2nd important detail)

_____

_____ the (author/writer) _____
(Transition)

_____ _____
(citation verb)   (3rd important detail)

_____

_____ the (author/writer) _____
(Transition)

_____ _____
(citation verb)   (4th important detail)

_____

C

_____ the (author/writer) _____
(Transition)
concludes that _____
                    (restate author's conclusion)

_____

Formal Summary
ASSESSING AND REVISING

Rate Your Summary

Scoring Guide
1	Insufficient
2	Developing
3	Sufficient
4	Exemplary

ASSESS YOUR DRAFT
Rate your formal summary. Then have a partner rate it.

1. Does the topic sentence state the title, author, and topic?	Self	1	2	3	4
	Partner	1	2	3	4
2. Did you paraphrase the most important details from the text?	Self	1	2	3	4
	Partner	1	2	3	4
3. Did you use citation verbs to credit the author?	Self	1	2	3	4
	Partner	1	2	3	4
4. Did you use transitions to introduce and sequence details?	Self	1	2	3	4
	Partner	1	2	3	4
5. Did you include precise topic words and high-utility academic words?	Self	1	2	3	4
	Partner	1	2	3	4
6. Did you restate the author's conclusion using your own words?	Self	1	2	3	4
	Partner	1	2	3	4

REFLECT AND REVISE
Record specific priorities and suggestions to help you and your partner revise.

(Partner) Positive Feedback: I appreciate how you (used/included) _____

_____

(Partner) Suggestion: As you revise your summary, focus on _____

_____

(Self) Priority 1: My summary paragraph needs _____

_____

(Self) Priority 2: I plan to improve my summary by _____

_____

CHECK AND EDIT
Use this checklist to proofread and edit your formal summary.

- ☐ Did you capitalize the title of the article and proper nouns?
- ☐ Did you put quotation marks around the title of the article?
- ☐ Did you use commas appropriately after transitions?
- ☐ Do simple present-tense verbs end in –s?
- ☐ Is each sentence complete?
- ☐ Are all words spelled correctly?

Building Concepts and Language

SPEAKING AND LISTENING

Academic Discussion

What are some examples of responsible and irresponsible financial behavior?

BRAINSTORM IDEAS
Briefly record at least two ideas in each column using everyday English.

Responsible Behaviors	Irresponsible Behaviors
• not overspending • •	• missing credit card payments • •

ANALYZE WORDS
Complete the chart with precise words to discuss and write about the topic.

Everyday	Precise
keep to *(verb)*	adhere to,
check *(verb)*	monitor,
habit *(noun)*	routine,

MAKE A CLAIM
Rewrite two ideas using the frames and precise words. Then prepare to elaborate verbally.

1. **Frame:** An example of (responsible/irresponsible) financial behavior is _____ (**verb + –ing:** minimizing expenses, saving for the future, building debt)

   Response: _____

2. **Frame:** Young adults show (responsible/irresponsible) financial behavior when they _____ (**verb phrase:** avoid fees, save income, pay bills late)

   Response: _____

> **Language to ELABORATE**
> As an illustration, _____.
> I have discovered that _____.

COLLABORATE
Listen attentively, restate, and record your partner's ideas.

Classmate's Name	Ideas
	1.
	2.

> **Language to RESTATE**
> So your point of view is that _____.
> Yes, that's correct.
> No, not quite. What I (expressed/suggested) is that _____.

134 Issue 4

SPEAKING AND WRITING

Ten-Minute Response

A **ten-minute response** begins with a **claim**, followed by **two detail sentences** that elaborate with relevant examples and precise words.

Language to AGREE/DISAGREE

I (agree/disagree) with _____'s point of view about _____.

🎤 PRESENT IDEAS
Listen, compare ideas, and take notes. Then indicate whether you agree (+) or disagree (−).

Classmate's Name	Idea	+/−

✏️ ELABORATE IN WRITING
Work with the teacher to write a ten-minute response.

Language to COLLABORATE

What should we write?

We could choose _____. What do you think fits logically?

Another possibility is _____.

    An example of _____ financial behavior is forgetting to pay credit card bills on time. For example, the _____ forgave my friend for his first late payment, but then he _____ _____.

As a result, the bank raised the interest rate on his account, and now he _____ _____.

Work with a partner to write a ten-minute response.

    Young adults show _____ financial behavior when they make it a practice to _____ _____.

For example, _____ _____ _____.

As a result, _____ _____ _____.

Money Matters

Analyzing and Discussing Text

ACADEMIC VOCABULARY

Words to Go

📖 BUILD WORD KNOWLEDGE
Complete the meanings and examples for this high-utility academic word.

Word to Go	Meaning	Example
restructure re•struc•ture *verb*	to _____ the way something is organized; to _____ the terms of debts	By borrowing money from _____, I was able to **restructure** my debt. The new _____ plans to **restructure** the school's _____ so that it's more efficient.

💬 DISCUSS AND WRITE EXAMPLES
Discuss your response with a partner. Then complete the sentence in writing.

The club decided to **restructure** its leadership so that _____

_____

Write your response and read it aloud to a partner.

I may not be able to eliminate the money I owe on my credit card, but I can

_____ the debt so that I can _____

📖 BUILD WORD KNOWLEDGE
Complete the meanings and examples for these high-utility academic words.

Word to Go	Meaning	Example
promote pro•mote *verb*	to help something become more _____ or well known	I _____ to **promote** myself when I ran for class president.
promotion pro•mo•tion *noun*	an activity to help something become more successful or _____	As part of the **promotion** for a new movie, the company that made it is giving away _____

💬 DISCUSS AND WRITE EXAMPLES
Discuss your response with a partner. Then complete the sentence in writing.

Magazine advertisements **promoting** _____ often use enhanced photos so that people will _____

Write your response and read it aloud to a partner.

The local grocery store is giving away tote bags as part of a _____

for _____

Text ③ • Magazine Article

RESPONDING TO TEXT

Close Reading

📖 BUILD FLUENCY
Read the text "In Debt by 25" (*Issues*, pp. 67–69).

💬 IDENTIFY KEY IDEAS AND DETAILS
Take turns asking and answering questions with a partner. Then write brief notes.

Discussion Frames	Text Notes
Q: What is the author's **main idea**? **A:** The author's **main idea** is _____.	• many young adults are getting into _____
Q: What are the **key details** in this text? **A:** (One/Another) **key detail** in this text is _____.	• some experts say rise due to _____ • others blame increasing _____ _____ and using student loan money for _____ • some colleges and organizations teach young adults _____

✏️ RESPOND WITH EVIDENCE
Use the frames and evidence from the text to construct a formal written response.

1. According to the author, how can the college experience contribute to the potential for young adults to accumulate debt?

   According to the author, _____

   _____ can increase the likelihood for them to accumulate debt.

   In addition, the high cost of tuition forces many students to _____

   _____

Use the frames to analyze the author's word choice.

2. How does the author use the word *stain* in paragraph 5? What is its effect?

   The author uses the word *stain* (literally/figuratively) _____

   because _____

   Using *stain* in this context suggests that bankruptcy _____

   _____

🔍 IDENTIFY PRECISE WORDS
Review Text 3 and your *Portfolio* (pp. 134–137) to identify words for your writing.

Topic Words	High-Utility Academic Words
• financial literacy	• aggressive
•	•
•	•

Money Matters **137**

Presenting Ideas

Take a Stand

Debate Are adolescents prepared to take on the responsibilities of using credit cards?

COLLABORATE
Read the debate question about teens and money. Then take turns using a frame to respond with your initial reaction.

Language to RESPOND
So _____, what's your initial reaction?
My initial reaction is _____.
My initial reaction is (the same/somewhat different).

ANALYZE SOURCES
Read a quote that either supports or opposes the debate question. Then paraphrase.

Quote	Paraphrase
Model: "75% [of teens report that they] lack confidence in their knowledge of personal finance" (Annuity.org 52).	This quote reinforces the idea that more than _____ of teens are not confident they can _____ their _____.
1. "Buying a home, purchasing a car, starting a business, and getting a student loan for college are smart uses of credit" (Stephens 54).	In this quote, the author states that people should use credit for major _____ such as going to college or purchasing _____.
2. "'Many young people don't take the time to check their receipts or make the necessary phone calls or write letters to correct a problem'" ("If at First" 65).	This quote reinforces the idea that adolescents often fail to _____ their receipts or contact _____ to correct _____.
3. "But many teens find that it takes only a year or two for their newfound financial freedom to turn into a big liability. Some even turn to a last resort: filing for bankruptcy" (Smillie 67).	In this quote, the author states that some _____ have to _____ when they find themselves in _____.
4. "Some students resort to using student-loan money to pay off debt, notably credit-card balances, which is often against the terms of loan agreements" (Smillie 68).	This quote reinforces the idea that some _____ students are improperly using student loan money for _____ _____ instead of _____.

138 Issue 4

Debate Ideas

SYNTHESIZE IDEAS

Write a response to the debate question, including a paraphrase of a text quote and elaboration on the quote.

Claim: My position is that adolescents (are/are not) _____ prepared to take on the responsibilities of using a credit card.

Transitional Statement: I have (one key reason/a compelling reason) _____ _____ for taking this stance.

Quote Paraphrase: (According to _____,/The author points out _____)

_____
_____
_____

Quote Elaboration: (As a result, _____/Consequently, _____)

_____
_____
_____

PRESENT EVIDENCE

Speaking at an Appropriate Pace

When presenting ideas during class or in a meeting, speak at an **appropriate pace**. Speak slowly, stop to breathe, and pause briefly to emphasize a point or to avoid inserting fillers such as *um, so,* or *like*.

LISTEN AND TAKE NOTES

Listen attentively and take notes. Then indicate whether you agree (+) or disagree (−).

> **Language to AFFIRM AND CLARIFY**
> That's an intriguing perspective.
> I don't quite understand _____.

Classmate's Name	Idea	+/−

Money Matters 139

Academic Writing

ANALYZING TEXT ELEMENTS

Student Writing Model

Academic Writing Type

A **justification essay** states a claim and supports it with logical reasons and relevant evidence from texts.

A. The **thesis statement** clearly states the writer's claim and tells what the writer will explain about the topic.

B. **Supporting paragraphs** support the claim with reasons and evidence from texts.

C. The **conclusion statement** restates the writer's claim about the issue.

ANALYZE TEXT
Read this student model to analyze elements of a justification essay.

A
After analyzing research on teens and money, I agree strongly that adolescents are prepared to take on the responsibilities of using credit cards.

B
One reason I maintain this position is because the majority of teens are not at risk for going into credit card debt. A survey by Lexington Law presents convincing statistics about teens' incomes. The survey reveals that 61% of teens making money have started saving their money in a bank account (52). This is significant because, while some people may argue that teens don't have the resources to stay out of debt if they use a credit card, the reality is that many teens are earning their own money to pay their bills and managing their finances responsibly.

Another important reason I hold this position is that even if teens start out with minimal financial know-how, many tools are available to help them. According to Dirk Smillie, numerous organizations offer free financial advice and education (69). This evidence underscores the seriousness of using credit cards while showing that teens have the potential to become responsible credit card users.

In addition, my own relevant experience as the relative of someone who is in debt has made me critically aware that financial responsibility has little to do with age. As an illustration, my uncle went bankrupt because he overspent with credit cards. Conversely, my 19-year-old sister uses a credit card, but her first priority is adding to her savings account each month. This is proof that teens can be trusted with credit cards.

C
For these reasons, I contend that teens can handle the responsibilities that come with using credit cards.

Justification Essay
ANALYZING TEXT ELEMENTS

💬 MARK AND DISCUSS ELEMENTS
Mark the justification elements and use the frames to discuss them with your partner.

1. **Circle the writer's claim within the thesis statement.** *The writer's claim is _____.*

2. **Draw a box around five transition words or phrases.**
   One transition (word/phrase) is _____.

3. **Underline and label three reasons that support the writer's claim with the letter *R*.**
   One reason that supports the writer's claim is _____.

4. **Underline and label three pieces of evidence that support the writer's claim with the letter *E*.**
   One piece of evidence that supports the writer's claim is _____.

5. **Star four precise topic words and check four high-utility academic words.**
   An example of a (precise topic word/high-utility academic word) is _____.

✅ ASSESS A STUDENT SAMPLE
Read an additional student writing sample and rate it.

Scoring Guide			
1	Insufficient	3	Sufficient
2	Developing	4	Exemplary

1. Does the thesis statement clearly state the claim?	1	2	3	4
2. Do supporting paragraphs begin with a topic sentence that specifies a reason?	1	2	3	4
3. Did the writer give evidence drawn primarily from sources to support the claim?	1	2	3	4
4. Did the writer explain why the evidence is relevant and significant?	1	2	3	4
5. Did the writer use strong verbs to state and restate the claim?	1	2	3	4
6. Did the writer use transitions to introduce reasons and evidence?	1	2	3	4
7. Did the writer include precise topic words and high-utility words?	1	2	3	4
8. Does the conclusion statement strongly restate the claim using new wording?	1	2	3	4

👥 REFLECT AND REVISE
Record specific priorities and suggestions to help the writer.

The writer did an effective job of (organizing/including/stating) _____
_____
_____

One way the writer could make the justification essay stronger is _____
_____
_____

I noticed that the writer (forgot to/included/used) _____
_____
_____

This will support me with writing a justification essay because I will remember to
_____
_____
_____

Money Matters 141

Academic Writing
FRONTLOADING LANGUAGE

Transitions to Introduce Evidence

Transitions	Examples
According to (Source), _____.	**In the text, Jackson explains** that more than one-quarter of all vehicle crashes each year involved phone use.
In the text, (Author's Name) explains _____.	
The (Source) points out _____.	**The National Center for Education Statistics points out** that more schools are offering courses in Arabic and Chinese.
(Author's Name) emphasizes _____.	
In addition, the text states _____.	
In my experience, _____.	**In my experience,** lack of sleep has caused me to forget crucial test material.
Based on my experience as a _____.	
Drawing from my experience as a _____.	**As an illustration,** many people in my community are bilingual, which allows them to interact with more people.
As an illustration, _____.	

IDENTIFY TRANSITIONS
Review the transitions that writers use to introduce evidence that supports a claim. Then complete each sentence below with an appropriate transition.

1. _____ only about one-fourth of teenagers feel confident in their knowledge of personal finance.

2. _____ that "credit repair clinics" charge steep fees and rarely help.

3. _____ teen with very little income, I am critically aware that credit cards can make overspending tempting.

WRITE SUPPORTING EVIDENCE
Write four sentences using transitions to introduce evidence that supports the claim.

1. _____

2. _____

3. _____

4. _____

Justification Essay
FRONTLOADING CONVENTIONS

Simple and Complex Sentences

Guidelines for Writing Simple and Complex Sentences
A **simple sentence** contains a subject and a predicate to express a complete thought.
A **complex sentence** contains a simple sentence and one or more dependent clauses.
A dependent clause cannot stand on its own as a sentence and often begins with a word such as *because, since,* or *that*.

Presenting Reasons	Examples
One reason I maintain this position is that _____.	**One reason I maintain this position is that** establishing good credit can make it easier to acquire an important loan later in life.
Another fundamental reason I hold this position is that _____.	**Another fundamental reason I hold this position is that** so many young people are getting themselves into serious debt.
Due to my own experience as (a/an) _____, I am critically aware that _____.	**Due to my own experience as** an impulsive shopper, **I am critically aware that** many teens cannot use credit cards responsibly.
Presenting Evidence	**Examples**
For instance, _____.	**For instance,** people with poor credit may only qualify for small, high-interest loans.
This is (important/significant) because _____.	**This is significant because** young people can quickly go from financial independence to debt.
Based on (current data/recent findings) that show _____, I maintain my position that _____.	**Based on current data that show** most teens don't understand how credit works, **I maintain my position that** teens should not be trusted with credit cards.

PRESENT REASONS AND EVIDENCE
Write simple and complex sentences to present reasons and evidence.

Claim: Schools should start later to accommodate teens' sleep schedules.

Reason: One reason why I firmly believe that _____
is the fact that _____

Evidence: For instance, _____
_____

Claim: Schools _____ require students to study a world language.

Reason: A fundamental reason I hold this position is that _____
_____
so I am certain that _____

Evidence: This is important because _____
_____

Money Matters 143

Academic Writing
PLANNING TO WRITE

Organize a Justification Essay

Prompt Are adolescents prepared to take on the responsibilities of using credit cards? Write a justification that states and supports your claim.

Thesis Starters	Examples
After analyzing the research on . . .	**After analyzing the research on** teens and driving, I strongly disagree that states should raise the driving age.
After reviewing the (evidence/data) on . . .	
After examining the issues surrounding . . .	**After reviewing the evidence on** vehicle crashes due to teen drivers, I am convinced that the driving age should be raised.

Conclusion Starters	Examples
For these reasons,	**For these reasons,** I conclude that a second language should be a requirement to graduate.
In light of this evidence,	**In light of this evidence,** I still maintain that students should not be required to study a word language to earn a diploma.

✏️ WRITE A THESIS STATEMENT
Describe your claim.

My claim: _____

_____

Use academic language to restate your claim as a thesis statement.

_____ adolescents and financial responsibility,

I (agree/disagree) _____ (strongly/firmly) _____

that _____
(your claim)

💡 CHOOSE SUPPORTING TOPICS
List each topic you will write about to support your claim.

Supporting Paragraph 1

Topic: _____

_____

Supporting Paragraph 2

Topic: _____

_____

Supporting Paragraph 3

Topic: _____

_____

Justification Essay
PLANNING TO WRITE

📋 PLAN SUPPORTING PARAGRAPHS
List reasons and evidence that support your claim. You may draw from texts, your experience, or a classmate's experience.

Supporting Paragraph 1

Reason 1: _____

Evidence: _____

Source: _____

Author: _____

Elaboration on this evidence: _____

Supporting Paragraph 2

Reason 2: _____

Evidence: _____

Source: _____

Author: _____

Elaboration on this evidence: _____

Supporting Paragraph 3

Reason 3: _____

Relevant personal experience: _____

Relevant personal connection: _____

Elaboration on this evidence: _____

✏️ WRITE A CONCLUSION
Plan a conclusion statement that restates your claim.

_____ I contend that
(Conclusion starter)

_____

Money Matters 145

Academic Writing

WRITING A DRAFT

Write a Justification Essay

Prompt | Are adolescents prepared to take on the responsibilities of using credit cards? Write a justification that states and supports your claim.

✎ WRITE AN ESSAY

Use the frame to write your thesis statement, supporting paragraphs, and conclusion statement.

A

_____
(Thesis starter)
adolescents and financial responsibility, I (agree/disagree) _____
(strongly, firmly) _____ that _____
(claim)
_____
_____
_____

B1

One reason I maintain this position is _____
(1st reason that supports your claim)
_____
_____
_____

In _____
(Title of Source)
_____ presents (strong/convincing/compelling)
(Author's Name)
_____ (data/statistics/evidence) _____
regarding the (positive/negative/serious) _____ consequences
of _____
(topic)
_____
_____

The author points out that _____
(text evidence)
_____
_____
_____

This is significant because _____
(elaborate on text evidence)
_____
_____
_____

Issue 4

JUSTIFICATION ESSAY
ASSESSING AND REVISING

B2

Another (important/fundamental/critical) _____ reason I hold this position is that _____
_(2nd reason that supports your claim)
_____
_____
_____

According to _____
_(source or author's name)
_____
_(text evidence)
_____
_____

This (data/evidence) _____ underscores (the need for/the impact of/the seriousness of) _____
_____
_(elaborate on text evidence)
_____
_____

B3

In addition, my own relevant experience as _____
_(relevant personal connection)
_____
has made me critically aware that _____
_(claim)
_____
_____
_____

As an illustration, _____
_(relevant personal experience)
_____
_____
_____

This is (evidence/proof) _____ that _____
_(elaborate on personal experience)
_____
_____
_____

C

_____ I contend that
_(Conclusion starter)
_____
_(restate your claim)
_____
_____

Money Matters **147**

Presenting Ideas

60-Second Speech

IDENTIFY TOPIC
Choose one of the questions below to address in a 60-second speech.

☐ Should our state require teen drivers to display "new driver" decals on their cars?

☐ Should our school offer personal finance courses?

BRAINSTORM IDEAS
Write your position and two reasons that support it.

My Claim: _____

Reason 1: _____

Reason 2: _____

SYNTHESIZE IDEAS
Take notes on supporting evidence and a counterclaim.

Evidence 1: _____
_____

Evidence 2: _____
_____

Counterclaim: _____
_____

Response: _____
_____

WRITE A SPEECH
Write a 60-second speech that states your claim and includes reasons, evidence, and a counterclaim.

From my point of view, _____
_____

One reason is that _____
_____

Secondly, _____
_____

For example, _____
_____

Critics might claim that _____
_____

However, _____
_____

For these reasons, I _____ that _____
_____

Present and Rate Your Speech

Speaking at an Appropriate Pace
When presenting ideas during class or in a meeting, speak at an **appropriate pace**. Speak slowly, stop to breathe, and pause briefly to emphasize a point or to avoid inserting fillers such as *um, so,* or *like*.

PRESENT YOUR SPEECH
Present your speech to the small group. Make sure to speak at an appropriate pace.

LISTEN AND TAKE NOTES
Listen attentively and take notes. Then indicate whether you agree (+) or disagree (−).

Language to AFFIRM AND CLARIFY
That's an intriguing perspective.
I don't quite understand _____.

Classmate's Name	Idea	+/−

ASSESS YOUR SPEECH
Use the scoring guide to rate your speech.

Scoring Guide				
1	Insufficient		3	Sufficient
2	Developing		4	Exemplary

1. Did your topic sentence clearly state your claim?	1	2	3	4
2. Did you include strong reasons and evidence to support your speech?	1	2	3	4
3. Did you include precise topic words?	1	2	3	4
4. Were you easy to understand?	1	2	3	4
5. Did you speak at an appropriate pace?	1	2	3	4

REFLECT
Think of two ways you can improve for your next speech.

Priority 1: I can strengthen my next speech by _____

Priority 2: In my next speech, I will include _____

Issue 5 Virtual vs. Reality

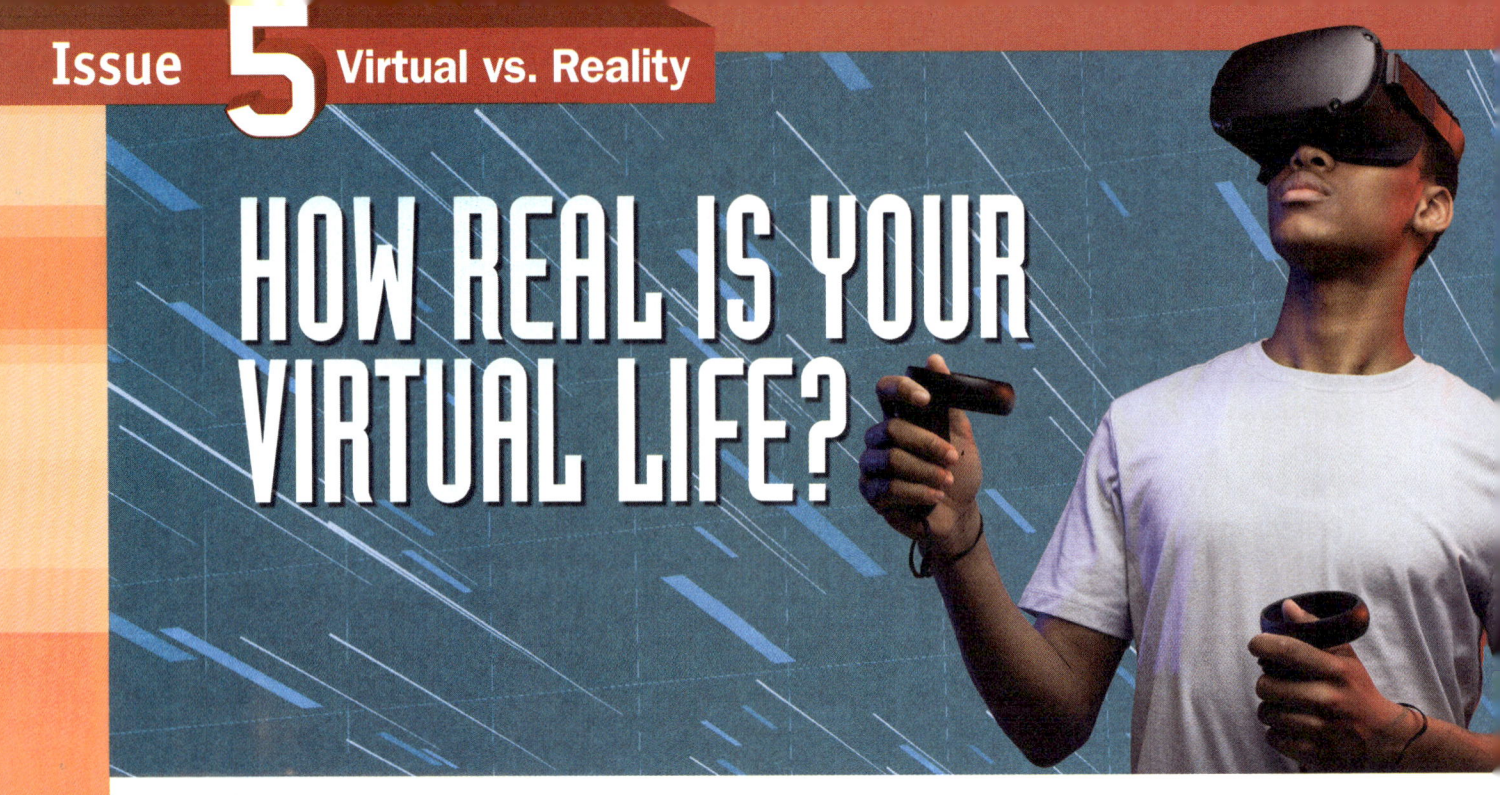

HOW REAL IS YOUR VIRTUAL LIFE?

📖 BUILD KNOWLEDGE
Read and respond to the Data File (*Issues,* p. 70).

💡 BRAINSTORM IDEAS
Write a brief list of the ways people can use virtual reality.

- field trips
- _____
- _____
- _____

🎤 PRESENT IDEAS
Use the frames to discuss ideas with your group. Listen attentively and record the strongest ideas to complete the concept map.

Language to FACILITATE DISCUSSION
So _____, what's your suggestion?
_____, what examples did you come up with?

1. One way to use virtual reality is to _____ (**base verb:** learn)
2. Virtual reality can help people _____ (**base verb:** experience)
3. We can also use virtual reality to _____ (**base verb:** explore)
4. Virtual reality is useful for its ability to _____ (**base verb:** create)

WAYS TO USE VIRTUAL REALITY
- practice medical procedures
- _____
- _____
- _____
- _____

Words to Know

BUILD WORD KNOWLEDGE

Rate your word knowledge. Then discuss word meanings and examples with your group.

① Don't Know   ② Recognize   ③ Familiar   ④ Know

Word to Know	Meaning	Example
1 **avatar** *noun* ① ② ③ ④	an _____ that represents a _____ online or in a game	The **avatar** I created for the game has _____ just like me.
2 **virtual** *adjective* ① ② ③ ④	made, done, or seen on a _____ rather than in the _____	You can take a **virtual** tour of a _____ to help you decide if you want to _____
3 **authentic** *adjective* ① ② ③ ④	reflecting one's _____ character or _____	Posting **authentic** content online means showing the real you, not just _____
4 **interact** *verb* ① ② ③ ④	to _____ with someone or something and receive a _____	I like to **interact** with my friends _____
1 **reality** *noun* ① ② ③ ④	what actually happens or is true, not what is _____ or thought	I love to _____ as an escape from **reality**.
2 **access** *verb* ① ② ③ ④	to _____ something, such as a _____	I use my smartphone to **access** _____
3 **agency** *noun* ① ② ③ ④	the _____ to make your own choices and do things your _____	Choosing your _____ can give you a sense of **agency** over your life.
4 **digital** *adjective* ① ② ③ ④	involving the use of electronic or _____ technology	My dad is amazed by the high quality of the **digital** _____ produced today.

Virtual vs. Reality 151

Building Concepts and Language

SPEAKING AND LISTENING

Academic Discussion

What are the benefits and drawbacks of using virtual reality?

BRAINSTORM IDEAS
Briefly record at least two ideas in each column using everyday English.

Benefits	Drawbacks
• connect with people far away • •	• feel motion sickness • •

ANALYZE WORDS
Complete the chart with precise words to discuss and write about the topic.

Everyday	Precise
easy *(adjective)*	comfortable,
alone *(adjective)*	lonely,
negative result *(noun)*	ramification,

MAKE A CLAIM
Rewrite two ideas using the frames and precise words.

1. **Frame:** One (benefit/drawback) of virtual reality is the (ability/potential) to _____ (**base verb:** explore, meet, spend)

   Response: _____

   _____

2. **Frame:** Using virtual reality can be (beneficial/harmful) when you _____ (**present-tense verb:** learn, isolate, interact)

   Response: _____

   _____

Language to ELABORATE

To illustrate, _____.

I have observed that _____.

COLLABORATE
Listen attentively, restate, and record your partner's ideas.

Classmate's Name	Ideas
	1.
	2.

Language to RESTATE

If I understand correctly, your opinion is that _____.

Yes, that's accurate.

Actually, what I (suggested/related) is that _____.

152 Issue 5

SPEAKING AND WRITING

Ten-Minute Response

A **ten-minute response** begins with a **claim**, followed by **two detail sentences** that elaborate with relevant examples and precise words.

Language to COMPARE IDEAS

My opinion is (similar to/different from) _____'s.

🎤 PRESENT IDEAS

Listen, compare ideas, and take notes. Then indicate whether you agree (+) or disagree (–).

Classmate's Name	Idea	+/−

✏️ ELABORATE IN WRITING
Work with a partner to write a ten-minute response.

Language to COLLABORATE

What should we write?

We could choose _____. What do you think is a strong choice?

In addition, we could write _____.

One benefit of virtual reality is the ability to _____

For example, in virtual worlds you can _____

As a result, you gain a _____

_____ without even leaving home.

Write a ten-minute response.

Using virtual reality can be _____ when you

_____

For example, _____

As a result, _____

Analyzing and Discussing Text
ACADEMIC VOCABULARY

Words to Go

BUILD WORD KNOWLEDGE
Complete the meanings and examples for these high-utility academic words.

Words to Go	Meaning	Example
physical phy•si•cal *adjective*	of the _____ or material things, rather than the mind, spirit, or virtual	She noticed a big improvement in her **physical** health after _____ _____ _____
physically phy•si•cal•ly *adverb*	relating to the _____ or _____ things	He felt **physically** exhausted after the long run and _____ _____ to feel better.

DISCUSS AND WRITE EXAMPLES
Discuss your response with a partner. Then complete the sentence in writing.

Some of the **physical** features of my area include _____
_____

Write your response and read it aloud to a partner.

One of the most _____ challenging activities of this year was when I
_____

BUILD WORD KNOWLEDGE
Complete the meanings and examples for these high-utility academic words.

Word to Go	Meaning	Example
represent rep•re•sent *verb*	to symbolize or _____ for someone or something	Your _____ _____ can **represent** your personal style and individuality.
representation rep•re•sen•ta•tion *noun*	the _____ in which something or someone is presented or _____	The flag is a **representation** of a country, often using colors and symbols to reflect its _____

DISCUSS AND WRITE EXAMPLES
Discuss your response with a partner. Then complete the sentence in writing.

In art, colors can be used to **represent** different _____

Write your response and read it aloud to a partner.

Accurate and respectful _____ of _____
_____ in television and movies is extremely important.

Text 1 • Opinion Article
RESPONDING TO TEXT

Close Reading

📖 BUILD FLUENCY
Read the text "Metaverse Threatens Human Connection, Offers More Problems Than Solutions" (*Issues*, pp. 71–75).

💬 IDENTIFY KEY IDEAS AND DETAILS
Take turns asking and answering questions with a partner. Then write brief notes.

Discussion Frames	Text Notes
Q: What is the text **primarily about**? **A:** The text is **primarily about** _____.	• potential negative impact of _____ _____
Q: What are the **most important details** in this text? **A:** One **essential detail** in this text is _____. **A:** An additional **essential detail** in this text is _____.	• virtual environments cannot compare to _____; we need face-to-face _____ • the virtual world and social media can have _____ effects on _____ • the metaverse offers benefits, such as _____ for disabled people • it also presents challenges, such as _____ of diversity and the blurring of _____ and virtual experiences

✏️ RESPOND WITH EVIDENCE
Use the frames and evidence from the text to construct formal written responses.

1. According to the text, what are one pro and one con of the metaverse?

According to the text, one pro of the metaverse is _____
_____

One con is the potential _____
_____

Use the frame to analyze Emily Samuel's point of view.

2. How does Samuel's use of descriptive language enhance her argument? What does it tell you about her point of view?

By using descriptive language, with the phrase "flesh-and-blood human beings," Samuel vividly illustrates physical qualities of the real world compared to that of the _____. This descriptive language tells readers that the author has a _____ point of view toward virtual reality experiences.

🔍 IDENTIFY PRECISE WORDS
Review Text 1 and your *Portfolio* (pp. 150–155) to identify words for your writing.

Topic Words	High-Utility Academic Words
• metaverse • •	• underrepresented • •

Virtual vs. Reality 155

Building Concepts and Language

SPEAKING AND LISTENING

Academic Discussion

How are virtual experiences similar to and different from real-life?

BRAINSTORM IDEAS
Briefly record at least two ideas in each column using everyday English.

Similar	Different
• uses multiple senses	• requires internet
•	•
•	•

ANALYZE WORDS
Complete the chart with precise words to discuss and write about the issue.

Everyday	Precise
grab *(verb)*	engage,
move *(verb)*	motivate,
carry *(verb)*	convey,

MAKE A CLAIM
Rewrite two ideas using the frames and precise words. Then prepare to elaborate verbally.

1. **Frame:** Virtual experiences are (similar to/different from) real-life experiences because you (are/are not) able to _____ (**base verb:** learn, visit, touch)

   Response: _____

2. **Frame:** Virtual experiences (can/cannot) replicate real-life experiences such as _____ (**verb + –ing:** meeting, playing, touching)

   Response: _____

Language to ELABORATE
To illustrate, _____.
I have observed that _____.

COLLABORATE
Listen attentively, restate, and record your partner's ideas.

Classmate's Name	Ideas
	1.
	2.

Language to RESTATE
If I understand correctly, your opinion is that _____.
Yes, that's accurate.
Actually, what I (suggested/related) is that _____.

SPEAKING AND WRITING

Ten-Minute Response

A **ten-minute response** begins with a **claim**, followed by **two detail sentences** that elaborate with relevant examples and precise words.

Language to COMPARE IDEAS

My opinion is (similar to/different from) _____'s.

🎤 PRESENT IDEAS

Listen, compare ideas, and take notes. Then indicate whether you agree (+) or disagree (–).

Classmate's Name	Idea	+/–

✏️ ELABORATE IN WRITING

Work with a partner to write a ten-minute response.

Language to COLLABORATE

What should we write?

We could choose _____. What do you think is a strong choice?

In addition, we could write _____.

Virtual experiences are similar to real-life experiences because you are able to learn new skills. For example, virtual reality learning offers the ability to _____ _____ and _____ _____ from just about anywhere. As a result, students can build _____ before applying them in _____ scenarios, which enhances their _____

Write a ten-minute response.

Virtual experiences _____ replicate real-life experiences such as _____

_____

For example, _____

_____

_____

As a result, _____

_____

Virtual vs. Reality 157

Analyzing and Discussing Text

ACADEMIC VOCABULARY

Words to Go

BUILD WORD KNOWLEDGE
Complete the meanings and examples for these high-utility academic words.

Word to Go	Meaning	Example
anonymity a•non•y•mi•ty *noun*	when other people do not know _____ _____ or what your name is	The _____ _____ I wore to the party gave me **anonymity**.
anonymous a•non•y•mous *adjective*	describing a person who is not identified by _____	He made an **anonymous** comment on the online post by _____

DISCUSS AND WRITE EXAMPLES
Discuss your response with a partner. Then complete the sentence in writing.

She valued her **anonymity** online to _____
_____ without judgment.

Write your response and read it aloud to a partner.

They submitted their feedback _____ to ensure that _____
_____

BUILD WORD KNOWLEDGE
Complete the meanings and examples for these high-utility academic words.

Word to Go	Meaning	Example
experiment ex•per•i•ment *verb*	to _____ something new	The teens decided to **experiment** with new _____ for their cooking club meeting.
experimentation ex•per•i•men•ta•tion *noun*	the process of trying new ideas or methods to _____ if they work	Through our **experimentation** with coding, we were able to create _____

DISCUSS AND WRITE EXAMPLES
Discuss your response with a partner. Then complete the sentence in writing.

I like to **experiment** with my _____ to _____
_____

Write your response and read it aloud to a partner.

Through careful _____, the scientists were able to _____
_____

Text ❷ • Section 1 • News Article

SUMMARIZING TEXT

Section Shrink

BUILD FLUENCY
Read the introduction and Section 1 of the text "How Avatars Are Helping Gen Z Find Themselves" (*Issues,* pp. 76–77).

IDENTIFY KEY IDEAS AND DETAILS
Take turns asking and answering questions with a partner. Then write brief notes.

Discussion Frames	Text Notes
Q: What does this section **focus on**? **A:** This section **focuses on** _____.	• avatars in the _____ attracting younger generations; they can show their true _____
Q: What are the **significant details** in this section? **A:** (One/An additional) **significant detail** in this section is _____. **A:** Perhaps the **most significant detail** in this section is _____.	• many members of _____ and _____ prefer to spend their time in digital spaces • users find a sense of _____ in online spaces • _____ online gives people more freedom to _____

SUMMARIZE
"Shrink" Section 1 of the text by writing a summary in 40 or fewer words.

CLASS SUMMARY   **WORD COUNT:** _____

The metaverse attracts _____ because it allows them to use avatars for _____ and provides _____ so that they can freely _____ their identities without _____ judgment.

PARTNER SUMMARY   **WORD COUNT:** _____

It is popular among young users of _____
to express their _____ through their
_____, which give them the opportunity to
_____ with their identities, often
_____ and without judgment.

IDENTIFY PRECISE WORDS
Review Section 1 and your *Portfolio* (pp. 156–159) to identify words for your writing.

Topic Words	High-Utility Academic Words
• platforms • •	• sole • •

Virtual vs. Reality 159

Analyzing and Discussing Text

ACADEMIC VOCABULARY

Words to Go

📗 BUILD WORD KNOWLEDGE
Complete the meaning and example for this high-utility academic word.

Word to Go	Meaning	Examples
as a result as a re•sult *conjunction*	indicates the _____ of something that happened _____ it	I decided not to take pre-calculus this year and, **as a result**, _____ _____ **As a result** of my dedication and patience, I have finally _____ _____ after years of practice.

💬 DISCUSS AND WRITE EXAMPLES
Discuss your response with a partner. Then complete the sentence in writing.

I followed a strict training regimen, and **as a result**, I _____

Write your response and read it aloud to a partner.

_____ of their behavior at the football game, my friend was _____

📗 BUILD WORD KNOWLEDGE
Complete the meaning and example for this high-utility academic word.

Word to Go	Meaning	Examples
unique u•nique *adjective*	being the _____ one of its kind; _____ anything else	Every snowflake is **unique**, each with a _____ _____ Something that makes my school **unique** is its _____ _____

💬 DISCUSS AND WRITE EXAMPLES
Discuss your response with a partner. Then complete the sentence in writing.

I have a truly **unique** clothing style; no one else _____

Write your response and read it aloud to a partner.

My _____

sets me apart from the crowd and highlights my _____

Text ❷ • Section 2 • News Article

SUMMARIZING TEXT

Section Shrink

📖 BUILD FLUENCY
Read Section 2 of "How Avatars Are Helping Gen Z Find Themselves" (*Issues*, p. 78).

💬 IDENTIFY KEY IDEAS AND DETAILS
Take turns asking and answering questions with a partner. Then write brief notes.

Discussion Frames	Text Notes
Q: What does this section **focus on**? **A:** This section **focuses on** _____.	• the metaverse being fun for _____, _____ but not a _____ space for everyone
Q: What are the **significant details** in this section? **A:** (One/An additional) **significant detail** in this section is _____. **A:** Perhaps the **most significant detail** in this section is _____.	• some users make their avatar look _____ from themselves; they feel they can be more _____ with their appearance in virtual spaces • the metaverse feels _____, but it often is not • a user shared that he _____ discrimination because of his avatar and user name

✏️ SUMMARIZE
"Shrink" Section 2 of the text by writing a summary in 40 or fewer words.

CLASS SUMMARY   **WORD COUNT:** _____

Virtual spaces like _____ can feel safe by providing

opportunities for creative _____ through experimenting with your

_____ yet issues such as _____

and judgment can still arise and affect the user's _____

PARTNER SUMMARY   **WORD COUNT:** _____

The ability to _____ an avatar to _____

oneself in a virtual space enables users to be _____

in their self-presentation, though they may still face _____ based on

their _____

🔍 IDENTIFY PRECISE WORDS
Review Section 2 and your *Portfolio* (pp. 160–161) to identify words for your writing.

Topic Words	High-Utility Academic Words
• gaming • •	• likeness • •

Virtual vs. Reality **161**

Analyzing and Discussing Text

ACADEMIC VOCABULARY

Words to Go

📖 BUILD WORD KNOWLEDGE

Complete the meanings and examples for these high-utility academic words.

Word to Go	Meaning	Example
customize cus·tom·ize *verb*	to _____ something to make it just right for you	I can **customize** my phone's home screen by _____ _____
customization cus·tom·i·za·tion *noun*	the process of changing something to meet specific _____ or preferences	The app offers **customization**, allowing users to adjust the _____ _____ they like.

💬 DISCUSS AND WRITE EXAMPLES

Discuss your response with a partner. Then complete the sentence in writing.

The team **customized** their homecoming jerseys by _____
_____

Write your response and read it aloud to a partner.

Many teens enjoy _____ in fashion, such as _____
_____ to match their personal style.

📖 BUILD WORD KNOWLEDGE

Complete the meaning and example for this high-utility academic word.

Word to Go	Meaning	Examples
option op·tion *noun*	a _____ among several possibilities	I like having the **option** to _____ _____ because it suits my learning style best. I wish that the school cafeteria had more _____ **options** for lunch.

💬 DISCUSS AND WRITE EXAMPLES

Discuss your response with a partner. Then complete the sentence in writing.

Every year, our school gives students the **option** to _____
_____

Write your response and read it aloud to a partner.

I have several _____ for _____
_____ that can help me prepare for my future.

162 Issue 5

Section Shrink

Text 2 • Section 3 • News Article
SUMMARIZING TEXT

📖 BUILD FLUENCY
Read Section 3 of "How Avatars Are Helping Gen Z Find Themselves" (*Issues*, pp. 79–80).

💬 IDENTIFY KEY IDEAS AND DETAILS
Take turns asking and answering questions with a partner. Then write brief notes.

Discussion Frames	Text Notes
Q: What does this section **focus on**? **A:** This section **focuses on** _____.	• the merging of _____ and _____ worlds through avatar customization and fashion
Q: What are the **significant details** in this section? **A:** (One/An additional) **significant detail** in this section is _____. **A:** Perhaps the **most significant detail** in this section is _____.	• nearly half of Gen Z seeks digital fashion brands to experiment with _____ they wouldn't try in real life • users also want _____ for skin color, hair, and body types • popular items in the virtual world are then _____ for the real world • for Gen Z, owning an item digitally feels _____ to owning a physical item

✏️ SUMMARIZE
"Shrink" Section 3 of the text by writing a summary in 40 or fewer words.

CLASS SUMMARY   **WORD COUNT:** _____

Many users are excited to _____ brand name
_____ items and _____ with
digital clothing they typically wouldn't try in _____ highlighting the
growing demand for options and _____

PARTNER SUMMARY   **WORD COUNT:** _____

The growing _____ of digital _____
gives users an outlet for _____ allowing them to explore a range
of style _____ they might not have considered wearing in the
_____ world.

🔍 IDENTIFY PRECISE WORDS
Review Section 3 and your *Portfolio* (pp. 162–163) to identify words for your writing.

Topic Words	High-Utility Academic Words
• digital fashion • •	• ownership • •

Virtual vs. Reality 163

Academic Writing

ANALYZING TEXT ELEMENTS

Student Writing Model

Academic Writing Type

A **formal written summary** provides an objective overview of the topic and important details from an informational text. The writer credits the author but writes in primarily their own words, without including personal opinions.

A. The **topic sentence** includes the text type, title, author, and topic.

B. **Detail sentences** include the important details from the summarized text.

C. The **concluding sentence** restates the author's conclusion in the writer's own words.

ANALYZE TEXT

Read this student model to analyze the elements of a formal summary.

A
In the opinion article titled "Metaverse Threatens Human Connection, Offers More Problems Than Solutions," Emily Samuels argues that the metaverse could diminish authentic human experiences.

B
Samuels begins by pointing out that virtual spaces might replace real-world interactions, affecting students and employees. The writer continues to report that online environments limit opportunities for personal and intellectual growth. She describes further how avatars can obscure true identities, potentially harming self-perception. Moreover, the author discusses that mental health issues, such as depression and anxiety, are linked to screen time and virtual spaces.

C
Samuels concludes by emphasizing the importance of prioritizing real-life connections.

MARK AND DISCUSS ELEMENTS

Mark the summary elements and use the frames to discuss them with your partner.

1. **Number (1–4) the four elements of the topic sentence.**
   The topic sentence includes the _____.

2. **Draw a box around four transition words or phrases.**
   One transition (word/phrase) is _____.

3. **Underline four important details.** *One important detail in this summary is _____.*

4. **Circle four citation verbs.** *One citation verb that the writer uses is _____.*

5. **Star four precise topic words and check four high-utility academic words.**
   An example of a (precise topic word/high-utility academic word) is _____.

164 Issue 5

Formal Summary
PLANNING TO WRITE

Organize a Formal Summary

Prompt: Write a formal summary of "How Avatars Are Helping Gen Z Find Themselves."

Guidelines for Paraphrasing Multiple Sentences
Paraphrase related details from a source text by combining key information into one sentence. Replace key words and phrases with synonyms and keep important topic words.

Text Detail 1	Text Detail 2	Text Detail 3
"The freedom to express yourself through an avatar . . . has provided an irresistible lure for Gen Z and Gen Alpha to embody their true selves" (Cutrone 76).	"According to a Razorfish study, 52 percent of Gen Z gamers feel more like themselves in the metaverse than in real life" (Cutrone 77).	"One of the really exciting things about the metaverse is that it allows people to experiment with new identities that don't necessarily reflect the agency they were born with" (Cutrone 77).

PARAPHRASE IDEAS
Combine key information from the three text details above into one detail sentence.

The metaverse can give users the freedom to express themselves, which can help them

(text detail 1) _____

(text detail 2) _____ and

(text detail 3) _____

PLAN KEY IDEAS AND DETAILS
State the text information to write a topic sentence.

In the news article titled (Title) _____

(Author's Full Name) _____ (citation verb: examines, discusses)

_____ (topic) _____

List four important details from the article primarily using your own words.

1. _____
   _____

2. _____
   _____

3. _____
   _____

4. _____
   _____

Restate the author's conclusion in your own words.

_____
_____

Academic Writing

WRITING A DRAFT

Write a Formal Summary

Prompt Write a formal summary of "How Avatars Are Helping Gen Z Find Themselves."

✏️ WRITE A PARAGRAPH
Use the frame to write your topic sentence, detail sentences, and concluding sentence.

A

In the _____ titled _____
  (text type)   (Title)

_____ _____ _____
  (Author's full name)   (present-tense citation verb)

_____
  (topic)

_____

_____

B

_____ begins by _____
  (Author's Last Name)   (citation verb + –ing: presenting, arguing)

_____
  (1st important detail)

_____

_____

The (author/writer/researcher) _____ continues to _____
                                                                      (citation verb, base form: describe, report)

_____
  (2nd important detail)

_____

_____

_____ further that _____
  (Author's Last Name)   (present-tense citation verb)

_____
  (3rd important detail)

_____

_____

_____

Moreover, the (author/writer/researcher) _____ _____
                                                                   (present-tense citation verb)

_____
  (4th important detail)

_____

_____

C

_____ concludes by _____
  (Author's Last Name)   (citation verb + –ing: suggesting, emphasizing)

_____
  (restate author's conclusion)

_____

Formal Summary
ASSESSING AND REVISING

Rate Your Summary

Scoring Guide
1	Insufficient
2	Developing
3	Sufficient
4	Exemplary

ASSESS YOUR DRAFT
Rate your formal summary. Then have your partner rate it.

1. Does the topic sentence state the title, author, and topic?	Self	1	2	3	4
	Partner	1	2	3	4
2. Did you paraphrase the most important details from the text?	Self	1	2	3	4
	Partner	1	2	3	4
3. Did you use citation verbs to credit the author?	Self	1	2	3	4
	Partner	1	2	3	4
4. Did you use transitions to introduce and sequence details?	Self	1	2	3	4
	Partner	1	2	3	4
5. Did you include precise topic words and high-utility academic words?	Self	1	2	3	4
	Partner	1	2	3	4
6. Did you restate the author's conclusion using your own words?	Self	1	2	3	4
	Partner	1	2	3	4

REFLECT AND REVISE
Record specific priorities and suggestions to help you and your partner revise.

(Partner) Positive Feedback: I appreciate how you (used/included) _____

_____

_____

(Partner) Suggestion: As you revise your summary, focus on _____

_____

_____

(Self) Priority 1: My summary paragraph needs _____

_____

_____

(Self) Priority 2: I plan to improve my summary by _____

_____

_____

CHECK AND EDIT
Use this checklist to proofread and edit your summary.

- ☐ Did you capitalize the title of the news article and proper nouns?
- ☐ Did you put quotation marks around the title of the article?
- ☐ Did you use commas appropriately after transitions?
- ☐ Do simple present-tense verbs end in –s?
- ☐ Is each sentence complete?
- ☐ Are all words spelled correctly?

Analyzing and Discussing Text

ACADEMIC VOCABULARY

Words to Know

BUILD WORD KNOWLEDGE
Rate your word knowledge. Then discuss word meanings and examples with your group.

① Don't Know ② Recognize ③ Familiar ④ Know

Word to Know	Meaning	Examples
1 **simulation** *noun*	an imitation or _____ of a real-world process or system	During our driving course, we practiced in a **simulation** before _____ _____. The virtual reality **simulation** allowed us to explore famous landmarks from around the world _____ _____.
2 **differentiate** *verb*	to identify ways in which two or more things or people are _____ _____	Identical twins may _____ _____ so people can **differentiate** between them. My baby brother still can't **differentiate** between _____ _____.
3 **effective** *adjective*	having the ability to bring about a _____ that is wanted	I doubted how **effective** begging my parents to let me _____ _____ would be, but they actually agreed. _____ _____ can be very **effective** when trying to get a good night's sleep.
4 **contributing factor** *noun phrase*	an action or element that _____ to make something happen	_____ _____ was a **contributing factor** in my failure to remember what I had studied the night before. Stress is a **contributing factor** of _____ _____.

168 Issue 5

Text ❸ • Novel Excerpt
RESPONDING TO TEXT

Close Reading

📖 READ THE TEXT
Read an excerpt from *Ready Player One* (*Issues*, pp. 81–87).

🔍 IDENTIFY KEY IDEAS AND DETAILS

Making Inferences
To make an **inference**, the reader combines various facts and points of information from the text with their own prior knowledge to figure out something the author has not explicitly stated.

Use the frames to analyze the text and make inferences.

1. What inference can you make about the state of the real world outside the OASIS based on the author's use of the phrase "in these dark times" on page 81?

    Based on the author's use of the phrase "in these dark times," I can infer _____

    _____

    _____

2. What inferences can you make based on Wade3's encounter with Todd13?

    When Wade3 retorts, or responds to, Todd13's insults, he never even _____

    _____

    This reveals that Wade3 _____

    _____

✏️ ANALYZE CRAFT AND STRUCTURE

Analyzing Figurative Language
Authors use **figurative language**, words and phrases with a meaning that is different from their literal interpretation, to help the reader visualize what is happening.

Use the frames to analyze the author's use of figurative language.

3. Wade3 says, "I nearly broke my neck sprinting to the office to submit my application" for OASIS's public schools. What does the figurative language "nearly broke my neck" emphasize about Wade3's desire to attend school in the OASIS?

    The author uses the figurative language _____

    to emphasize that Wade3 _____

    _____

4. What does Wade3 mean when he says, "At this school, the only real weapons are words"?

    Since _____ is forbidden on Ludus, the only way students can

    _____ one another is by _____

    _____

Virtual vs. Reality 169

Analyzing and Discussing Text
SPEAKING AND LISTENING

Academic Discussion

What effects can virtual worlds have on a person?

BRAINSTORM IDEAS
Briefly record at least two ideas in each column using everyday English.

Positive Effects	Negative Effects
• interactive learning	• limited socialization
•	•
•	•

ANALYZE WORDS
Complete the chart with precise words to discuss and write about the topic.

Everyday	Precise
hide *(verb)*	camouflage,
hurt *(verb)*	wound,
disrespect *(noun)*	indignity,

MAKE A CLAIM
Rewrite two ideas using the frames and precise words. Then prepare to elaborate verbally.

Language to ELABORATE
To illustrate, _____.
I have observed that _____.

1. **Frame:** Virtual worlds can have a (positive/negative) effect on a person's _____ (**noun:** self-esteem, mental health, behavior)

   Response: _____

   _____

2. **Frame:** One potential (positive/negative) effect of virtual worlds is that they _____ (**base verb:** enhance, contribute, create)

   Response: _____

   _____

COLLABORATE
Listen attentively, restate, and record your partner's ideas.

Language to RESTATE
If I understand correctly, your opinion is that _____.

Yes, that's accurate.

Actually, what I (suggested/related) is that _____.

Classmate's Name	Ideas
	1.
	2.

170 Issue 5

Text ❸ • Novel Excerpt
SPEAKING AND WRITING

Ten-Minute Response

A **ten-minute response** begins with a **claim**, followed by **two detail sentences** that elaborate with relevant examples and precise words.

Language to COMPARE IDEAS
My opinion is (similar to/different from) _____'s.

🎙 PRESENT IDEAS
Listen, compare ideas, and take notes. Then indicate whether you agree (+) or disagree (−).

Classmate's Name	Idea	+/−

✏ ELABORATE IN WRITING
Work with a partner to write a ten-minute response.

Language to COLLABORATE
What should we write?
We could choose _____. What do you think is a strong choice?
In addition, we could write _____.

Virtual worlds can have a negative effect on a person's perception of reality. For example, spending too much time in virtual worlds can make it harder to _____
_____

As a result, a person can begin _____
_____

which can lead to _____
_____

Write a ten-minute response.

One potential _____ effect of virtual worlds is that they
_____

For example, _____
_____
_____

As a result, _____
_____
_____

Virtual vs. Reality **171**

Presenting Ideas

Take a Stand

Debate | Which is more authentic: life online or offline?

💬 COLLABORATE
Read the debate question about authenticity online. Then take turns using a frame to respond with your initial reaction.

Language to RESPOND
So _____, what is your initial reaction?
My initial reaction is _____.
_____ and I had (similar/somewhat different) initial reactions.

🔍 ANALYZE SOURCES
Read a quote that either supports or opposes the debate topic. Then paraphrase.

Quote	Paraphrase
Model: "60% of Gen Z [adult] participants said how you present yourself online is more important than how you present yourself in person" (Squarespace 70).	To put it another way, many young adults think that _____ self-presentation is more important than _____ self-presentation.
1. "If people can hide behind artificially created avatars, they never have to learn to embrace their identities—flaws and all" (Samuels 72).	To put it another way, the use of an avatar, which is an inauthentic _____ of a person, _____ the user's ability to _____ themselves as they are.
2. "So long as humans are breathing, we will remain social creatures that crave an intimacy that is impossible to achieve through a screen" (Samuels 75).	This quote clarifies that humans will seek _____ with other humans, which online experiences cannot _____
3. "The freedom to express yourself through an avatar—a digital representation of a user as they inhabit these virtual spaces—may not be the sole purpose of these games, but it has provided an irresistible lure for Gen Z and Gen Alpha to embody their true selves" (Cutrone 76).	This quote clarifies that younger _____ are drawn to online spaces because they can _____ their true selves through the _____ of virtual _____
4. "'Anonymity is obviously necessary in order to give people the ability to express themselves fully without being tied to whatever baggage they have coming from the real world'" (Cutrone 77).	To put it another way, being _____ online gives people the _____ to be themselves since they are disconnected from their _____

172 Issue 5

Debate Ideas

SYNTHESIZE IDEAS

Write a response to the debate question, including a paraphrase of a text quote and elaboration on the quote.

Claim: My position is that life (online/offline) _____

is more authentic than life (online/offline) _____

Transition Statement: I have (one key reason/a compelling reason) _____

_____ for taking this stance.

Quote Paraphrase: (For example,/According to (author),) _____.

_____

_____

_____

Quote Elaboration: (As a result,/Consequently,) _____.

_____

_____

_____

PRESENT EVIDENCE

Exuding Confidence
When presenting ideas during class or in a meeting, **exude confidence**. Take a deep breath before speaking, maintain a self-assured posture, and focus your attention on your audience.

LISTEN AND TAKE NOTES

Listen attentively and take notes.
Then indicate whether you agree (+) or disagree (−).

Language to AFFIRM AND CLARIFY
I hadn't thought of that.
What do you mean by _____ ?

Classmate's Name	Idea	+/−

Virtual vs. Reality 173

Academic Writing

ANALYZING TEXT ELEMENTS

Student Writing Model

Academic Writing Type

An **argument** states a claim and supports it with logical reasons and relevant evidence from sources.

A. The **thesis statement** clearly states the writer's claim and tells what the writer will explain about the topic.

B. **Supporting paragraphs** support the claim with reasons and evidence from sources. The writer also presents counterclaims and responds with strong evidence.

C. The **conclusion statement** restates the writer's claim about the issue.

ANALYZE TEXT
Read this student model to analyze elements of an argument research paper.

A
After examining the issues surrounding virtual reality, I am convinced that life online is more authentic than life offline.

B
One reason I maintain this position is that online spaces offer individuals the freedom to explore and express their identities without the limitations of physical appearances or societal norms. In "How Avatars Are Helping Gen Z Find Themselves," Carolyn Cutrone presents strong data regarding the positive effects of virtual environments on self-expression. For example, a study of Gen Z gamers revealed that more than half felt more like themselves in the metaverse than in real life (76). Opponents of online spaces often argue that being online can cause people to neglect their real lives. However, current data shows that people actually spend more time online than offline, blurring the line between the physical and virtual realms.

I am also in favor of the belief that life online is more authentic due to the genuine community these spaces foster. Emily Samuels points out in "Metaverse Threatens Human Connection, Offers More Problems Than Solutions" that online communities can be lifesaving for people who may not have the same access in real life (74). One particularly compelling statistic is that 29 percent of young Roblox users believe expressing themselves in immersive spaces helps to build connections with others (77).

C
Whether or not life online is more authentic than life offline will remain a controversial issue. After reviewing relevant data, I contend that life online is the more authentic experience.

Argument
ANALYZING TEXT ELEMENTS

💬 MARK AND DISCUSS ELEMENTS
Mark the argument elements and use the frames to discuss them with your partner.

1. **Circle the writer's claim within the thesis statement.**
   The writer's claim is _____.

2. **Underline and label two reasons that support the writer's claim with the letter *R*.**
   One reason that supports the writer's claim is _____.

3. **Underline and label four pieces of evidence that support the writer's claim with the letter *E*.**
   One piece of evidence that supports the writer's claim is _____.

4. **Draw a box around a counterclaim.** *One counterclaim is _____.*

5. **Star four precise topic words and check four high-utility academic words.**
   An example of a (precise topic word/high-utility academic word) is _____.

📝 ASSESS A STUDENT SAMPLE
Read an additional student writing sample and rate it.

Scoring Guide	
1	Insufficient
2	Developing
3	Sufficient
4	Exemplary

1. Does the thesis statement clearly state the claim?	1	2	3	4
2. Do supporting paragraphs begin with a topic sentence that specifies a reason?	1	2	3	4
3. Did the writer give evidence drawn primarily from sources to support the claim?	1	2	3	4
4. Did the writer explain why the evidence is relevant and significant?	1	2	3	4
5. Did the writer include complex sentences to present and respond to counterclaims?	1	2	3	4
6. Did the writer use strong verbs and verb phrases to express opinions?	1	2	3	4
7. Did the writer use transitions to introduce reasons and evidence?	1	2	3	4
8. Did the writer use precise adjectives to describe evidence?	1	2	3	4
9. Did the writer include citation information for text evidence?	1	2	3	4
10. Did the writer include precise topic words and high-utility words?	1	2	3	4
11. Does the conclusion statement strongly restate the claim using new wording?	1	2	3	4

👥 REFLECT AND REVISE
Record specific priorities and suggestions to help the writer.

The writer did an effective job of (organizing/including/stating) _____
_____
_____

One way the writer could make the argument stronger is _____
_____
_____

I noticed that the writer (forgot to/included/used) _____
_____
_____

This will support me with writing an argument because I will remember to _____
_____
_____

Virtual vs. Reality

Academic Writing

FRONTLOADING LANGUAGE

Paraphrasing Text

Guidelines for Paraphrasing Text
Look for text evidence that supports your position. Then **paraphrase** it by replacing key words and phrases with precise synonyms and your own words. Remember to keep important topic words in your paraphrase.

Source Text	Key Words and Phrases	→	Precise Synonyms	Paraphrasing
"Despite obstacles that exist, users' penchant for experimentation— both for identity exploration and play—are getting noticed" (Cutrone 79).	despite obstacles	→	in spite of challenges	In spite of challenges, people's interest in experimentation—both for self-discovery and play—are being recognized.
	users' penchant	→	people's interest	
	identity exploration	→	self-discovery	
	getting noticed	→	being recognized	

IDENTIFY PRECISE SYNONYMS
Read these statements and replace the words in parentheses with precise synonyms.

1. (Over 171,000,000) _____ people use VR technology and (at least) _____ one-third of users believe VR will positively impact society.

2. The number of universities with digital campuses in the metaverse, where students (experience) _____ their campus grounds in virtual reality, is steadily (rising) _____.

3. Immersive environments, such as virtual reality, (can improve) _____ student (outcomes) _____.

4. (Supporters) _____ of metaverse schools say that online classes help (train) _____ students for the digital world.

PARAPHRASE IDEAS
Paraphrase the four statements above using your own words and phrasing.

1. Recent surveys show that _____

2. The latest findings indicate that _____

3. Statistics show that _____

4. As a result, _____

Conditional Verbs

Guidelines for Using Conditional Verbs
Conditional verbs describe what might or could happen. They show what conditions would be like if a recommendation became reality.

A real future possibility: will, shall, can, may (+ base verb)
  Virtual reality can revolutionize remote learning by enhancing collaboration.

An uncertain future possibility: would, should, could, might (+ base verb)
  If virtual reality headsets become more affordable, they might become a household staple.

A past impossibility: would have, should have, could have, might have (+ past participle)
  Without advancements in technology, immersive gaming would have remained a dream.

IDENTIFY CONDITIONAL VERBS
Read the argument and circle the conditional verbs.

> After examining the issues surrounding virtual reality fatigue and eye pain, I believe developers should implement more user-friendly features. One reason I maintain this position is that users may continue to experience discomfort without proper adjustments. In "Don't Fight Your Eyes: Reducing Eye Strain from Screen Time," Julie Wood presents compelling data on the negative effects of prolonged VR use. For instance, users could suffer from eye strain if they do not take regular breaks from the screen. Additionally, those who might have enjoyed VR experiences could become discouraged due to persistent motion sickness. Whether developers can mitigate these issues will remain a controversial topic. After reviewing recent data, I conclude that they should at least make an effort.

WRITE CONDITIONAL VERBS
Use a conditional verb to complete each sentence.

1. Teens spending even more time online than they already do _____
   _____

2. If there were no demand for online communities, _____
   _____

3. Concerned parents and teachers claim that virtual spaces _____
   _____

4. Spending too much time in virtual reality _____
   _____

Academic Writing

PLANNING TO WRITE

Organize an Argument

Prompt Which is more authentic: life online or offline? Write an argument that states your claim and supports it with text evidence.

Guidelines for Crediting an Author
Paraphrase significant blocks of text evidence to avoid having too many quotes and to maintain your own voice in the argument. Credit the author when you paraphrase to avoid plagiarizing and to show that your argument is valid and supported by an authority.

Source Text	Paraphrased Idea
"To achieve real, face-to-face connection, students need to physically be in class and employees need to be in an office. Online environments do not provide the same opportunities for personal and intellectual growth" (Samuels 71).	Genuine connection requires students to attend class in person and employees to be physically present in the office, where people can grow in ways that are impossible virtually (Samuels 71).

✏ WRITE A THESIS STATEMENT
Describe your claim.

My claim: _____

_____

Use academic language to restate your claim as a thesis statement.

_____ virtual reality
(Thesis starter)
I (strongly/firmly) _____ believe _____
_____
(your claim)
_____

💡 CHOOSE SUPPORTING TOPICS
List each topic you will write about to support your claim.

Supporting Paragraph 1

Topic: _____

_____

Supporting Paragraph 2

Topic: _____

_____

Argument
PLANNING TO WRITE

📋 PLAN SUPPORTING PARAGRAPHS
List reasons and text evidence that support your claim. Include a counterclaim and a response supported with strong evidence.

Supporting Paragraph 1:

Reason 1: _____

_____

Evidence: _____

_____

Source: _____

Author: _____

Counterclaim: _____

_____

Response to counterclaim: _____

_____

Source: _____

Author: _____

Supporting Paragraph 2:

Reason 2: _____

_____

Evidence: _____

_____

_____

Source: _____

Author: _____

Statistical Evidence: _____

_____

_____

Source: _____

✏️ WRITE A CONCLUSION
Plan a conclusion that restates your claim.

Whether _____
         (restate the issue)
will remain a controversial issue. After reviewing (recent/relevant/substantial)

_____ data, I _____ that _____
                            (verb/verb phrase to express opinion)   (restate your claim)

_____

Virtual vs. Reality **179**

Academic Writing

WRITING A DRAFT

Write an Argument

Prompt Which is more authentic: life online or offline? Write an argument that states your claim and supports it with text evidence.

✏️ WRITE A RESEARCH PAPER
Use the frame to write your thesis statement, supporting paragraphs, and conclusion statement.

A

_____
(Thesis starter)

_____
(topic)

I _____
(verb/verb phrase to express opinion)

that _____
(strongly state your claim)

B1

One reason I maintain this position is that _____
(1st reason that supports your claim)

_____

_____

In _____
(Title of Source)

_____ presents (convincing/strong) _____
(Author's Full Name)

data regarding the (positive/negative) _____ consequences of

_____
(topic)

_____

For example, _____
(evidence from source)

_____

_____

(Opponents/Proponents) _____ of _____
(topic)

tend to (emphasize/point out/highlight) _____
(counterclaim)

_____

However, (current data/research) _____ actually

demonstrates that _____
(your response to counterclaim)

_____

_____

180 Issue 5

Argument
ASSESSING AND REVISING

B2

I am also (in favor of/opposed to) _____ _____
(topic)

_____

due to _____
(2nd reason that supports your claim)

_____

_____

_____

_____ emphasizes in _____
(Author's Full Name)   (Title of Source)

that _____
(evidence from a different source)

_____

_____

_____

One particularly (convincing/alarming/compelling) _____

statistic is _____
(statistic from a source)

_____

_____

_____

_____

C

Whether _____
(restate the issue)

_____

will remain a controversial issue. After reviewing (recent/relevant/substantial)

_____ data, I _____ that
                                      (verb/verb phrase to express opinion)

_____
(restate your claim)

_____

Virtual vs. Reality **181**

Issue 6 Ready to Work

ARE TEENS READY TO GET TO WORK?

📖 BUILD KNOWLEDGE
Read and respond to the Data File (*Issues,* p. 88).

💡 BRAINSTORM IDEAS
Write a brief list of what can help teens prepare for a good career.

- responsibility
- _____
- _____
- _____

🎤 PRESENT IDEAS
Use the frames to discuss ideas with your group. Listen attentively and record the strongest ideas to complete the organizer.

> **Language to FACILITATE DISCUSSION**
> So, _____, what's your point of view?
> _____, what example did you come up with?

1. A teen looking for a good career should _____ (**present-tense verb:** develop)
2. In school, a teen concerned about work should _____ (**present-tense verb:** strive for)
3. Teens will be well positioned for careers if they _____ (**present-tense verb:** obtain)
4. Teens' career plans could also _____ (**present-tense verb:** include)

CAREER DEVELOPMENT

PERSONAL
- dedication
-
-
-

ACADEMIC
- excellence in school
-
-
-

OTHER
- connections in business
-
-
-

Building Concepts and Language
ACADEMIC VOCABULARY

Words to Know

BUILD WORD KNOWLEDGE
Rate your word knowledge. Then discuss word meanings and examples with your group.

① Don't Know ② Recognize ③ Familiar ④ Know

Word to Know	Meaning	Example
1 prepare *verb* ①②③④	to get _____; to help make someone or something _____	I will **prepare** for the test by _____
2 focus *verb* ①②③④	to give special _____ to something or someone	_____ can make it difficult for teens to **focus** in class.
3 mentor *noun* ①②③④	someone who _____ another person with less knowledge or experience	A **mentor** could be very helpful for someone new at _____
4 field *noun* ①②③④	a person's area of _____; a subject of study	_____ can be useful if you want to work in an international **field**.
1 expertise *noun* ①②③④	special _____ or _____ in a particular subject	My father relies on my help because of my **expertise** with _____
2 professional *noun* ①②③④	someone who _____ in a job that requires special education or training	Becoming a medical **professional** requires _____
3 resilience *noun* ①②③④	the ability to return to _____ after a difficult _____	The people affected by the hurricane showed great **resilience** by _____
4 specialty *noun* ①②③④	a person's particular _____ or area of study	Olympic athletes have many **specialties**, such as _____

Ready to Work 183

Building Concepts and Language

SPEAKING AND LISTENING

Academic Discussion

How should school prepare students for the future?

BRAINSTORM IDEAS
Briefly record at least two ideas in each column using everyday English.

Experiences	Academics
• bring in professionals to teach/lecture • •	• offer technical classes • •

ANALYZE WORDS
Complete the chart with precise words to discuss and write about the topic.

Everyday	Precise
set up *(verb)*	arrange,
job *(noun)*	occupation,
bring in *(verb)*	enlist,

MAKE A CLAIM
Rewrite two ideas using the frames and precise words. Then prepare to elaborate verbally.

> **Language to ELABORATE**
> To demonstrate, _____.
> In my experience, _____.

1. **Frame:** In my opinion, schools should prepare students for the future by _____ (**verb + –ing:** teaching, offering, providing)

   Response: _____
   _____

2. **Frame:** From my perspective, schools should teach students _____ (**adjective:** technical, academic, professional) skills that develop _____ (**noun:** expertise, knowledge, experience)

   Response: _____
   _____

COLLABORATE
Listen attentively, restate, and record your partner's ideas.

> **Language to RESTATE**
> So, if I understand you correctly, your perspective is that _____.
> Yes, that's accurate.
> Actually, what I (related/ specified) is that _____.

Classmate's Name	Ideas
	1.
	2.

184 Issue 6

Ten-Minute Response

A **ten-minute response** begins with a **claim**, followed by **two detail sentences** that elaborate with relevant examples and precise words.

Language to COMPARE IDEAS

My perspective on _____ is (similar to/different from) _____'s.

🎤 PRESENT IDEAS
Listen, compare ideas, and take notes. Then indicate whether you agree (+) or disagree (−).

Classmate's Name	Idea	+/−

✏️ ELABORATE IN WRITING
Work with a partner to write a ten-minute response.

Language to COLLABORATE

What should we write?

We could select _____. What do you think seems reasonable?

Additionally, we could write _____.

    In my opinion, schools should prepare students for the future by engaging professionals to share their work experiences. For example, a professional in the field of _____ could visit a school and _____ _____ about the _____ and _____ students need to succeed in that field. As a result, teens can take _____ that will _____ those skills, and become better prepared for _____

Write a ten-minute response.

    From my perspective, schools should teach students _____ skills that develop _____.

For example, students interested in _____ could spend several hours a week at _____ where they would help _____

As a result, they will understand _____ and the experience they gain will make them more _____ to _____

Ready to Work **185**

Analyzing and Discussing Text
ACADEMIC VOCABULARY

Words to Go

BUILD WORD KNOWLEDGE
Complete the meaning and examples for this high-utility academic word.

Word to Go	Meaning	Example
principle prin•ci•ple *noun*	a basic rule or _____	Our family meetings work on the **principle** that each person _____ _____ _____ The **principle** of _____ _____ is important in my friendships.

DISCUSS AND WRITE EXAMPLES
Discuss your response with a partner. Then complete the sentence in writing.

Peer assessment is based on the **principle** that personal _____ _____ play no part in judgments.

Write your response and read it aloud to a partner.

When school officials announced locker searches, we staged a protest about the _____ of _____

BUILD WORD KNOWLEDGE
Complete the meaning and examples for this high-utility academic word.

Word to Go	Meaning	Examples
adapt a•dapt *verb*	to _____ so that you can _____ in a different situation	After moving last year, I found it hard to **adapt** to _____ _____ _____ My _____ has been waking me up earlier, but I've **adapted** to the new schedule.

DISCUSS AND WRITE EXAMPLES
Discuss your response with a partner. Then complete the sentence in writing.

Some students complained when the cafeteria stopped _____ _____ but most of us **adapted** to the new diet.

Write your response and read it aloud to a partner.

The boys on the baseball team are _____ to having girls _____

186 Issue 6

Text ① • Magazine Article
RESPONDING TO TEXT

Close Reading

BUILD FLUENCY
Read the text "Look to the Future" (*Issues,* pp. 89–93).

IDENTIFY KEY IDEAS AND DETAILS
Take turns asking and answering questions with a partner. Then write brief notes.

Discussion Frames	Text Notes
Q: What is the text **primarily about**? **A:** The text is **primarily about** _____. **Q:** What are the **most essential details** in this text? **A:** (One/An additional) **essential detail** in this article is _____.	• how teens can _____ for their future _____ • teens should begin _____ careers as early as _____ • spending time with _____ and _____ can help students figure out what they want to do • prospective employers look for _____ so teens should look for _____

RESPOND WITH EVIDENCE
Use the frames and evidence from the text to construct a formal written response.

1. According to the author, what do career counselors consider when helping teens?

   According to the author, career counselors look at teens' favorite _____ _____ when helping them decide on a career.

   Counselors also consider students' _____

Use the frame to analyze the author's development of ideas.

2. What is the purpose of the vacation analogy in paragraph 10?

   The purpose of the analogy is to compare _____ to _____ When packing for a vacation, you need to know _____ When preparing for a career, you need to know _____

IDENTIFY PRECISE WORDS
Review Text 1 and your *Portfolio* (pp. 182–187) to identify words for your writing.

Topic Words	High-Utility Academic Words
• career • •	• groundwork • •

Ready to Work 187

Building Concepts and Language

SPEAKING AND LISTENING

Academic Discussion

How can adolescents develop skills for the workplace?

BRAINSTORM IDEAS
Briefly record at least two ideas in each column using everyday English.

Knowledge	Communication Skills
• internships	• practice public speaking
•	•
•	•

ANALYZE WORDS
Complete the chart with precise words to discuss and write about the issue.

Everyday	Precise
figure out *(verb)*	determine,
needed *(adjective)*	obligatory,
watch *(verb)*	observe,

MAKE A CLAIM
Rewrite two ideas using the frames and precise words. Then prepare to elaborate verbally.

Language to ELABORATE
To demonstrate, _____.
In my experience, _____.

1. **Frame:** One way that adolescents can develop skills for the workplace is by _____ (**verb + –ing:** acquiring, identifying, taking)

   Response: _____

2. **Frame:** To develop skills for the workplace, adolescents can _____ (**base verb:** focus, locate, participate)

   Response: _____

COLLABORATE
Listen attentively, restate, and record your partner's ideas.

Language to RESTATE
So, if I understand you correctly, your perspective is that _____.
Yes, that's accurate.
Actually, what I (related/specified) is that _____.

Classmate's Name	Ideas
	1.
	2.

Issue 6

SPEAKING AND WRITING

Ten-Minute Response

A **ten-minute response** begins with a **claim**, followed by **two detail sentences** that elaborate with relevant examples and precise words.

> **Language to COMPARE IDEAS**
>
> My perspective on _____ is (similar to/different from) _____'s.

🎤 PRESENT IDEAS

Listen, compare ideas, and take notes. Then indicate whether you agree (+) or disagree (–).

Classmate's Name	Idea	+/–

✏️ ELABORATE IN WRITING

Work with a partner to write a ten-minute response.

> **Language to COLLABORATE**
>
> What should we write?
>
> We could select _____. What do you think seems reasonable?
>
> Additionally, we could write _____.

    One way that adolescents can develop skills for the workplace is by applying for internships. For example, teens who are interested in _____ _____ can look for internships at _____ or _____ As a result, interns will learn about _____ and will gain _____ that future employers may require.

Write a ten-minute response.

    To develop skills for the workplace, adolescents can _____ _____

For example, a teen who has ambitions of working in the field of _____ might _____

As a result, the adolescent will _____

what it takes to _____ and can

begin to _____

Ready to Work 189

Analyzing and Discussing Text
ACADEMIC VOCABULARY

Words to Go

📘 BUILD WORD KNOWLEDGE
Complete the meanings and examples for these high-utility academic words.

Word to Go	Meaning	Example
persist per•sist *verb*	to _____ doing something difficult	If you **persist** in _____ _____ _____ you will probably do better on the math test.
persistence per•sis•tence *noun*	the determination to _____ doing something difficult	My parents let me _____ _____ _____ because my **persistence** wore them down.

💬 DISCUSS AND WRITE EXAMPLES
Discuss your response with a partner. Then complete the sentence in writing.

The cyberbully **persisted** in _____

_____ until the school investigated the threats.

Write your response and read it aloud to a partner.

The students' _____ paid off when the principal agreed to let students

_____

📘 BUILD WORD KNOWLEDGE
Complete the meaning and examples for this high-utility academic word.

Word to Go	Meaning	Examples
technical tech•ni•cal *adjective*	of or having to do with _____ engineering, mechanics, or _____ things work	I called customer service because I needed **technical** support for my _____ _____ **Technical** training helped my brother become (a/an) _____ _____

💬 DISCUSS AND WRITE EXAMPLES
Discuss your response with a partner. Then complete the sentence in writing.

The _____

in math class was having **technical** problems, so we had to use paper and pens.

Write your response and read it aloud to a partner.

Someone with little _____ knowledge will probably not be able to help

you with your _____

Text ② • Section ① • Magazine Article

SUMMARIZING TEXT

Section Shrink

📖 BUILD FLUENCY
Read Section 1 of "Learning That Works" (*Issues,* pp. 94–95).

💬 IDENTIFY KEY IDEAS AND DETAILS
Take turns asking and answering questions with a partner. Then write brief notes.

Discussion Frames	Text Notes
Q: What does this section **focus on**? **A:** This section **focuses on** _____.	• hands-on _____ science classes that prepare students for _____
Q: What are the **significant details** in this section? **A:** (One/An additional) **significant detail** in this section is _____. **A:** Perhaps the **most significant detail** in this section is _____.	• McBride wanted to teach _____ skills; at first, superintendent thought _____ were more important • now superintendent thinks it's a great way to teach _____ • almost all students in the program _____ state tests; less than _____ of kids in _____ classes passed

✏️ SUMMARIZE
"Shrink" Section 1 of the text by writing a summary in 40 or fewer words.

CLASS SUMMARY **WORD COUNT:** _____

In Clyde McBride's program, classes that _____ in teaching _____ and _____ skills _____ students for careers in those fields and provide _____ in fundamental subjects.

PARTNER SUMMARY **WORD COUNT:** _____

Clyde McBride's agricultural sciences program _____ the _____ students will need for careers in _____ while also teaching the _____ for academic success.

🔍 IDENTIFY PRECISE WORDS
Review Section 1 and your *Portfolio* (pp. 188–191) to identify words for your writing.

Topic Words	High-Utility Academic Words
• technicians	• hands-on
•	•
•	•

Analyzing and Discussing Text

ACADEMIC VOCABULARY

Words to Go

📘 BUILD WORD KNOWLEDGE
Complete the meanings and examples for these high-utility academic words.

Word to Go	Meaning	Example
establish es•tab•lish *verb*	to _____ something that will last for some time	Teens who **establish** _____ _____ _____ habits are more likely to become healthy adults.
establishment es•tab•lish•ment *noun*	the people who are in _____ of a society or _____	Graffiti is often seen as _____ _____ by the art **establishment**.

💬 DISCUSS AND WRITE EXAMPLES
Discuss your response with a partner. Then complete the sentence in writing.

When our school **established** _____

last year, I signed up right away.

Write your response and read it aloud to a partner.

Many people claim that the beauty _____ promotes _____

_____

📘 BUILD WORD KNOWLEDGE
Complete the meaning and examples for this high-utility academic word.

Word to Go	Meaning	Examples
notion no•tion *noun*	an _____ or belief	My grandfather's **notion** of technology is _____ _____ Parents and teens seem to have different **notions** about the purpose of _____

💬 DISCUSS AND WRITE EXAMPLES
Discuss your response with a partner. Then complete the sentence in writing.

The **notion** of putting most of my allowance into savings seems _____

_____

Write your response and read it aloud to a partner.

Many people once had mistaken _____ about _____

_____ but now people know better.

Text ❷ • Section ❷ • Magazine Article

SUMMARIZING TEXT

Section Shrink

BUILD FLUENCY
Read Section 2 of "Learning That Works" (*Issues,* pp. 95–98).

IDENTIFY KEY IDEAS AND DETAILS
Take turns asking and answering questions with a partner. Then write brief notes.

Discussion Frames	Text Notes
Q: What does this section **focus on**? **A:** This section **focuses on** _____.	• the benefits of _____
Q: What are the **significant details** in this section? **A:** (One/An additional) **significant detail** in this section is _____. **A:** Perhaps the **most significant detail** in this section is _____.	• high _____ for high school graduates not in school • _____ provides skills that focus on teens' _____ and lead to _____ • 98.5% of East Valley Institute of Technology students _____ • Arizona's state superintendent praises _____ learning

SUMMARIZE
"Shrink" Section 2 of the text by writing a summary in 40 or fewer words.

CLASS SUMMARY   **WORD COUNT:** _____

The _____ education students receive on the _____
_____ can improve _____
_____ and provide better preparation for _____

PARTNER SUMMARY   **WORD COUNT:** _____

_____ education gives students _____
_____ in fields that _____
which results in _____ and graduates who are
_____ for work.

IDENTIFY PRECISE WORDS
Review Section 2 and your *Portfolio* (pp. 192–193) to identify words for your writing.

Topic Words	High-Utility Academic Words
• certified skills	• suited
•	•
•	•

Analyzing and Discussing Text
ACADEMIC VOCABULARY

Words to Go

📚 BUILD WORD KNOWLEDGE
Complete the meanings and examples for these high-utility academic words.

Word to Go	Meaning	Example
reluctant re•luc•tant *adjective*	not _____ to do something	I was **reluctant** to let my brother _____ _____ _____
reluctantly re•luc•tant•ly *adverb*	in a _____ or _____ way	After I promised to _____ _____ my mother **reluctantly** gave me permission to attend the party.

💬 DISCUSS AND WRITE EXAMPLES
Discuss your response with a partner. Then complete the sentence in writing.

Some students are **reluctant** to _____
_____ even though it is a school rule.

Write your response and read it aloud to a partner.

I wanted to go to the movies with my friends, but I _____ agreed
to _____

📚 BUILD WORD KNOWLEDGE
Complete the meaning and examples for this high-utility academic word.

Word to Go	Meaning	Examples
bias bi•as *noun*	an _____ about whether a person, group, or idea is _____ or _____	My cousin has a **bias** against my new friend just because she _____ _____ My music playlist shows my **bias** for _____

💬 DISCUSS AND WRITE EXAMPLES
Discuss your response with a partner. Then complete the sentence in writing.

Statistics on car accidents suggest that **biases** against _____
are valid.

Write your response and read it aloud to a partner.

The debate about changes in the athletic department showed that school officials have

several _____ against allowing _____
_____

Text ❷ • Section ❸ • Magazine Article

SUMMARIZING TEXT

Section Shrink

BUILD FLUENCY
Read Section 3 of "Learning That Works" (*Issues,* pp. 98–101).

IDENTIFY KEY IDEAS AND DETAILS
Take turns asking and answering questions with a partner. Then write brief notes.

Discussion Frames	Text Notes
Q: What does this section **focus on**? **A:** This section **focuses on** _____.	• _____ to voc-ed and its _____
Q: What are the **significant details** in this section? **A:** (One/An additional) **significant detail** in this section is _____. **A:** Perhaps the **most significant detail** in this section is _____.	• hard to _____ vocational schools; Democrats push for _____ and Republicans _____ to spend money • home high schools often _____ voc-ed participation • many say schools have a responsibility to create good _____; voc-ed proponents say it teaches _____ and how to be _____

SUMMARIZE

"Shrink" Section 3 of the text by writing a summary in 40 or fewer words.

CLASS SUMMARY   **WORD COUNT:** _____

_____ may prepare students for _____

cost less, and create _____ but vocational education

gives students the _____ and _____ skills to be

exceptional employees who _____ to their communities.

PARTNER SUMMARY   **WORD COUNT:** _____

Opponents of _____ cite

the _____ and need to develop good _____ but

supporters say they involve _____

and emphasize _____

IDENTIFY PRECISE WORDS
Review Section 3 and your *Portfolio* (pp. 194–195) to identify words for your writing.

Topic Words	High-Utility Academic Words
• tech-track	• ideological
•	•
•	•

Ready to Work 195

Academic Writing

ANALYZING TEXT ELEMENTS

Student Writing Model

Academic Writing Type

A **formal written summary** provides an objective overview of the topic and important details from an informational text. Writers credit the author but write in primarily their own words, without including personal opinions.

    A. The **topic sentence** includes the text type, title, author, and topic.
    B. **Detail sentences** include the important details from the summarized text.
    C. The **concluding sentence** restates the author's conclusion in the writer's own words.

ANALYZE TEXT

Read this student model to analyze the elements of a formal summary.

A
    In the magazine article titled "Look to the Future," Betsy O'Donovan discusses how teens can prepare for careers.

B
O'Donovan begins by reporting that the government expects the number of jobs in the United States to increase by 2030. The writer continues to point out that teens should establish their career paths early on so they can focus on the courses they need and find mentors. She explains further that career interest tests can help teens identify fields they may want to pursue. Moreover, the writer notes that teens should shadow professionals so that they can experience particular jobs.

C
O'Donovan concludes by emphasizing that employers want workers who are resilient and can adapt to unfamiliar situations.

MARK AND DISCUSS ELEMENTS

Mark the summary elements and use the frames to discuss them with your partner.

1. **Number (1–4) the four elements of the topic sentence.** *The topic sentence includes the* _____.

2. **Draw a box around four transition words or phrases.** *One transition (word/phrase) is* _____.

3. **Underline four important details.** *One important detail in this summary is* _____.

4. **Circle four citation verbs.** *One citation verb that the writer uses is* _____.

5. **Star four precise topic words and check four high-utility academic words.** *An example of a (precise topic word/high-utility academic word) is* _____.

Formal Summary
PLANNING TO WRITE

Organize a Formal Summary

Prompt Write a formal summary of "Learning That Works."

Guidelines for Paraphrasing Multiple Sentences
Paraphrase related details from a source text by combining key information into one sentence. Replace keywords and phrases with synonyms and keep important topic words.

Text Detail 1	Text Detail 2	Text Detail 3
"High school dropout rates continue to be a national problem" (Klein 96).	"The unemployment rate for recent high school graduates who are not in school is nearly 20 percent" (Klein 96).	"'But according to the Bureau of Labor Statistics, less than a quarter of new job openings will require a bachelor of arts degree'" (Klein 96).

PARAPHRASE IDEAS
Combine key information from the text details above into one detail sentence.

Klein argues that college prep for all students has resulted in

(text detail 1) _____

(text detail 2) _____ and

(text detail 3) _____

PLAN KEY IDEAS AND DETAILS
State the text information to write a topic sentence.

In the magazine article titled (title) _____

(author's full name) _____ (citation verb: *presents, examines, investigates*)

_____ (topic) _____

List four important details from the text using primarily your own words.

1. _____
   _____

2. _____
   _____

3. _____
   _____

4. _____
   _____

Restate the conclusion in your own words.

_____
_____

Academic Writing
WRITING A DRAFT

Write a Formal Summary

Prompt Write a formal summary of "Learning That Works."

✏️ **WRITE A PARAGRAPH**
Use the frame to write your topic sentence, detail sentences, and concluding sentence.

A
In the _____ titled _____
       (text type)   (Title)

_____ _____ _____
(Author's Full Name)   (citation verb)   (topic)

_____

B
_____ begins by _____
(Author's Last Name)   (citation verb + –ing: presenting, arguing)

_____
(1st important detail)

_____

_____

The (author/writer/researcher) _____ continues to

_____ _____
(citation verb, base form: describe, report)   (2nd important detail)

_____

_____

_____ _____ further that
(Pronoun)   (present-tense citation verb)

_____
(3rd important detail)

_____

_____

Moreover, the (author/writer/researcher) _____

_____ _____
(present-tense citation verb)   (4th important detail)

_____

_____

C
_____ concludes by _____ that
(Author's Last Name)   (citation verb + –ing: suggesting, emphasizing)

_____
(restate conclusion)

_____

Formal Summary
ASSESSING AND REVISING

Rate Your Summary

ASSESS YOUR DRAFT
Rate your formal summary. Then have a partner rate it.

Scoring Guide	
1	Insufficient
2	Developing
3	Sufficient
4	Exemplary

1. Does the topic sentence state the text type, title, author, and topic?	Self	1	2	3	4
	Partner	1	2	3	4
2. Did you paraphrase the most important details from the text?	Self	1	2	3	4
	Partner	1	2	3	4
3. Did you use citation verbs to credit the author?	Self	1	2	3	4
	Partner	1	2	3	4
4. Did you include precise topic words and high-utility academic words?	Self	1	2	3	4
	Partner	1	2	3	4
5. Did you use transitions to introduce and sequence details?	Self	1	2	3	4
	Partner	1	2	3	4
6. Did you accurately restate the author's conclusion?	Self	1	2	3	4
	Partner	1	2	3	4

REFLECT AND REVISE
Record specific priorities and suggestions to help you and your partner revise.

(Partner) Positive Feedback: I appreciate how you (used/included) _____
_____
_____

(Partner) Suggestion: As you revise your summary, focus on _____
_____
_____

(Self) Priority 1: My summary paragraph needs _____
_____
_____

(Self) Priority 2: I plan to improve my summary by _____
_____
_____

CHECK AND EDIT
Use this checklist to proofread and edit your formal summary.

- ☐ Did you capitalize the title of the magazine article and proper nouns?
- ☐ Did you put quotation marks around the title of the magazine article?
- ☐ Did you use commas appropriately after transitions?
- ☐ Do simple present-tense verbs end in –s?
- ☐ Is each sentence complete?
- ☐ Are all words spelled correctly?

Building Concepts and Language

SPEAKING AND LISTENING

Academic Discussion

What are the arguments supporting and opposing career and technical education?

BRAINSTORM IDEAS
Briefly record at least two ideas in each column using everyday English.

Supporting Arguments	Opposing Arguments
• gives hands-on experience	• loses focus on academics
•	•
•	•

ANALYZE WORDS
Complete the chart with precise words to discuss and write about the topic.

Everyday	Precise
pay no attention to *(verb phrase)*	disregard,
help *(verb)*	encourage,
mess with *(verb)*	disrupt,

MAKE A CLAIM
Rewrite two ideas using the frames and precise words. Then prepare to elaborate verbally.

1. **Frame:** (Proponents/Opponents) argue that career and technical education _____ (**present-tense verb:** develops, prepares, wastes, segregates)

   Response: _____
   _____

2. **Frame:** One (supporting/opposing) argument is that career and technical education (benefits/harms) students by _____ (**verb + –ing**: training, building, preventing, denying)

   Response: _____

Language to ELABORATE
To demonstrate, _____.
In my experience, _____.

COLLABORATE
Listen attentively, restate, and record your partner's ideas.

Classmate's Name	Ideas
	1.
	2.

Language to RESTATE
So, if I understand you correctly, your perspective is that _____.
Yes, that's accurate.
Actually, what I (related/specified) is that _____.

Building Concepts and Language
SPEAKING AND WRITING

Ten-Minute Response

A **ten-minute response** begins with a **claim**, followed by **two detail sentences** that elaborate with relevant examples and precise words.

Language to COMPARE IDEAS

My perspective on _____ is (similar to/different from) _____'s.

PRESENT IDEAS
Listen, compare ideas, and take notes. Then indicate whether you agree (+) or disagree (–).

Classmate's Name	Idea	+/–

ELABORATE IN WRITING
Work with a partner to write a ten-minute response.

Language to COLLABORATE

What should we write?

We could select _____. What do you think seems reasonable?

Additionally, we could write _____.

Proponents argue that career and technical education contributes to higher graduation rates. For example, at East Valley Institute of Technology in Arizona, students are _____
_____
As a result, _____
of the students _____

Write a ten-minute response.

One _____ argument is that career and technical education _____ students by _____
_____

For example, _____
_____
_____

As a result, _____
_____
_____

Ready to Work 201

Analyzing and Discussing Text

ACADEMIC VOCABULARY

Words to Go

📖 BUILD WORD KNOWLEDGE

Complete the meanings and examples for these high-utility academic words.

Word to Go	Meaning	Example
innovate in•no•vate *verb*	to introduce _____ ideas or methods of doing something	If our soccer team wants to win more games, we need to **innovate** and _____ _____
innovation in•no•va•tion *noun*	the introduction of _____ ideas or methods	A new _____ _____ won an award for **innovation** in technology.

💬 DISCUSS AND WRITE EXAMPLES

Discuss your response with a partner. Then complete the sentence in writing.

Before Henry Ford **innovated** the assembly line system for building automobiles, cars were _____

Write your response and read it aloud to a partner.

Older generations can be reluctant to accept _____ such as _____ and _____

📖 BUILD WORD KNOWLEDGE

Complete the meaning and examples for this high-utility academic word.

Word to Go	Meaning	Examples
passive pas•sive *adjective*	tending to _____ conditions; not taking _____	_____ is an example of a **passive** character. My **passive** dog just sits there when _____ _____

💬 DISCUSS AND WRITE EXAMPLES

Discuss your response with a partner. Then complete the sentence in writing.

Environmental activists are not **passive** about _____
_____

Write your response and read it aloud to a partner.

Rather than being _____, victims of bullying should _____
_____

Text 3 • Essay
RESPONDING TO TEXT

Close Reading

📖 BUILD FLUENCY
Read the text "Educating the Next Steve Jobs" (*Issues,* pp. 102–105).

💬 IDENTIFY KEY IDEAS AND DETAILS
Take turns asking and answering questions with a partner. Then write brief notes.

Discussion Frames	Text Notes
Q: What is the text **primarily about**? **A:** The text is **primarily about** _____.	• preparing students to _____
Q: What are the **most essential details** in this text? **A:** (One/An additional) **essential detail** in this text is _____.	• students learn to be _____ through _____ • innovative schools are _____ not _____ like conventional schools • being _____ is more important than _____

✏️ RESPOND WITH EVIDENCE
Use the frame and evidence from the text to construct a formal written response.

1. According to the author, which practices do innovative schools reject?

   According to the author, practices that innovative schools reject are _____

   _____

   _____

   Moreover, innovative schools teach students to _____

   _____

Use the frame to analyze how the author develops ideas.

2. What is the author's claim? How does the author support his claim in paragraphs 3–6? The author's claim is that _____

   _____

   The author supports his claim by _____

   _____

   _____ to show how innovative schools succeed.

🔍 IDENTIFY PRECISE WORDS
Review Text 3 and your *Portfolio* (pp. 200–203) to identify words for your writing.

Topic Words	High-Utility Academic Words
• conventional	• persevere
•	•
•	•

Ready to Work **203**

Presenting Ideas

Take a Stand

Debate | Does school prepare students for their future careers?

💬 COLLABORATE
Read the debate question about preparation for work. Then take turns using a frame to respond with your initial reaction.

Language to RESPOND

So, _____, what's your initial reaction?

My initial reaction is _____.

_____ and I had (similar/somewhat different) initial reactions.

🔍 ANALYZE SOURCES
Read a quote that either supports or opposes the debate topic. Then paraphrase.

Quote	Paraphrase
Model: "82% of employers report that workers who are recent high school graduates do not know what they need to know to do typical jobs at their companies" (All4Ed 88).	To paraphrase, a _____ of bosses surveyed _____ high school graduates do not have _____
1. "School counselors often have access to career interest tests that they like to use with students too. Students can review the results with their school counselors, who can help them figure out the next steps" (O'Donovan 91).	The author seems to be saying that schools have _____ to help students identify _____ and assist them in _____ their chosen fields.
2. "The unemployment rate for recent high school graduates who are not in school is nearly 20 percent" (Klein 96).	To paraphrase, _____ of high school graduates not pursuing further _____ are _____
3. "'It's easier to learn engineering by actually building a house—which my family did when I was a kid, by the way—than sitting in a classroom figuring out the process in the abstract'" (Klein 98).	To paraphrase, students who receive _____ learn _____ skills such as _____ more thoroughly.
4. "...the most important thing educators can do to prepare students for work in companies like [Google] is to teach them that problems can never be understood or solved in the context of a single academic discipline" (Wagner 103).	The author seems to be saying that _____ want students who have learned to _____ by working on _____ at the same time.

204 Issue 6

Debate Ideas

SYNTHESIZE IDEAS

Write a response to the debate question, including a paraphrase of a text quote and elaboration on the quote.

Claim: My position is that school (does/does not) _____ prepare students for their future careers.

Transitional Statement: I have (one key reason/a compelling reason) _____ _____ for taking this stance.

Quote Paraphrase: (According to _____,/The author points out _____.)

_____
_____
_____

Quote Elaboration: (As a result, _____./Consequently, _____.)

_____
_____
_____

PRESENT EVIDENCE

Including Visual Displays

When presenting ideas during class or in a meeting, include a **visual display**. Consider including images or graphics to express information, strengthen claims and evidence, and add interest.

LISTEN AND TAKE NOTES

Listen attentively and take notes. Then indicate whether you agree (+) or disagree (−).

> **Language to AFFIRM AND CLARIFY**
> That's a compelling stance.
> What exactly do you mean by _____?

Classmate's Name	Idea	+/−

Ready to Work 205

Academic Writing

ANALYZING TEXT ELEMENTS

Student Writing Model

Academic Writing Type

An **argument** states a claim and supports it with logical reasons and relevant evidence from sources.

A. The **thesis statement** clearly states the writer's claim and tells what the writer will explain about the topic.

B. **Supporting paragraphs** support the claim with reasons and evidence from sources. The writer also presents counterclaims and responds with strong evidence.

C. The **conclusion statement** restates the writer's claim about the issue.

ANALYZE TEXT
Read this student model to analyze elements of an argument research paper.

A After examining the issues surrounding schools and job skills, I am convinced that school does prepare students for their future careers.

B One reason I maintain this position is that most students have access to valuable career guidance in their own schools. In "Look to the Future," Betsy O'Donovan presents compelling data regarding the positive consequences of providing job skills to students. For example, counselors can give students interest tests and advise them on a course of study (91). Opponents of relying on conventional schools to prepare students for their professional lives tend to highlight the need for innovative programs that provide technical training. However, high school students have access to guidance counselors who can help them with career exploration and ensure they are well prepared for both college and the workforce (91).

I am also in favor of current career training due to the advantages of offering students choices. Joe Klein emphasizes in "Learning That Works" that vocational education can improve test scores and graduation rates. One particularly convincing statistic is that 27 percent of students in Arizona participate in career and technical education (97).

C Whether school teaches the skills required for work after graduation will remain a controversial issue. After reviewing relevant data, I maintain that students are learning what they need to know for their future careers.

Argument
ANALYZING TEXT ELEMENTS

💬 MARK AND DISCUSS ELEMENTS
Mark the argument elements and use the frames to discuss them with your partner.

1. **Circle the writer's claim within the thesis statement.** *The writer's claim is _____.*

2. **Underline and label two reasons that support the writer's claim with the letter *R*.**

   One reason that supports the writer's claim is _____.

3. **Underline and label four pieces of evidence that support the writer's claim with the letter *E*.**

   One piece of evidence that supports the writer's claim is _____.

4. **Draw a box around a counterclaim.** *One counterclaim is _____.*

5. **Star four precise topic words and check four high-utility academic words.**

   An example of a (precise topic word/high-utility academic word) is _____.

✍️ ASSESS A STUDENT SAMPLE
Read an additional student sample and rate it.

Scoring Guide			
1	Insufficient	3	Sufficient
2	Developing	4	Exemplary

1. Does the thesis statement clearly state the claim?	1	2	3	4
2. Do supporting paragraphs begin with a topic sentence that specifies a reason?	1	2	3	4
3. Did the writer give evidence drawn primarily from sources to support the claim?	1	2	3	4
4. Did the writer explain why the evidence is relevant and significant?	1	2	3	4
5. Did the writer include complex sentences to present and respond to counterclaims?	1	2	3	4
6. Did the writer use strong verbs and verb phrases to express opinions?	1	2	3	4
7. Did the writer use transitions to introduce reasons and evidence?	1	2	3	4
8. Did the writer use precise adjectives to describe evidence?	1	2	3	4
9. Did the writer include citation information for text evidence?	1	2	3	4
10. Did the writer include precise topic words and high-utility words?	1	2	3	4
11. Does the conclusion statement strongly restate the claim using new wording?	1	2	3	4

🗣️ REFLECT AND REVISE
Record specific priorities and suggestions to help the writer.

I appreciated the student's (effort to/use of/skillful) _____

_____

_____

One suggestion I have to revise this argument research paper is to _____

_____

_____

Another suggestion I have to strengthen this argument research paper is to _____

_____

_____

Ready to Work 207

Academic Writing

FRONTLOADING LANGUAGE

Precise Adjectives

Guidelines for Using Precise Adjectives to Describe Evidence
Precise adjectives describe nouns vividly and make your writing more interesting. Use precise adjectives to describe the data, statistics, and other evidence you present to support your claim.

Everyday Adjectives	Precise Adjectives
good	convincing, strong, compelling, relevant, striking
scary	alarming, distressing, unnerving, striking, disturbing
interesting	fascinating, intriguing, thought-provoking, provocative, controversial
hard	difficult, troubling, challenging, complex, complicated, perplexing
new	recent, current, up-to-date
enough/true-sounding	sufficient, adequate, substantial, believable, convincing
silly	absurd, preposterous, ridiculous, unreasonable
untrue	unfounded, groundless, baseless, unsubstantiated

WRITE PRECISE ADJECTIVES
Complete the sentences with precise adjectives.

1. (A/An) _____ argument against mandating teen drivers display decals on their license plate is that it could pose a safety risk.

2. _____ evidence proves that the number of young people accumulating debt is increasing.

3. Although a common argument against later school start times is that bus schedules would need to change, I don't find the evidence _____

Use precise adjectives to complete the sentences about the claim.

Claim: Virtual experiences better enable individuals to express their authentic selves.

1. **Evidence:** In "How Avatars Help Gen Z Find Themselves," Carolyn Cutrone presents _____ data regarding the positive consequences of self-expression through avatars.

2. **Evidence:** One particularly _____ statistic is that 40 percent of Gen-Z users say it is easier to be authentic in the metaverse than in the physical world.

3. **Counterclaim:** Although a common argument against virtual experiences is that they are not comparable to face-to-face interactions, I don't find the evidence _____

4. **Response to Counterclaim:** Clearly, there is _____ evidence that proves virtual experiences are not as authentic as those in person.

5. **Restating Claim:** After reviewing _____ data, I contend that life online is more authentic than life offline.

Simple and Complex Sentences

Guidelines for Using Simple and Complex Sentences
Use **simple and complex sentences** to present and respond to counterclaims in your argument.

Presenting Counterclaims

A _____ (adjective: common, pervasive, consistent) argument (in favor of/against) _____ is _____.

(Opponents/Proponents) of _____ tend to _____. (verb: emphasize, point out, highlight)

Although a common argument (in favor of/against) _____ is _____, I don't find the evidence _____. (adjective: compelling, substantial, believable)

Examples

A consistent argument in favor of raising the driving age is that it will reduce fatal crashes.

Opponents of changing school start times **tend to emphasize** the inconvenience of adjusting bus schedules.

Although a common argument in favor of mandating online courses is that they prepare students for college, **I don't find the evidence compelling**.

Responding to Counterclaims

(Current data/Recent findings/Studies) actually demonstrate that _____.

Clearly, there is (sufficient/adequate/striking) evidence that (shows/proves) _____.

Examples

Studies actually demonstrate that bilingual people are cognitively flexible.

Clearly, there is sufficient evidence that proves credit cards can be dangerous for teenagers.

✎ WRITE COUNTERCLAIMS

Work with the teacher to write a counterclaim and response.

Claim: Schools should not change start times.

Counterclaim: (A/An) (**adjective**: common, pervasive, consistent) _____ argument in favor of starting school later is that it improves attendance.

Response: Clearly, there is (sufficient/adequate/striking) _____ evidence that _____

Work with a partner to write a counterclaim and response.

Claim: Schools should require world-language study.

Counterclaim: Although a common argument _____ is _____ I don't find the evidence _____

Response: _____ actually demonstrate that _____
_____

Work on your own to write a counterclaim and response.

Claim: Our state should not change the driving age.

Counterclaim: _____
_____

Response: _____
_____

Academic Writing

PLANNING TO WRITE

Organize an Argument

Prompt Does school prepare students for their future careers? Write an argument that states your claim and supports it with text evidence.

Guidelines for Using Direct Quotes to Cite Text Evidence
Use a direct quote from an authority on a topic to reinforce your argument or to accentuate an idea. Avoid quotes that are longer than three lines, and enclose the exact words of the source in quotation marks (" "). Include a citation that indicates the source of the quote.

Incorporating Quotes	Examples
Introduce the quote with a complete sentence and a colon.	Joe Klein argues that vocational education can still breed good citizens: "But people with jobs, especially skilled jobs, tend to be better citizens than those without them" (100).
Use an introductory phrase.	According to Tony Wagner, "at the most innovative schools, classes are 'hands-on,' and students are creators, not mere consumers" (103).
Blend the quote into your own sentence.	The advice that students "research, job shadow, and ask for informational interviews" strongly suggests that schools may not provide students the career experiences they need (O'Donovan 91).

WRITE A THESIS STATEMENT
Describe your claim.

My claim: _____

_____

Use academic language to restate your claim as a thesis statement.

_____ high schools and jobs,
(Thesis starter)
I (agree/disagree) _____ (strongly/firmly) _____
that _____
(your claim)

CHOOSE SUPPORTING TOPICS
List each topic you will write about to support your claim.

Supporting Paragraph 1

Topic: _____

Supporting Paragraph 2

Topic: _____

Find a quote from the texts that supports your claim and incorporate it into a sentence.

_____

_____

_____

_____

Argument
PLANNING TO WRITE

📋 PLAN SUPPORTING PARAGRAPHS
List reasons and evidence that support your claim. You may draw from texts, your experience, or a classmate's experience.

Supporting Paragraph 1

Reason 1: _____

_____

Evidence: _____

_____

Source/Page Number: _____

Author: _____

Counterclaim: _____

_____

Response to Counterclaim: _____

_____

Source: _____

Author: _____

Supporting Paragraph 2

Reason 2: _____

_____

Evidence: _____

_____

Source/Page Number: _____

Author: _____

Statistical Evidence: _____

_____

Source: _____

✏️ WRITE A CONCLUSION
Plan a conclusion that restates your claim.

Whether _____

_____ will remain a controversial issue.

After reviewing _____ data, I _____
                                                                  (verb/verb phrase to express opinion)

that _____

_____

_____

Ready to Work **211**

Academic Writing

WRITING A DRAFT

Write an Argument

Prompt | Does school prepare students for their future careers? Write an argument that states your claim and supports it with text evidence.

✏️ WRITE A RESEARCH PAPER
Use the frame to write your thesis statement, supporting paragraphs, and conclusion statement.

A

_____ (Thesis starter)

(topic)
I _____ that _____
　(your claim)　　　　　　　　　　(your claim)

_____

B1

One reason I maintain this position is that _____
　　　　　　　　　　　　　　　　　　　　(1st reason that supports your claim)

_____

_____

_____

In _____
　(Title of Source)

_____ presents _____ data
(Author's Full Name)　　　　　　　(precise adjective)
regarding the (positive/negative) _____ consequences of

_____
(topic)

For example, _____
　　　　　　　(evidence from source)

_____

_____

(Opponents/Proponents) _____ of _____
　　　　　　　　　　　　　　　　　　　　　　　　　　　　　(topic)

tend to (verb: emphasize, point out, highlight) _____

_____
(counterclaim)

However, (current data/studies) _____ actually demonstrate
that _____
　　(your response to counterclaim)

_____

_____

212 Issue 6

Argument
ASSESSING AND REVISING

B2

I am also (in favor of/opposed to) _____
_____
(topic)
due to _____
            (2nd reason that supports your claim)
_____
_____

_____ emphasizes in _____
(Author's full Name)   (Title of Source)
_____
that _____
      (evidence from a different source)
_____
_____

One particularly _____ statistic is _____
                   (precise adjective)   (statistic from a source)
_____
_____
_____

C

Whether _____
         (restate the issue)
_____
_____
_____ will remain a controversial issue.

After reviewing _____ data, I _____
                   (precise adjective)   (verb/verb phrase to express opinion)
that _____
      (restate your claim)
_____
_____

Ready to Work 213

Presenting Ideas

Two-Minute Speech

IDENTIFY TOPIC
Choose one of the questions below to address in a two-minute speech.
- ☐ Should our school integrate virtual reality experiences into the curriculum?
- ☐ Should our school provide internships for career education?

BRAINSTORM IDEAS
Write your claim and two reasons that support it.

My Claim: _____

Reason 1: _____

Reason 2: _____

SYNTHESIZE IDEAS
Take notes on supporting evidence and a counterclaim.

Evidence 1: _____

_____

Evidence 2: _____

_____

Counterclaim: _____

_____

Response: _____

_____

WRITE A SPEECH
Write a two-minute speech that states your claim and includes reasons, evidence, and a counterclaim.

From my point of view, _____

_____

One reason is that _____

_____

_____

Secondly, _____

_____

For example, _____

_____

_____

Critics might claim that _____

_____

However, _____

_____

For these reasons, I _____ that _____

_____

Present and Rate Your Speech

Including Visual Displays
When presenting ideas during class or in a meeting, include a **visual display.** Consider including images or graphics to express information, strengthen claims and evidence, and add interest.

PRESENT YOUR SPEECH
Present your speech to the small group. Make sure to include a visual display and explain it.

LISTEN AND TAKE NOTES
Listen attentively and take notes. Then indicate whether you agree (+) or disagree (–).

Language to AFFIRM AND CLARIFY

That's a compelling stance.

What exactly do you mean by _____?

Classmate's Name	Idea	+/–

ASSESS YOUR SPEECH
Use the Scoring Guide to rate your speech.

Scoring Guide
1	Insufficient	3	Sufficient
2	Developing	4	Exemplary

1. Did your topic sentence clearly state your claim?	1	2	3	4
2. Did you include strong reasons and evidence to support your speech?	1	2	3	4
3. Did you include precise topic words?	1	2	3	4
4. Were you easy to understand?	1	2	3	4
5. Did you include a visual display?	1	2	3	4

REFLECT
Think of two ways you can improve for your next speech.

Priority 1: I can enhance my next speech by _____

_____

_____

Priority 2: In my next speech, I will incorporate _____

_____

_____

Issue 7: Your Vote, Your Voice

SHOULD EVERYONE HAVE TO TURN OUT TO VOTE?

📖 BUILD KNOWLEDGE
Read and respond to the Data File (*Issues*, p. 106).

💡 BRAINSTORM IDEAS
Write a brief list of the benefits of voting.

- voice your opinion
- _____
- _____
- _____

🎤 PRESENT IDEAS
Use the frames to discuss ideas with your group. Listen attentively and record the strongest ideas to complete the concept web.

Language to FACILITATE DISCUSSION
So _____, what's your suggestion?
_____, what benefit did you come up with?

1. When you vote, you are able to _____ (**base verb:** voice)
2. Your vote can also _____ (**base verb:** affect)
3. A vote sends a message that you want to _____ (**base verb:** change)
4. Voting gives you the power to _____ (**base verb:** impact)

Concept web — center: **BENEFITS OF VOTING**; one node: elect trusted politicians

Building Concepts and Language

ACADEMIC VOCABULARY

Words to Know

BUILD WORD KNOWLEDGE

Rate your word knowledge. Then discuss word meanings and examples with your group.

① Don't Know   ② Recognize   ③ Familiar   ④ Know

Word to Know	Meaning	Example
1 duty *noun* ①②③④	a thing a person _____ do because it is morally or _____ right	It is my **duty** as an older brother to _____ my younger brother.
2 democratic *adjective* ①②③④	referring to the idea that _____ should be involved in making _____	If _____ were more **democratic**, decisions would reflect the wishes of _____ instead of _____
3 citizen *noun* ①②③④	a person who has _____ as well as full _____ in a particular country or place	As a tax-paying **citizen**, my father feels that he shouldn't have to _____
4 civic *adjective* ①②③④	of or having to do with a _____ or the _____ who live there	The _____ in our town is a source of **civic** pride.
1 obligation *noun* ①②③④	something you _____ because it is your responsibility or because you have promised	_____ is an **obligation** that I take seriously.
2 constitutional *adjective* ①②③④	of or relating to the written document containing the basic _____ of the United States	I believe that _____ are a violation of my **constitutional** right to privacy.
3 representative *adjective* ①②③④	describing a system of _____ made up of people who act and speak for the people who _____ for them	When Americans were under British rule, they had to _____ even though they didn't have a **representative** government.
4 contribution *noun* ①②③④	something that a person _____ or _____ to help something succeed	I only _____ but I know that my **contribution** helped make the school play a success.

Your Vote, Your Voice 217

Building Concepts and Language
SPEAKING AND LISTENING

Academic Discussion

What are the reasons why some people do not vote?

BRAINSTORM IDEAS
Briefly record at least two ideas in each column using everyday English.

Personal Reasons	Political Reasons
• work long hours • •	• dislike the candidates • •

ANALYZE WORDS
Complete the chart with precise words to discuss and write about the topic.

Everyday	Precise
expect *(verb)*	anticipate,
boredom *(noun)*	indifference,
out of the way *(adjective)*	inaccessible,

MAKE A CLAIM
Rewrite two ideas using the frames and precise words. Then prepare to elaborate verbally.

1. **Frame:** From my point of view, one (personal/political) reason why some people do not vote is because they _____ (**present-tense verb:** have, forget, believe)

   Response: _____

   _____

2. **Frame:** I imagine that some people do not vote due to _____ (**noun phrase:** lack of time, other responsibilities, registration difficulties).

   Response: _____

   _____

Language to ELABORATE
To clarify, _____.

Based on my experience, _____.

COLLABORATE
Listen attentively, restate, and record your partner's ideas.

Classmate's Name	Ideas
	1. 2.

Language to RESTATE
In other words, your point of view is that _____.

Yes, that's accurate.

No. What I intended to say was _____.

SPEAKING AND WRITING

Ten-Minute Response

A **ten-minute response** begins with a **claim**, followed by **two detail sentences** that elaborate with relevant examples and precise words.

Language to COMPARE IDEAS

My point of view on _____ is (similar to/somewhat different from) _____'s.

🎤 PRESENT IDEAS

Listen, compare ideas, and take notes. Then indicate whether you agree (+) or disagree (−).

Classmate's Name	Idea	+/−

✏️ ELABORATE IN WRITING

Work with a partner to write a ten-minute response.

Language to COLLABORATE

What should we write?

We could select _____. What do you think is a strong selection?

As an alternative, we could write _____.

From my point of view, one personal reason why some people do not vote is because they forget to reregister to vote when they move. For example, when my friend's family _____ last year,

her parents forgot to _____

their _____ registration.

As a result, when it was _____

they discovered that they were not _____

and they couldn't participate in that _____

Write a ten-minute response.

I imagine that some people do not vote due to _____

_____

For example, _____

_____

_____

As a result, _____

_____

_____

Your Vote, Your Voice **219**

Analyzing and Discussing Text
ACADEMIC VOCABULARY

Words to Go

BUILD WORD KNOWLEDGE
Complete the meaning and examples for this high-utility academic word.

Word to Go	Meaning	Examples
institution in•sti•tu•tion *noun*	a large _____ _____ that has a certain kind of work or purpose, especially of a public nature	Many financial **institutions** try to provide consumers with help in _____ _____ People who want to _____ _____ should think about a career in a political **institution**.

DISCUSS AND WRITE EXAMPLES
Discuss your response with a partner. Then complete the sentence in writing.

Environmental **institutions** educate the public about the dangers of certain actions such as

_____

Write your response and read it aloud to a partner.

A health issue such as _____

is a major concern of the medical _____

BUILD WORD KNOWLEDGE
Complete the meaning and examples for this high-utility academic word.

Word to Go	Meaning	Examples
incentive in•cen•tive *noun*	something that _____ you to do something	The chance to _____ _____ was an **incentive** for me to rake the leaves in the yard. Joining the _____ _____ had certain social **incentives** for me.

DISCUSS AND WRITE EXAMPLES
Discuss your response with a partner. Then complete the sentence in writing.

I believe that driving privileges should not be used as an **incentive** to convince students

to _____

Write your response and read it aloud to a partner.

The musical director told us that as an added _____ we would each receive

a _____ if our glee club won the contest.

Text 1 • Op-Ed
RESPONDING TO TEXT

Close Reading

📖 BUILD FLUENCY
Read the text "Telling Americans to Vote, or Else" (*Issues,* pp. 107–111).

💬 IDENTIFY KEY IDEAS AND DETAILS
Take turns asking and answering questions with a partner. Then write brief notes.

Discussion Frames	Text Notes
Q: What is a **central idea** in this text? **A:** A **central idea** in this text is _____.	• the United States should have _____

Q: What are the **relevant supporting details** in this text?
A: (One/An additional) **relevant supporting detail** in this text is _____.
	• voting _____ in 31 countries, like Australia, where turnout is about _____
	• pros: voters better _____;
	  more citizens _____;
	  less _____
	• many _____ mandated voting; need to try and observe _____

✏️ RESPOND WITH EVIDENCE
Use the frames and evidence from the text to construct a formal written response.

1. According to the author, what are two ways mandatory voting would affect politics?

According to the author, mandatory voting would _____

_____

and _____

_____

Use the frame to analyze the author's purpose.

2. What is the effect of describing the success of mandatory voting in Australia? Why does the author include the information?

One effect of describing the success of mandatory voting in Australia is to _____

_____

The author includes this information to _____

_____

🔍 IDENTIFY PRECISE WORDS
Review Text 1 and your *Portfolio* (pp. 216–221) to identify words for your writing.

Topic Words	High-Utility Academic Words
• partisan • •	• prevalence • •

Your Vote, Your Voice

Building Concepts and Language

SPEAKING AND LISTENING

Academic Discussion

What are some ways in which people can engage in democracy?

BRAINSTORM IDEAS
Briefly record at least two ideas in each column using everyday English.

Individual	Collaborative
• learn about the issues • •	• join campaigns • •

ANALYZE WORDS
Complete the chart with precise words to discuss and write about the issue.

Everyday	Precise
sign up *(verb phrase)*	enroll,
try to get votes *(verb phrase)*	canvass,
back *(verb)*	advocate for,

MAKE A CLAIM
Rewrite two ideas using the frames and precise words. Then prepare to elaborate verbally.

1. **Frame:** One (individual/collaborative) way in which people can engage in democracy is to _____
   (**base verb:** vote, volunteer, serve, plan)

   Response: _____

2. **Frame:** (Individually/Collaboratively), people can make a contribution to democracy by _____ (**verb + -ing:** joining, writing, discussing, organizing)

   Response: _____

Language to ELABORATE
To clarify, _____.
Based on my experience, _____.

COLLABORATE
Listen attentively, restate, and record your partner's ideas.

Classmate's Name	Ideas
	1. 2.

Language to RESTATE
In other words, your point of view is that _____.
Yes, that's accurate.
No. What I intended to say was _____.

Issue 7

SPEAKING AND WRITING

Ten-Minute Response

A **ten-minute response** begins with a **claim**, followed by **two detail sentences** that elaborate with relevant examples and precise words.

> **Language to COMPARE IDEAS**
> My point of view on _____ is (similar to/somewhat different from) _____'s.

🎤 PRESENT IDEAS

Listen, compare ideas, and take notes. Then indicate whether you agree (+) or disagree (–).

Classmate's Name	Idea	+/–

✏️ ELABORATE IN WRITING

Work with a partner to write a ten-minute response.

> **Language to COLLABORATE**
> What should we write?
> We could select _____. What do you think is a strong selection?
> As an alternative, we could write _____.

One collaborative way in which people can engage in democracy is to canvass for the candidate they support. For example, people can go door-to-door _____ the residents of a particular _____ or _____ about the _____ and where they stand on the _____ As a result, some previously _____ _____ voters may decide to _____ the candidate.

Write a ten-minute response.

_____ people can make a contribution to democracy by _____
_____

For example, _____
_____
_____

As a result, _____
_____
_____

Analyzing and Discussing Text
ACADEMIC VOCABULARY

Words to Go

📗 BUILD WORD KNOWLEDGE
Complete the meaning and examples for this high-utility academic word.

Word to Go	Meaning	Examples
dynamic dy•nam•ic *adjective*	constantly _____ _____ due to many influences	After seeing my mother work at a job that _____ I'm hoping for a career in a more **dynamic** field. Carla's varied _____ _____ make our friendship rather **dynamic**.

💬 DISCUSS AND WRITE EXAMPLES
Discuss your response with a partner. Then complete the sentence in writing.

My personality becomes more **dynamic** when I _____

_____

Write your response and read it aloud to a partner.

Some people feel that traditional courses are not _____ enough to keep

up with _____

📗 BUILD WORD KNOWLEDGE
Complete the meaning and examples for this high-utility academic word.

Word to Go	Meaning	Examples
precede pre•cede *verb*	to come _____ something else	The principal's speech will **precede** our _____ _____ The movie was **preceded** by _____ _____

💬 DISCUSS AND WRITE EXAMPLES
Discuss your response with a partner. Then complete the sentence in writing.

Many young people's overuse of _____

preceded their problems with excessive debt.

Write your response and read it aloud to a partner.

Because I stayed up late video chatting with friends the night _____

the exam, I _____

224 Issue 7

Text ❷ • Section ❶ • Speech

SUMMARIZING TEXT

Section Shrink

📖 BUILD FLUENCY
Read Section 1 of the speech "What Does It Mean to Be an American Citizen?" (*Issues*, pp. 112–113).

💬 IDENTIFY KEY IDEAS AND DETAILS
Take turns asking and answering questions with a partner. Then write brief notes.

Discussion Frames	Text Notes
Q: What is a **central idea** in this section? **A:** A **central idea** in this section is _____.	• the debt of _____ owed by American _____
Q: What are the **relevant supporting details** in this section? **A:** (One/An additional) **relevant supporting detail** in this section is _____. **A:** Perhaps, the **most relevant supporting detail** in this section is _____.	• _____ justice, and opportunity given by those who _____ • Americans trade _____ for _____ to protect democracy • citizens should be _____ for the country left to them, and leave a _____ _____ for those who follow us

✏️ SUMMARIZE
"Shrink" Section 1 of the speech by writing a summary in 40 or fewer words.

CLASS SUMMARY: **WORD COUNT:** _____

_____ should recognize the _____ _____ they owe for their _____ and feel _____ for the _____ inherited, while attempting to improve it for _____

PARTNER SUMMARY: **WORD COUNT:** _____

Americans should have _____ for the _____ _____ and should _____ to _____ and _____ it so they can _____ a(n) _____ democracy.

🔍 IDENTIFY PRECISE WORDS
Review Section 1 and your *Portfolio* (pp. 222–225) to identify words for your writing.

Topic Words	High-Utility Academic Words
• liberty	• gratitude
•	•
•	•

Your Vote, Your Voice **225**

Analyzing and Discussing Text
ACADEMIC VOCABULARY

Words to Go

BUILD WORD KNOWLEDGE
Complete the meanings and examples for these high-utility academic words.

Word to Go	Meaning	Example
relevant rel•e•vant *adjective*	directly _____ _____ an issue or a matter	Mom told me that how I felt about _____ _____ _____ was not **relevant** to her decision.
relevance rel•e•vance *noun*	the condition of _____ an issue or a matter	Do _____ have **relevance** in this digital age?

DISCUSS AND WRITE EXAMPLES
Discuss your response with a partner. Then complete the sentence in writing.

It's important to include **relevant** _____
_____ when writing a justification or an argument essay.

Write your response and read it aloud to a partner.

The _____ of _____
_____ is clear when you consider how critical it is for college admissions.

BUILD WORD KNOWLEDGE
Complete the meanings and examples for these high-utility academic words.

Word to Go	Meaning	Example
responsive re•spon•sive *adjective*	_____ quickly and in a positive way	A good coach tries to be **responsive** to the _____ _____
responsiveness re•spon•sive•ness *noun*	the quality or state of _____ quickly and in a positive way	I was impressed by the **responsiveness** of the police when our community complained about _____ _____

DISCUSS AND WRITE EXAMPLES
Discuss your response with a partner. Then complete the sentence in writing.

A school administration should be especially **responsive** when it comes to important issues like _____

Write your response and read it aloud to a partner.

The _____ of a live teacher is _____
_____ that conventional classrooms have over online courses.

Text ❷ • Section ❷ • Speech

SUMMARIZING TEXT

Section Shrink

BUILD FLUENCY
Read Section 2 of the speech "What Does It Mean to Be an American Citizen?" (*Issues,* pp. 114–116).

IDENTIFY KEY IDEAS AND DETAILS
Take turns asking and answering questions with a partner. Then write brief notes.

Discussion Frames	Text Notes
Q: What is a **central idea** in this section? **A:** A **central idea** in this section is _____.	• creating a _____ government through _____
Q: What are the **relevant supporting details** in this section? **A:** (One/An additional) **relevant supporting detail** in this section is _____. **A:** Perhaps the **most relevant supporting detail** in this section is _____.	• people are _____ less and _____ more • _____ leads to power-hungry _____; may destroy _____ • put aside _____ interests; instead take _____ to improve the _____

SUMMARIZE
"Shrink" Section 2 of the speech by writing a summary in 40 or fewer words.

CLASS SUMMARY: **WORD COUNT:** _____

Without _____

such as _____ and putting aside

_____ to better support the common good,

_____ may fail.

PARTNER SUMMARY: **WORD COUNT:** _____

The _____ of U.S. citizens threatens _____

and the _____ of the government, so people

need to _____ and attend to the _____

_____ to fight for the _____

IDENTIFY PRECISE WORDS
Review Section 2 and your *Portfolio* (pp. 226–227) to identify words for your writing.

Topic Words	High-Utility Academic Words
• civic engagement • •	• endeavor • •

Analyzing and Discussing Text
ACADEMIC VOCABULARY

Words to Go

📖 BUILD WORD KNOWLEDGE
Complete the meanings and examples for these high-utility academic words.

Words to Go	Meanings	Examples
resolve re•solve *verb*	to find a _____ to a problem or to settle a _____	In order to **resolve** my transportation problems, I _____
resolution res•o•lu•tion *noun*	an agreed-upon _____ to a problem	My sister and I are working toward a **resolution** of _____

💬 DISCUSS AND WRITE EXAMPLES
Discuss your response with a partner. Then complete the sentence in writing.

My school **resolved** the problem of _____ by starting the school day later.

Write your response and read it aloud to a partner.

It seems obvious that the best _____ to the high number of _____ is to raise the driving age.

📖 BUILD WORD KNOWLEDGE
Complete the meaning and examples for this high-utility academic word.

Word to Go	Meaning	Examples
consensus con•sen•sus *noun*	an _____ among all the people in a group	It took a while, but my family finally reached a **consensus** on _____ There is a **consensus** among the students in Ms. Black's class that she is _____

💬 DISCUSS AND WRITE EXAMPLES
Discuss your response with a partner. Then complete the sentence in writing.

The student body couldn't reach a decision about _____ due to a lack of **consensus**.

Write your response and read it aloud to a partner.

The _____ of our class regarding school and job skills is that _____

Text ❷ • Section ❸ • Speech

SUMMARIZING TEXT

Section Shrink

📖 BUILD FLUENCY
Read Section 3 of the speech "What Does It Mean to Be an American Citizen?" (*Issues,* pp. 116–121).

💬 IDENTIFY KEY IDEAS AND DETAILS
Take turns asking and answering questions with a partner. Then write brief notes.

Discussion Frames	Text Notes
Q: What is a **central idea** in this section? **A:** A **central idea** in this section is _____.	• how citizens can _____ in democracy
Q: What are the **relevant supporting details** in this section? **A:** (One/An additional) **relevant supporting detail** in this section is _____. **A:** Perhaps the **most relevant supporting detail** in this section is _____.	• most can't _____ big problems, but all can make _____ changes • citizens engage when they are informed about _____ and the _____ faced • _____ makes people feel like _____; helps them _____ democracy

✏️ SUMMARIZE
"Shrink" Section 3 of the text by writing a summary in 40 or fewer words.

CLASS SUMMARY: **WORD COUNT:** _____

Most citizens will _____ to _____ small problems once they know _____ and doing so will _____

PARTNER SUMMARY: **WORD COUNT:** _____

People who _____ how their community works can engage to _____ and, as a result, _____ as an integral part of the _____

🔍 IDENTIFY PRECISE WORDS
Review Section 3 and your *Portfolio* (pp. 228–229) to identify words for your writing.

Topic Words	High-Utility Academic Words
• constituent	• insignificant
•	•
•	•

Your Vote, Your Voice   229

Academic Writing

ANALYZING TEXT FEATURES

Student Writing Model

Academic Writing Type

A **formal written summary** provides an objective overview of the topic and important details from an informational text. The writer credits the author, but writes in primarily their own words, without including personal opinions.

  A. The **topic sentence** includes the text type, title, author, and topic.
  B. **Detail sentences** include the important details from the summarized text.
  C. The **concluding sentence** restates the author's conclusion in the writer's own words.

ANALYZE TEXT
Read this student model to analyze the elements of a formal summary.

A
In the op-ed article titled "Telling Americans to Vote, or Else," William A. Galston examines voting and citizenship.

B
Galston begins by suggesting that mandatory voting is a requirement that would improve democracy. The writer continues to describe the dramatic increase to voter turnout in Australia after voting was changed from optional to mandatory. He discusses further that voting should be a civic responsibility for all American citizens, and that making voting mandatory would resolve the problem of policies that aren't representative of the entire citizenship. Moreover, the writer points out that a major incentive for making voting mandatory is that it would improve electoral politics and hold legislators accountable for their campaign promises.

C
Galston concludes by emphasizing that mandatory voting would force politicians to focus more on the issues and earn the trust of the Americans they represent.

MARK AND DISCUSS ELEMENTS
Mark the summary elements and use the frames to discuss them with your partner.

1. **Number (1–4) the four elements of the topic sentence.**
   The topic sentence includes the _____.

2. **Draw a box around four transition words or phrases.**
   One transition (word/phrase) is _____.

3. **Underline four important details.** *One important detail in this summary is _____.*

4. **Circle four citation verbs.** *One citation verb that the writer uses is _____.*

5. **Star four precise topic words and check four high-utility academic words.**
   An example of a (precise topic word/high-utility academic word) is _____.

Formal Summary
PLANNING TO WRITE

Organize a Formal Summary

Prompt Write a formal summary of "What Does It Mean to Be an American Citizen?"

Guidelines for Paraphrasing Multiple Sentences
Paraphrase related details from a source text by combining key information into one sentence. Replace key words and phrases with synonyms and keep important topic words.

Text Detail 1	Text Detail 2	Text Detail 3
"People are voting less; paying less attention to their civic responsibility; ignoring the great lessons of the American experiment . . ." (Hamilton 114).	"There is a sense, particularly among many young people, that being an American citizen is no big deal, with no obligation attached to it . . ." (Hamilton 114).	"People think [elected representatives] are not relevant to their day-to-day lives" (Hamilton 114).

PARAPHRASE IDEAS
Combine key information from the three text details above into one detail sentence.

Lack of understanding about the importance of democracy has led many Americans to

(text detail 1) _____

(text detail 2) _____ and

(text detail 3) _____

PLAN KEY IDEAS AND DETAILS
State the text information to write a topic sentence.

In the speech titled (Title) _____

(Speaker's Full Name) _____

(citation verb: presents, investigates, discusses) _____

(topic) _____

List four important details from the text using primarily your own words.

1. _____
_____

2. _____
_____

3. _____
_____

4. _____
_____

Restate the conclusion in your own words.

_____

_____

Academic Writing
WRITING A DRAFT

Write a Formal Summary

Prompt Write a formal summary of "What Does It Mean to Be an American Citizen?"

✏️ WRITE A PARAGRAPH
Use the frame to write your topic sentence, detail sentences, and concluding sentence.

A

In the _____ titled _____
     (text type)   (Title)

_____ _____
(Speaker's Full Name)   (citation verb)

_____
(topic)

B

_____ begins by _____
(Speaker's Last Name)   (citation verb + -ing: presenting, arguing)

_____
(1st important detail)

The speaker continues to _____
                        (citation verb, base form: describe, report)

_____
(2nd important detail)

_____ _____ further that
(Pronoun)   (present-tense citation verb)

_____
(3rd important detail)

Moreover, the speaker _____
                    (present-tense citation verb)

_____
(4th important detail)

C

_____ concludes by _____
(Speaker's Last Name)   (citation verb + -ing: suggesting, emphasizing)

_____
(restate conclusion)

Summary
ASSESSING AND REVISING

Rate Your Summary

ASSESS YOUR DRAFT
Rate your formal summary. Then have a partner rate it.

Scoring Guide	
1	Insufficient
2	Developing
3	Sufficient
4	Exemplary

1. Does the topic sentence state the title, speaker, and topic?	Self	1	2	3	4
	Partner	1	2	3	4
2. Did you paraphrase the most important details from the speech?	Self	1	2	3	4
	Partner	1	2	3	4
3. Did you use citation verbs to credit the speaker?	Self	1	2	3	4
	Partner	1	2	3	4
4. Did you use transitions to introduce and sequence details?	Self	1	2	3	4
	Partner	1	2	3	4
5. Did you include precise topic words and high-utility academic words?	Self	1	2	3	4
	Partner	1	2	3	4
6. Did you restate the speaker's conclusion using your own words?	Self	1	2	3	4
	Partner	1	2	3	4

REFLECT AND REVISE
Record specific priorities and suggestions to help you and your partner revise.

(Partner) Positive Feedback: I appreciate how you (used/included) _____

_____

_____

(Partner) Suggestion: As you revise your summary, focus on _____

_____

_____

(Self) Priority 1: My summary paragraph needs _____

_____

_____

(Self) Priority 2: I plan to improve my summary by _____

_____

_____

CHECK AND EDIT
Use this checklist to proofread and edit your summary.

- [ ] Did you capitalize the title of the speech and proper nouns?
- [ ] Did you put quotation marks around the title of the speech?
- [ ] Did you use commas appropriately after transitions?
- [ ] Do simple present-tense verbs end in –s?
- [ ] Is each sentence complete?
- [ ] Are all words spelled correctly?

Analyzing and Discussing Text

ACADEMIC VOCABULARY

Words to Know

📖 BUILD WORD KNOWLEDGE

Rate your word knowledge. Then discuss word meanings and examples with your group.

① Don't Know   ② Recognize   ③ Familiar   ④ Know

Word to Know	Meaning	Examples
1 **registered** *adjective* ① ② ③ ④	entered or recorded on an _____ list	As a **registered** student in a college-level class, I have access to _____ _____ _____. My mother had to pass a licensing exam to become a **registered** _____ _____.
2 **organize** *verb* ① ② ③ ④	to _____ _____ and manage an event or an activity	The prom committee will **organize** a _____ to help pay for the event. For Mother's Day, I **organized** a _____ _____ for my mom.
3 **eliminate** *verb* ① ② ③ ④	to completely _____ _____ an unnecessary or _____ item	Using _____ can **eliminate** the need for paper maps. Our school **eliminated** _____ _____ from the lunch menu so students would have healthier choices.
4 **barrier** *noun* ① ② ③ ④	a rule or a problem that _____ or limits people from doing something	_____ _____ was a **barrier** to my attendance at the after-school picnic in the park. After we _____ _____, I had to work hard to break down the **barriers** between _____ _____ and me.

234 Issue 7

Text 3 • Novel Excerpt

RESPONDING TO TEXT

Close Reading

📖 READ THE TEXT
Read the excerpt from *Countdown* (*Issues*, pp. 122–129).

🔍 IDENTIFY KEY IDEAS AND DETAILS
Use the frames to analyze the text and make inferences.

1. The author writes: "After three tries, Fannie successfully registered to vote." What can you infer about Fannie's character based on this text evidence?

   The fact that Fannie _____

   the first three times suggests that _____

   _____

   This reveals that Fannie was _____ because she

   _____

✏️ ANALYZE CRAFT AND STRUCTURE
Use the frames to analyze the author's use of literary devices.

> ### Literary Devices
> **Literary devices** are the methods and techniques authors use to convey their messages in literary texts. **Irony** is a literary device that contrasts what happens in a text with what the reader might expect to happen. **Mood** is the effect that a writer's words have on readers. The mood of a text describes how the writer's words make readers feel.

2. Why does the author point out some of the significant events of 1961, the year that Fannie learns she can vote?

   The author points out some of the significant events of 1961 to _____

   _____

   and to contrast _____

   with _____

   _____

3. How do the five indented lines on page 127 reflect the author's use of irony?

   The lines are ironic because the first four lines describe _____

   _____ but the last line lets

   the reader know that, in fact, the actions had the _____ effect

   and _____

4. What mood does the author create with the words *arrested, beaten, ridiculed,* and *shot at*? How does the mood change when the author uses the word *galvanized*?

   These words convey a mood of _____

   Because the word _____ suggests

   _____ the mood shifts from one of

   _____ to one of _____

Your Vote, Your Voice **235**

Analyzing and Discussing Text

SPEAKING AND LISTENING

Academic Discussion

How do citizens today perceive voting differently than those in the past?

BRAINSTORM IDEAS
Briefly record at least two ideas in each column using everyday English.

In the Past	In the Present
• a right	• a hassle
•	•
•	•

ANALYZE WORDS
Complete the chart with precise words to discuss and write about the topic.

Everyday	Precise
right *(noun)*	prerogative,
change *(verb)*	alter,
choose *(verb)*	elect,

MAKE A CLAIM
Rewrite two ideas using the frames and precise words. Then prepare to elaborate verbally.

1. **Frame:** Some citizens today view voting as _____ (**adjective:** inconvenient, corrupt, insignificant), whereas citizens in the past viewed voting as a(n) _____ (**noun:** obligation, duty, right)

   Response: _____
   _____

2. **Frame:** For Fannie Lou Hamer, voting was a way to _____ (**base verb:** have, fight, affect)

   Response: _____
   _____

Language to ELABORATE
To clarify, _____.
Based on my experience, _____.

COLLABORATE
Listen attentively, restate, and record your partner's ideas.

Classmate's Name	Ideas
	3.
	4.

Language to RESTATE
In other words, your point of view is that _____.
Yes, that's accurate.
No. What I intended to say was _____.

Text ❸ • Novel Excerpt
SPEAKING AND WRITING

Ten-Minute Response

A **ten-minute response** begins with a **claim**, followed by **two detail sentences** that elaborate with relevant examples and precise words.

Language to COMPARE IDEAS

My point of view on _____ is (similar to/somewhat different from) _____'s.

🎤 PRESENT IDEAS

Listen, compare ideas, and take notes. Then indicate whether you agree (+) or disagree (–).

Classmate's Name	Idea	+/–

✏️ ELABORATE IN WRITING

Work with a partner to write a ten-minute response.

Language to COLLABORATE

What should we write? We could select _____.

What do you think is a strong selection?

As an alternative, we could write _____.

Some citizens today view voting as an inconvenience, whereas citizens in the past viewed voting as a privilege. For example, it is often time consuming to _____ _____ especially when _____

As a result, many people _____

because they _____

or they _____

_____

Write a ten-minute response.

For Fannie Lou Hamer, voting was a way to _____

_____

For example, _____

_____

_____

As a result, _____

_____

Your Vote, Your Voice

Presenting Ideas

Take a Stand

Debate | Should voting be made compulsory in all countries?

COLLABORATE
Read the debate question about voting. Then take turns using a frame to respond with your initial reaction.

Language to RESPOND
So _____, what's your initial reaction?
My initial reaction is _____.
My initial reaction is related to _____'s.

ANALYZE SOURCES
Read a quote that either supports or opposes the debate question. Then paraphrase.

Quote	Paraphrase
Model: "If American citizens increasingly become disengaged, then the entire American democratic enterprise is at risk" (Hamilton 114–115).	This quote makes it evident that _____ will be _____ if citizens aren't _____ in civic duties.
1. "Requiring people to vote in national elections once every two years would reinforce the principle of reciprocity at the heart of citizenship" (Galston 108).	The author seems to be saying that even demanding _____ in national elections is a responsibility of _____ that counters the _____ provided by governments.
2. "Mandatory voting would tend to even out disparities stemming from income, education and age, enhancing our system's inclusiveness" (Galston 109).	This quote makes it evident that making voting _____ would result in more balanced _____ of voters, despite their different _____.
3. "Mandating voting nationwide would go counter to our traditions (and perhaps our Constitution) and would encounter strong state opposition" (Galston 111).	This quote makes it evident that states in the U.S. would _____ mandatory voting, because it goes against U.S. _____ and maybe even _____.
4. "You and I are concerned because we know that if we are apathetic, passive, and cynical about our democracy, then we will invite leaders who abuse power" (Hamilton 114).	The author seems to be saying that if U.S. residents don't _____ _____ then corrupt _____ may be elected.

Debate Ideas

✏️ SYNTHESIZE IDEAS

Write a response to the debate question, including a paraphrase of a text quote and elaboration on the quote.

Claim: My position is that voting (should/should not) _____ be made compulsory in all countries.

Transitional Statement: I have (one key reason/a compelling reason) _____
_____ for taking this stance.

Quote Paraphrase: (For example,/According to [author],) _____.
_____
_____
_____

Quote Elaboration: (As a result,/Consequently,) _____.
_____
_____
_____

🎤 PRESENT EVIDENCE

Using Gestures for Emphasis
When presenting ideas during class or in a meeting, use **gestures for emphasis**. Move your hands when you make an important point or present a surprising piece of evidence.

📋 LISTEN AND TAKE NOTES

Listen attentively and take notes. Then indicate whether you agree (+) or disagree (−).

> **Language to AFFIRM AND CLARIFY**
> I can understand why you *see* it this way.
> Could you explain what you mean by _____?

Classmate's Name	Idea	+/−

Your Vote, Your Voice

Academic Writing

ANALYZING TEXT ELEMENTS

Student Writing Model

Academic Writing Type

An **argument** states a claim and supports it with logical reasons and relevant evidence from sources.

- **A.** The **thesis statement** clearly states the writer's claim and tells what the writer will explain about the topic.
- **B.** **Supporting paragraphs** support the claim with reasons and evidence from sources. The writer also presents counterclaims and responds with strong evidence.
- **C.** The **conclusion statement** restates the writer's claim about the issue.

🔍 ANALYZE TEXT
Read this student model to analyze elements of an argument research paper.

A
After examining the issues surrounding voting and citizenship, I am convinced that voting should not be mandatory in all countries.

B
One reason I maintain this position is that many people are likely to rebel against voting if it's presented as an obligation. In "Telling Americans to Vote, or Else," William A. Galston emphasizes that when Australia made voting mandatory, some feared that spite would be an incentive to destroy ballots (108). As a teen, I have firsthand experience with actions fueled by spite. As an illustration, when we were forced to wear school uniforms, organizers staged a protest in which students cut off their sleeves and pant legs. In contrast, proponents of mandatory voting believe that it would resolve the problem of apathy among U.S. citizens (Galston 108). However, I am not convinced that forcing people to vote would make them more responsive.

The Honorable Lee H. Hamilton's analysis of U.S. citizenship and the institution of democracy in "What Does It Mean to Be an American Citizen?" has strengthened my perspective that compulsory voting is a fruitless effort. According to Hamilton, many U.S. citizens believe that elected officials are the puppets of interest groups rather than the people (114). Although a common argument in favor of compulsory voting is that it would give typically underrepresented voters a greater voice in government (Galston 109), I don't find the evidence compelling. Clearly, there is adequate evidence that shows that those are the people who would be least able to pay the fines imposed if they failed to turn up to vote (Galston 109).

C
The question of whether or not to make voting mandatory is provocative. My analysis of this issue has left me with little doubt that compulsory voting should not be implemented in all countries.

Argument
ANALYZING TEXT ELEMENTS

💬 MARK AND DISCUSS ELEMENTS
Mark the argument elements and use the frames to discuss them with your partner.

1. **Circle the writer's claim within the thesis statement.** *The writer's claim is _____.*
2. **Underline and label two reasons that support the writer's claim with the letter *R*.**
   One reason that supports the writer's claim is _____.
3. **Underline and label four pieces of evidence that support the writer's claim with the letter *E*.**
   One piece of evidence that supports the writer's claim is _____.
4. **Draw boxes around two counterclaims.** *One counterclaim is _____.*
5. **Star four precise topic words and check four high-utility academic words.**
   An example of a (precise topic word/high-utility academic word) is _____.

📝 ASSESS A STUDENT SAMPLE
Read an additional student model and rate it.

Scoring Guide			
1	Insufficient	3	Sufficient
2	Developing	4	Exemplary

1. Does the thesis statement clearly state the claim?	1	2	3	4
2. Do supporting paragraphs begin with a topic sentence that specifies a reason?	1	2	3	4
3. Did the writer give evidence drawn primarily from sources to support the claim?	1	2	3	4
4. Did the writer explain why the evidence is relevant and significant?	1	2	3	4
5. Did the writer include complex sentences to present and respond to counterclaims?	1	2	3	4
6. Did the writer use strong verbs and verb phrases to express opinions?	1	2	3	4
7. Did the writer use transitions to introduce reasons and evidence?	1	2	3	4
8. Did the writer use precise adjectives to describe evidence?	1	2	3	4
9. Did the writer include citation information for text evidence?	1	2	3	4
10. Did the writer include precise topic words and high-utility words?	1	2	3	4
11. Does the conclusion statement strongly restate the claim using new wording?	1	2	3	4

👥 REFLECT AND REVISE
Record specific priorities and suggestions to help the writer.

The writer did an effective job of (organizing/including/stating) _____
_____
_____

One way the writer could make the argument stronger is _____
_____
_____

I noticed that the writer (forgot to/included/used) _____
_____
_____

This will support me with writing an argument because I will remember to _____
_____
_____

Academic Writing

FRONTLOADING LANGUAGE

Verbs and Verb Phrases to Express Opinion

Opinion	Verbs/Verb Phrases to Express an Opinion	Argument Examples
agree	*believe, conclude, contend, support, maintain, concur* *agree wholeheartedly that* *still maintain that* *still contend that* *am convinced that*	After examining the issues surrounding citizenship and voting, I **believe** that voting should be mandatory. One reason I **am convinced that** U.S. residents will reject mandatory voting is that it may be unconstitutional.
disagree	*contend, reject, maintain, challenge, conclude, oppose* *disagree entirely that* *cannot support the opinion that* *am not convinced that*	However, I **reject** that U.S. residents would deliberately destroy ballots. One reason I still **contend** that politicians would work harder is that they would have to please more voters.
undecided	*am uncertain, am unsure, am unconvinced, hesitate* *am undecided about whether* *see both sides of the issue* *am more inclined to believe*	Although the text includes some interesting evidence, I **am unsure** that voting should be compulsory. Due to the evidence presented, I **see both sides of the issue**.

🔍 IDENTIFY VERB PHRASES

Circle the verbs and verb phrases in the chart that you plan to use in your argument. Then complete each sentence with a verb or verb phrase to express an opinion.

1. After reviewing the evidence, I _____ more Americans should participate in local politics.

2. Despite the evidence presented, I _____ mandatory voting would lessen the power of special interests.

3. For these reasons, I _____ that civic engagement will improve with compulsory voting.

✏️ WRITE OPINIONS

Write sentences that express the opinion in parentheses. Include details from texts.

1. **(agree)** After analyzing the research on and voting, I _____
   _____

2. **(disagree)** However, I _____
   _____

3. **(undecided)** Although the article presents interesting evidence, I _____
   _____

Present Perfect–Tense Verbs

Guidelines for Using Present Perfect–Tense Verbs

Present perfect–tense verbs show action that happened sometime in the past or action that has happened and is still happening. Use present perfect–tense verbs to provide data and anecdotal evidence from the text or your experience that supports your claim.

I **have heard** people who don't vote complaining about the government.	hear → have heard
Studies **have shown** that voters are more involved citizens.	show → have shown
My uncle **has voted** in every election, but still feels unrepresented.	vote → has voted
Research **has proven** that voter turnout in Australia is near 95 percent.	prove → has proven

IDENTIFY PRESENT PERFECT–TENSE

Read the paragraph from an argument and circle the present perfect–tense verbs.

> After examining the issues surrounding voter turnout, I am convinced that same-day registration is the solution to the challenge of motivating voters to go to the polls.
>
> One reason I maintain this position is that people may decide at the last minute that they want to vote. In "Same-Day Registration," Marion Just emphasizes that people who have shown little interest in voting may be tempted to cast a ballot after they have witnessed two weeks of intense campaign ads leading up to Election Day (1). As a teen, I have firsthand experience with deciding to do something at the last minute. As an illustration, I have applied for a spot in a summer internship just before the deadline, because I could do so online. In contrast, some people I know have claimed that last-minute voters aren't well informed. However, I reject that notion because those voters have reacted strongly enough to something in the campaign ads to make them get out and vote.

WRITE PRESENT PERFECT–TENSE VERBS

Complete the sentences with the present perfect–tense of the verbs in parentheses.

1. Australia (mandate) _____ compulsory voting since 1924.
2. Laws there (yield) _____ voting by almost 95 percent of citizens, with only the threat of small fines for nonvoters.
3. The law (establish) _____ permissible excuses for not voting, like illness or travel out of the country.
4. The laws (change) _____ the way people in Australia feel about voting.

Academic Writing
PLANNING TO WRITE

Organize an Argument

Prompt Should voting be made compulsory in all countries? Write an argument that states your claim and supports it with text evidence.

Guidelines for Citing Text Evidence
Paraphrase text evidence when you want to summarize a longer section of text or multiple ideas. Use **direct quotes** when the author has used strong wording that is difficult to improve or simplify.

Quote	Paraphrase or Incorporate Quote
"The law also changed civic norms. Australians are more likely than before to see voting as an obligation." (Galston 108).	In "Telling Americans to Vote, or Else," William Galston emphasizes that mandatory voting in Australia transformed voting into a civic duty (108).
". . . an endeavor not particularly worthy of their time and talent" (Hamilton 114)	Young people feel that U.S. citizenship, of which voting is an integral part, is "an endeavor not particularly worthy of their time and talent" (Hamilton 114).

✏️ WRITE A THESIS STATEMENT
Describe your claim.

My claim: _____

Use academic language to restate your claim as a thesis statement.

_____ voting, I
(Thesis starter)

_____
(verb/verb phrase to express opinion)

that _____
(strongly state your claim)

💡 CHOOSE SUPPORTING TOPICS
List each topic you will write about to support your claim.

Supporting Paragraph 1

Topic: _____

_____

Supporting Paragraph 2

Topic: _____

_____

Find text evidence that supports your claim and write a sentence that paraphrases it or incorporates a direct quote.

_____

_____

_____

Argument
PLANNING TO WRITE

📋 PLAN SUPPORTING PARAGRAPHS
List reasons and evidence that support your claim. You may draw from texts, your experience, or a classmate's experience.

Supporting Paragraph 1:

Reason 1: _____

_____

Evidence: _____

_____

_____

Source/Page Number: _____

Author: _____

Counterclaim 1: _____

_____

Response to Counterclaim: _____

_____

Source/Page Number: _____

Author: _____

Supporting Paragraph 2:

Reason 2: _____

_____

Evidence: _____

_____

_____

Source/Page Number: _____

Author: _____

Counterclaim 2: _____

_____

Response to Counterclaim: _____

_____

Source/Page Number: _____

Author: _____

✏️ WRITE A CONCLUSION
Write a conclusion statement that restates your claim.

The question of whether or not to _____
　　　　　　　　　　　　　　　　　　(restate the issue)

is _____ My analysis of this issue has left me with little
　(precise adjective to respond)

doubt that _____
　　　　　　(restate your claim)

_____

Your Vote, Your Voice **245**

Academic Writing

WRITING A DRAFT

Write an Argument

Prompt Should voting be made compulsory in all countries? Write an argument that states your claim and supports it with text evidence.

✏️ **WRITE A RESEARCH PAPER**
Use the frame to write your thesis statement, supporting paragraphs, and conclusion statement.

A

_____
(Thesis starter)

I _____
(topic)
 (verb/verb phrase to express opinion)
that _____
(strongly state your claim)

_____

B1

One reason I maintain this position is that _____
 (1st reason that supports your claim)

_____

In _____
(Title of Source)
_____ emphasizes that
(Author's Full Name)
_____
(evidence from source)

_____

As a teen, I have firsthand experience with _____
 (situation or issue)

_____

_____ _____
(Transition introducing evidence) (evidence from your experience)

_____

In contrast, _____
 (group with an opposing claim)
_____ that _____
(verb/verb phrase to express opinion) (counterclaim from source or your experience)

_____

However, I _____ that _____
 (verb/verb phrase to express opinion) (your response to the counterclaim)

_____

_____

246 Issue 7

Argument
ASSESSING AND REVISING

B2

_____ analysis of _____
(Author's Full Name + 's)   (topic)

_____

in _____
   (Title of a Different Source)
has strengthened my perspective that _____
                                     (2nd reason that supports your claim)
_____
_____

_____ _____
(Transition introducing evidence) (evidence from source or your experience)
_____
_____
_____

Although a common argument (in favor of/against) _____
_____
(issue)
is _____
   (counterclaim from source or your experience)
_____
_____
_____

I don't find the evidence (compelling/substantial/believable) _____

Clearly, there is (sufficient/adequate/striking) _____

evidence that (shows/proves) _____
                              (your response to the counterclaim)
_____
_____

C

The question of whether or not to _____
                                   (restate the issue)
_____

is _____ My analysis of this issue has left me with little doubt
   (precise adjective to respond)
that_____
     (restate your claim)
_____
_____

Your Vote, Your Voice **247**

Issue 8 Future Focus

SHOULD WE LIVE FOR TODAY OR LEAVE A LEGACY FOR LATER?

BUILD KNOWLEDGE
Read and respond to the Data File (*Issues,* p. 130).

BRAINSTORM IDEAS
Write a brief list of positive and negative ways people can impact the future.

- positive: inventing technology
- _____
- _____
- _____

PRESENT IDEAS
Use the frames to discuss ideas with your group. Listen attentively and record the strongest ideas to complete the T-chart.

Language to FACILITATE DISCUSSION
So _____, what's your suggestion?
_____, what example did you come up with?

1. One (positive/negative) way people can impact the future is by _____ (**verb + –ing:** creating)
2. Another way people can (positively/negatively) impact the future is by _____ (**verb + –ing:** protecting)
3. People can have a positive impact on the future by _____ (**verb + –ing:** investing)
4. People can negatively impact the future by _____ (**verb + –ing: destroying:** support)

POSITIVE WAYS	NEGATIVE WAYS
• recycling	• destroying animal habitats

248 Issue 8

Words to Know

BUILD WORD KNOWLEDGE
Rate your word knowledge. Then discuss word meanings and examples with your group.

① Don't Know ② Recognize ③ Familiar ④ Know

Word to Know	Meaning	Example
1 right noun ① ② ③ 256	a moral or _____ claim to have or do something	The **right** to _____ _____ _____ is essential for all people.
2 power noun ① ② ③ ④	the _____ or capacity to _____ something	Students have the **power** to make a difference by _____ _____ _____
3 action noun ① ② ③ ④	an activity done to _____ an _____	When a storm destroyed the park, our community took **action** by _____ _____ _____
4 policy noun ① ② ③ ④	a _____ or official way of doing something	Our school has a strict **policy** against _____ _____ _____
1 moral adjective ① ② ③ ④	_____ in a way most people consider to be _____	Acting in a **moral** way means _____ _____ _____
2 gratitude noun ① ② ③ ④	the feeling of being _____ for _____	I show **gratitude** to people who help me by _____ _____
3 sacrifice noun ① ② ③ ④	something _____ given up to get something else considered	I know that to _____ I might have to make a **sacrifice**, such as _____ _____
4 humanity noun ① ② ③ ④	the collective group of all _____ as a _____	_____ _____ is something that benefits all of **humanity**.

Building Concepts and Language

SPEAKING AND LISTENING

Academic Discussion

Do high school students have the power to make change?

BRAINSTORM IDEAS
Briefly record at least two ideas in each column using everyday English.

Yes	No
• are good with technology • •	• are too young • •

ANALYZE WORDS
Complete the chart with precise words to discuss and write about the topic.

Everyday	Precise
lack of skills (noun)	ignorance,
excitement (noun)	passion,
not caring (adjective)	indifferent,

MAKE A CLAIM
Rewrite two ideas using the frames and precise words. Then prepare to elaborate verbally.

Language to ELABORATE
To exemplify, _____.
Personally, _____.

1. **Frame:** From my perspective, high school students (have/do not have) the power to make change due to their _____ (**noun:** energy, inexperience, skills, time constraints)

   Response: _____

2. **Frame:** In my experience, high school students are often _____ (**adjective:** busy, passionate, uncaring), and that can _____ (**base verb:** help, limit, motivate, prevent)

   Response: _____

COLLABORATE
Listen attentively, restate, and record your partner's idea.

Language to RESTATE
In other words, your stance is that _____.
Yes, that's accurate.
No. What I intended to say was _____.

Classmate's Name	Ideas
	1.
	2.

SPEAKING AND WRITING

Ten-Minute Response

A **ten-minute response** begins with a **claim**, followed by **two detail sentences** that elaborate with relevant examples and precise words.

Language to COMPARE IDEAS

My stance on _____ is related to _____'s.

🎤 PRESENT IDEAS

Listen, compare ideas, and take notes. Then indicate whether you agree (+) or disagree (−).

Classmate's Name	Idea	+/−

✏️ ELABORATE IN WRITING

Work with a partner to write a ten-minute response.

Language to COLLABORATE

What should we write?

We could select _____. What do you think works effectively?

Alternatively, we could write _____.

From my perspective, high school students have the power to make change due their knowledge of social media. For example, many high school students know how to _____
_____

As a result, they have the power to _____
_____
_____

Write a ten-minute response.

In my experience, high school students are often _____ and that can _____

For example, _____
_____

As a result, _____
_____

Future Focus 251

Analyzing and Discussing Text

ACADEMIC VOCABULARY

Words to Go

📘 BUILD WORD KNOWLEDGE

Complete the meanings and examples for these high-utility academic words.

Words to Go	Meaning	Example
environment en•vi•ron•ment *noun*	the air, water, and land on _____, which is affected by human activities	Pollution hurts the **environment** because it can _____ _____ _____
environmental en•vi•ron•men•tal *adjective*	concerning or affecting the air, _____, or _____ on Earth	_____ _____ can be an **environmental** issue in cities.

💬 DISCUSS AND WRITE EXAMPLES

Discuss your response with a partner. Then complete the sentence in writing.

One way we can protect the **environment** is by _____

Write your response and read it aloud to a partner.

_____ factors such as _____ can negatively affect your sleep.

📘 BUILD WORD KNOWLEDGE

Complete the meaning and examples for this high-utility academic word.

Word to Go	Meaning	Examples
validate val•i•date *verb*	to _____ or prove that something is _____ or important	It is important to **validate** your sources when doing research to _____ _____ To stay safe online, make sure to **validate** _____ _____ to stay safe online.

💬 DISCUSS AND WRITE EXAMPLES

Discuss your response with a partner. Then complete the sentence in writing.

Winning the science fair **validated** my belief that I am _____

Write your response and read it aloud to a partner.

One way teachers can _____ student work is by _____

_____

252 Issue 8

Close Reading

BUILD FLUENCY
Read the text "The Kids Who Sued Montana Over Climate Change and Won Say It's Just the Start" (*Issues,* pp. 131–135).

IDENTIFY KEY IDEAS AND DETAILS
Take turns asking and answering questions with a partner. Then write brief notes.

Discussion Frames	Text Notes
Q: What is a **central idea** in this text? **A:** A **central idea** in this text is _____.	• young people have the power to _____
Q: What are the **relevant supporting details** in this text? **A:** (One/An additional) **relevant supporting detail** in this text is _____.	• the teens sued Montana for not doing enough to protect the _____ • they _____ their case in court and will continue seeking _____ • their victory may _____ other young people to _____

RESPOND WITH EVIDENCE
Use the frames and evidence from the text to construct a formal written response.

1. According to the text, how do Claire Vlases and Sariel Sandoval exemplify "a rising generation of young activists who know the power of speaking their minds?"

   According to the text, Claire Clases and Sariel Sandoval show that young activists can make a difference by _____

   and proving that _____

Use the frame to analyze the text structure of the interview.

2. What is Twumasi's purpose for asking Vlases "What about it got you?" on page 133, and how does Vlases' response show the importance of teens speaking out?

   The question "What about it got you?" gives Vlases an opportunity to _____

   _____

   Vlases' response shows the importance of teens speaking out because it tells how _____

   _____

   _____

IDENTIFY PRECISE WORDS
Review Text 1 and your *Portfolio* (pp. 248–253) to identify words for your writing.

Topic Words	High-Utility Academic Words
• generations	• impending
•	•
•	•

Future Focus **253**

Building Concepts and Language

SPEAKING AND LISTENING

Academic Discussion

What are some actions we take today that might impact the future?

BRAINSTORM IDEAS

Briefly record at least two ideas in each column using everyday English.

Actions with Positive Impact	Actions with a Negative Impact
• saving money	• leaving lights on all night
•	•
•	•

ANALYZE WORDS

Complete the chart with precise words to discuss and write about the issue.

Everyday	Precise
mean *(adjective)*	unkind,
care about others *(verb)*	empathize,
save *(verb)*	protect,

MAKE A CLAIM

Rewrite two ideas using the frames and precise words. Then prepare to elaborate verbally.

Language to ELABORATE

To exemplify, _____.

Personally, _____.

1. **Frame:** One action we take today that might have a (positive/negative) impact on the future is _____ (**verb + –ing:** helping, continuing, ignoring)

   Response: _____

   _____

2. **Frame:** If we (start/stop) _____ (**verb + –ing:** advocating, trying, saving) now, it will (positively/negatively) impact our _____ (**noun:** environment, rights, world) in the future.

   Response: _____

   _____

COLLABORATE

Listen attentively, restate, and record your partner's ideas.

Language to RESTATE

In other words, your stance is that _____.

Yes, that's accurate.

No. What I intended to say was _____.

Classmate's Name	Ideas
	1.
	2.

254 Issue 8

SPEAKING AND WRITING

Ten-Minute Response

A **ten-minute response** begins with a **claim**, followed by **two detail sentences** that elaborate with relevant examples and precise words.

Language to COMPARE IDEAS

My stance on _____ is related to _____'s.

🎙 PRESENT IDEAS

Listen, compare ideas, and take notes. Then indicate whether you agree (+) or disagree (–).

Classmate's Name	Idea	+/–

✏️ ELABORATE IN WRITING
Work with a partner to write a ten-minute response.

Language to COLLABORATE

What should we write?

We could select _____. What do you think works effectively?

Alternatively, we could write _____.

One action today that might have a negative impact on the future is ignoring endangered wildlife. For example, there are several species of animals, such as tigers, that need our _____ or else they _____

_____

As a result, we must _____

_____

now if we want to _____

_____ in the future.

Write a ten-minute response.

If we start _____

now, it will _____ impact

our _____ in the future.

For example, _____

_____

As a result, _____

_____

Future Focus 255

Analyzing and Discussing Text

ACADEMIC VOCABULARY

Words to Go

BUILD WORD KNOWLEDGE
Complete the meaning and examples for this high-utility academic word.

Word to Go	Meaning	Examples
incorporate in•cor•por•ate *verb*	to _____ or _____ something as part of a larger whole	The teacher decided to **incorporate** more _____ into his lessons to make learning more fun. You can _____ _____ to **incorporate** more exercise into your daily routine.

DISCUSS AND WRITE EXAMPLES
Discuss your response with a partner. Then complete the sentence in writing.

To stay healthy, I make sure to **incorporate** _____ into my diet each day.

Write your response and read it aloud to a partner.

Many students say that _____ music into their study routine can
_____

BUILD WORD KNOWLEDGE
Complete the meanings and examples for these high-utility academic words.

Word to Go	Meaning	Example
sustainable sus•tain•a•ble *adjective*	able to be _____ for a long time without causing harm	_____ is a **sustainable** habit that helps reduce pollution.
sustainability sus•tain•a•bil•i•ty *noun*	the practice of conserving what we use to avoid _____ the environment	The concept of **sustainability** encourages us to think about how our _____ affect Earth in the long run.

DISCUSS AND WRITE EXAMPLES
Discuss your response with a partner. Then complete the sentence in writing.

Using a _____ water bottle is a **sustainable** choice because it reduces plastic waste.

Write your response and read it aloud to a partner.

_____ in schools can be promoted by encouraging students to
_____

256 Issue 8

Text 2 • Section 1 • News Article
SUMMARIZING TEXT

Section Shrink

📖 BUILD FLUENCY
Read Section 1 of "What We Owe to Future Generations" (*Issues,* pp. 136–139).

💬 IDENTIFY KEY IDEAS AND DETAILS
Take turns asking and answering questions with a partner. Then write brief notes.

Discussion Frames	Text Notes
Q: What is a **central idea** in this section? **A:** A **central idea** in this section is _____.	• the importance of considering the long-term _____ and the well-being of future generations
Q: What are the **relevant supporting details** in this section? **A:** (One/An additional) **relevant supporting detail** in this section is _____. **A:** Perhaps the **most relevant supporting detail** in this section is _____.	• an experiment in Yahaba, Japan, led to citizens advocating for policies that benefited _____ • considering the effects of our actions on the long-term future can _____ humanity • we should _____ about people in the future, just like we care about about people _____

✏️ SUMMARIZE
"Shrink" Section 1 of the article by writing a summary in 40 or fewer words.

CLASS SUMMARY: **WORD COUNT:** _____

We should _____ about how what we do _____ people in the _____ It's important to consider the _____ effects, and not just focus on what we need right _____

PARTNER SUMMARY: **WORD COUNT:** _____

We should _____ the impact of our _____ on future _____ into our thinking. It is crucial to consider the _____ effects rather than focusing on our _____ interests.

🔍 IDENTIFY PRECISE WORDS
Review Section 1 and your *Portfolio* (pp. 254–257) to identify words for your writing.

Topic Words	High-Utility Academic Words
• temporal distance • •	• communities • •

Analyzing and Discussing Text
ACADEMIC VOCABULARY

Words to Go

📖 BUILD WORD KNOWLEDGE
Complete the meaning and example for this high-utility academic word.

Word to Go	Meaning	Example
purpose pur•pose *noun*	the _____ for doing or creating something	The **purpose** of the multicultural club is to encourage students to _____ _____

💬 DISCUSS AND WRITE EXAMPLES
Discuss your response with a partner. Then complete the sentence in writing.

When reading a text, it is important to know the writer's **purpose** so you can _____
_____

Write your response and read it aloud to a partner.

I often feel that my _____ in life is to _____
_____

📖 BUILD WORD KNOWLEDGE
Complete the meaning and example for this high-utility academic word.

Word to Go	Meaning	Example
resource re•source *noun*	a _____ that is used to meet a _____	The most valuable **resource** at our school to help a new student is the _____ _____

💬 DISCUSS AND WRITE EXAMPLES
Discuss your response with a partner. Then complete the sentence in writing.

Renewable natural **resources**, such as _____
provide alternatives to fossil fuels.

Write your response and read it aloud to a partner.

Water is a vital natural _____ that is essential for _____
_____

Text ❷ • Section ❷ • News Article

SUMMARIZING TEXT

Section Shrink

BUILD FLUENCY
Read Section 2 of "What We Owe to Future Generations" (*Issues,* pp. 139–141).

IDENTIFY KEY IDEAS AND DETAILS
Take turns asking and answering questions with a partner. Then write brief notes.

Discussion Frames	Text Notes
Q: What is a **central idea** in this section? **A:** A **central idea** in this section is _____.	• people can be _____ to act in ways that benefit _____
Q: What are the **relevant supporting details** in this section? **A:** (One/An additional) **relevant supporting detail** in this section is _____. **A:** Perhaps the **most relevant supporting detail** in this section is _____.	• eliciting feelings of _____ is effective in getting people to act in the best interests of _____ • creating a _____ future for humanity will require that we make _____ now • considering future generations can give people a sense of _____

SUMMARIZE
"Shrink" Section 2 of the article by writing a summary in 40 or fewer words.

CLASS SUMMARY: **WORD COUNT:** _____

To _____ people to care about the _____ future, it is effective to engage with them _____ by evoking feelings of _____ and a sense of _____

PARTNER SUMMARY: **WORD COUNT:** _____

Various _____, such as being _____ to ancestors and finding meaning in _____ for the future, can inspire people to adopt _____ thinking.

IDENTIFY PRECISE WORDS
Review Section 2 and your *Portfolio* (pp. 258–259) to identify words for your writing.

Topic Words	High-Utility Academic Words
• descendants • •	• extract • •

Future Focus **259**

Analyzing and Discussing Text
ACADEMIC VOCABULARY

Words to Go

📘 BUILD WORD KNOWLEDGE
Complete the meaning and examples for this high-utility academic word.

Word to Go	Meaning	Examples
feature fea•ture *noun*	an _____ or _____ part of something that stands out	The most impressive **feature** of the newly renovated library is the _____ _____ An attractive **feature** of the college is the _____ _____

💬 DISCUSS AND WRITE EXAMPLES
Discuss your response with a partner. Then complete the sentence in writing.

Our school app has many **features**, such as the ability to _____
_____

Write your response and read it aloud to a partner.

One unique _____ of our school's arts program is the
_____

📘 BUILD WORD KNOWLEDGE
Complete the meaning and examples for this high-utility academic word.

Word to Go	Meaning	Examples
shift shift *noun*	a _____ from one position or _____ to another	A **shift** in the class seating arrangement helped me to better _____ _____ The sudden **shift** in the weather meant that we _____ _____

💬 DISCUSS AND WRITE EXAMPLES
Discuss your response with a partner. Then complete the sentence in writing.

The **shift** from high school to college can be _____
for many students.

Write your response and read it aloud to a partner.

Recent _____ in the school's policies now allow for _____
_____

Text ② • Section ③ • News Article

SUMMARIZING TEXT

Section Shrink

📖 BUILD FLUENCY
Read Section 3 of "What We Owe to Future Generations" (*Issues,* pp. 141–145).

💬 IDENTIFY KEY IDEAS AND DETAILS
Take turns asking and answering questions with a partner. Then write brief notes.

Discussion Frames	Text Notes
Q: What is a **central idea** in this section? **A:** A **central idea** in this section is _____.	• longtermism, which prioritizes the _____ future, can influence our _____ today; balancing this with immediate needs remains a _____
Q: What are the **relevant supporting details** in this section? **A:** (One/An additional) **relevant supporting detail** in this section is _____. **A:** Perhaps the **most relevant supporting detail** in this section is _____.	• there will be _____ people alive in the future than there are in the _____ or have been in the _____ • strong longtermism says that the most _____ impacts are those on the far future • we can _____ future generations while also contributing to causes that address current _____

✏️ SUMMARIZE
"Shrink" Section 3 of the text by writing a summary in 40 or fewer words.

CLASS SUMMARY: **WORD COUNT:** _____

Strong _____ emphasizes focusing more

on the future _____ of our actions because there will be

many more people in the _____. At the same time, it is important to

_____ caring for the future with addressing today's needs.

PARTNER SUMMARY: **WORD COUNT:** _____

Thinking about the _____ future is a key principle of strong longtermism.

While it is _____ to think about the future, we should also consider

_____ needs to ensure benefits to both humans in present-day and

_____ generations.

🔍 IDENTIFY PRECISE WORDS
Review Section 3 and your *Portfolio* (pp. 260–261) to identify words for your writing.

Topic Words	High-Utility Academic Words
• longtermism • •	• convincing • •

Future Focus **261**

Academic Writing

ANALYZING TEXT FEATURES

Student Writing Model

Academic Writing Type

A **formal written summary** provides an objective overview of the topic and important details from an informational text. The writer credits the author, but writes in primarily their own words, without including personal opinions.

    A. The **topic sentence** includes the text type, title, author, and topic.

    B. Detail sentences include the important details from the summarized text.

    C. The **concluding sentence** restates the author's conclusion in the writer's own words.

ANALYZE TEXT
Read this student model to analyze the elements of a formal summary.

> **A** In the interview titled "The Kids Who Sued Montana Over Climate Change and Won Say It's Just the Start," Ninis Twumasi talks to Sariel Sandoval and Claire Vlases about their landmark climate change lawsuit. **B** Twumasi begins by explaining that 16 young plaintiffs sued Montana for violating their right to a clean environment, eventually winning their case. Twumasi continues to highlight through his questioning that their motivations for advocating for environmental justice are based in a desire to improve the future. Additionally, the interviewees assert further that, despite their age, their voices demanded attention and have a right to be heard. Moreover, the writer reports on the emotional impact and inspiration drawn from plaintiffs' stories during the trial. **C** Twumasi concludes by suggesting that this case is a significant step toward addressing climate change and that it can inspire future generations to take action.

MARK AND DISCUSS ELEMENTS
Mark the summary elements and use the frames to discuss them with your partner.

1. **Number (1–4) the four elements of the topic sentence.** *The topic sentence includes the _____.*

2. **Draw a box around four transition words or phrases.** *One transition (word/phrase) is _____.*

3. **Underline four important details.** *One important detail in this summary is _____.*

4. **Circle four citation verbs.** *One citation verb that the writer uses is _____.*

5. **Star four precise topic words and check four high-utility academic words.** *An example of a (precise topic word/high-utility academic word) is _____.*

Organize a Formal Summary

Prompt Write a formal summary of "What We Owe to Future Generations."

Guidelines for Paraphrasing Multiple Sentences
Paraphrase related details from a source text by combining key information into one sentence. Replace key words and phrases with synonyms and keep important topic words.

Text Detail 1	Text Detail 2	Text Detail 3
"Instead, he's found it more effective to highlight how acting altruistically toward future generations can actually bring us pleasure now" (Samuel 140).	"When we ask people if they want to be the great ancestor that the future needs them to be, as part of what gives them meaning and purpose, they are no longer under the spell of lifespan bias," he told me. "They see themselves as something larger" (Samuel 140).	"They are no longer being asked to sacrifice for the future, but to enhance their own sense of meaning and purpose in their present" (Samuel 140).

✎ PARAPHRASE IDEAS
Combine key information from the three text details above into one detail sentence.

Thinking about the future can benefit us now by

(text detail 1) _____

(text detail 2) _____ and

(text detail 3) _____

📋 PLAN KEY IDEAS AND DETAILS
State the text information to write a topic sentence.

In the news article titled (Title) _____

(Author's Full Name) _____ (citation verb: explores, examines,

discusses) _____ (topic) _____

_____

List four important details from the text using primarily your own words.

1. _____
   _____

2. _____
   _____

3. _____
   _____

4. _____
   _____

Restate the conclusion in your own words.

_____

_____

Academic Writing
WRITING A DRAFT

Write a Formal Summary

Prompt Write a formal summary of "What We Owe to Future Generations."

✎ WRITE A PARAGRAPH
Use the frame to write your topic sentence, detail sentences, and concluding sentence.

A

In the _____ titled _____
         (text type)   (Title)

_____

_____ _____
(Author's Full Name)   (citation verb)

_____
(topic)

_____

B

_____ begins by _____ that
(Author's Last Name)   (citation verb + -ing: presenting, arguing)

_____
(1st important detail)

_____

_____

_____

The (author/writer) _____ continues to _____
                                                          (citation verb, base form: describe, report)

_____
(2nd important detail)

_____

_____

(He/She) _____ _____ further that
(Pronoun)   (present-tense citation verb)

_____
(3rd important detail)

_____

_____

_____

_____ the (author/writer) _____
(Transition)

_____ _____
(present-tense citation verb)   (4th important detail)

_____

_____

C

_____ concludes by _____ that
(Author's Last Name)   (citation verb + -ing: suggesting, emphasizing)

_____
(restate conclusion)

_____

_____

Formal Summary
ASSESSING AND REVISING

Rate Your Formal Summary

Scoring Guide
1	Insufficient
2	Developing
3	Sufficient
4	Exemplary

ASSESS YOUR DRAFT
Rate your formal summary. Then have a partner rate it.

1. Does the topic sentence state the text type, title, author, and topic?	Self	1	2	3	4
	Partner	1	2	3	4
2. Did you paraphrase the most important details from the text?	Self	1	2	3	4
	Partner	1	2	3	4
3. Did you use citation verbs to credit the author?	Self	1	2	3	4
	Partner	1	2	3	4
4. Did you use transitions to introduce and sequence details?	Self	1	2	3	4
	Partner	1	2	3	4
5. Did you include precise topic words and high-utility academic words?	Self	1	2	3	4
	Partner	1	2	3	4
6. Did you accurately restate the author's conclusion?	Self	1	2	3	4
	Partner	1	2	3	4

REFLECT AND REVISE
Record specific priorities and suggestions to help you and your partner revise.

(Partner) Positive Feedback: I appreciate how you (used/included) _____

_____

(Partner) Suggestion: As you revise your summary, focus on _____

_____

(Self) Priority 1: My summary paragraph needs _____

_____

(Self) Priority 2: I plan to improve my summary by _____

_____

CHECK AND EDIT
Use this checklist to proofread and edit your summary.

☐ Did you capitalize the title of the article and proper nouns?

☐ Did you put quotation marks around the title of the article?

☐ Did you use commas appropriately after transitions?

☐ Do simple present-tense verbs end in –s?

☐ Is each sentence complete?

☐ Are all words spelled correctly?

Analyzing and Discussing Text

ACADEMIC VOCABULARY

Words to Know

BUILD WORD KNOWLEDGE
Rate your word knowledge. Then discuss word meanings and examples with your group.

① Don't Know ② Recognize ③ Familiar ④ Know

Words to Know	Meaning	Examples
1 **demonstration** *noun* ① ② ③ ④	a _____ or public gathering to _____ something	I went to a **demonstration** to protest _____. Peaceful **demonstrations** in the 1960s sometimes _____ when the police got involved.
2 **nonviolence** *noun* ① ② ③ ④	the use of _____ means to bring about political or social change	We learned about Martin Luther King Jr. and his belief in **nonviolence** as a way to _____. The police had no reason to _____ since the protestors relied on **nonviolence**.
3 **segregation** *noun* ① ② ③ ④	the act or practice of keeping people or groups _____	Some schools have **segregation** of male and female students, but others _____. The issue of **segregation** in schools highlights the need for _____.
4 **solidarity** *noun* ① ② ③ ④	_____ of feeling or action, especially among those with a _____	The students showed **solidarity** by _____ in support of their friend who is sick. We should stand together in **solidarity** with _____.

266 Issue 8

Text 3 • Drama

RESPONDING TO TEXT

Close Reading

📖 READ THE TEXT
Read the text *The Brave Boys of Greensboro* (*Issues*, pp. 146–153).

🔍 IDENTIFY STRUCTURE

Dramatic Elements and Structure
Most dramas have **scenes**. Each scene typically takes place in a different time or place or involves different characters. A **flashback** shows an event that happened earlier.

Use the frames to analyze the drama's structure.

1. What is the structure and purpose of Scene 2?

   Scene 2 is a _____ It shows why _____
   _____

2. What incident in the scene makes the boys take action?

   The incident that makes the boys take action is _____
   _____

✏️ ANALYZE CRAFT AND STRUCTURE
Use the frames to compare the novel excerpt from *Countdown* with the drama *The Brave Boys of Greensboro*.

3. How do both texts address "heroes of the civil rights movement"?

   Both texts address "heroes of the civil rights movement" by _____
   _____

4. In *Countdown,* why does the author put the text "This little light of mine, I'm gonna let it shine!" in all capital letters and center it?

   The author uses this text formatting to _____
   _____

5. In *The Brave Boys of Greensboro,* what does the dialogue with Mr. Harris in Scene 3 reveal about his character?

   The dialogue with Mr. Harris reveals that his character is _____
   _____

✏️ ANALYZE THEME
Use the frames to analyze the drama's theme.

6. How does the Greensboro Four's willingness to risk their freedom for the greater good contribute to the drama's theme, or overall message?

   The boys' willingness to risk their freedom for the greater good sends the message that _____
   _____
   _____

Future Focus **267**

Analyzing and Discussing Text

SPEAKING AND LISTENING

Academic Discussion

What are the risks and rewards of advocating for a more just society?

BRAINSTORM IDEAS
Briefly record at least two ideas in each column using everyday English.

Risks	Rewards
• facing criticism	• equality
•	•
•	•

ANALYZE WORDS
Complete the chart with precise words to discuss and write about the topic.

Everyday	Precise
miss out (verb)	overlook,
get hurt (verb)	experience harm,
risk (noun)	danger,

MAKE A CLAIM
Rewrite two ideas using the frames and precise words. Then prepare to elaborate verbally.

Language to ELABORATE
To exemplify, _____.
Personally, _____.

1. **Frame:** One (risk/reward) of advocating for a more just society is _____ (**verb + –ing:** improving, risking, ignoring)

   Response: _____

2. **Frame:** _____ (**Character's name**) in *The Brave Boys of Greensboro* _____ aims to improve society by _____ (**verb + –ing:** protesting, risking, leading), (risking/earning) _____ (**noun:** arrest, respect, violence)

   Response: _____

COLLABORATE
Listen attentively, restate, and record your partner's ideas.

Language to RESTATE
In other words, your stance is that _____.
Yes, that's accurate.
No. What I intended to say was _____.

Classmate's Name	Ideas
	1.
	2.

Text ③ • Drama

SPEAKING AND WRITING

Ten-Minute Response

A **ten-minute response** begins with a **claim**, followed by **two detail sentences** that elaborate with relevant examples and precise words.

Language to COMPARE IDEAS

My stance on _____ is related to _____'s.

🎤 **PRESENT IDEAS**

Listen, compare ideas, and take notes. Then indicate whether you agree (+) or disagree (–).

Classmate's Name	Idea	+/–

✏️ **ELABORATE IN WRITING**

Work with a partner to write a ten-minute response.

Language to COLLABORATE

What should we write?

We could select _____. What do you think works effectively?

Alternatively, we could write _____.

One risk of advocating for a more just society is facing resistance, or even harm.

For example, in *The Brave Boys of Greensboro*, David aims to improve society by _____

_____

As a result, he _____

proving that _____

_____

Write a ten-minute response

One reward of advocating for a more just society is _____

_____

For example, _____

_____

_____

As a result, _____

_____

Future Focus **269**

Presenting Ideas

Take a Stand

Debate | Is it more important to prioritize the present or make sacrifices for the future?

🗨 COLLABORATE
Read the debate question about the present and future. Then take turns using a frame to respond with your initial reaction.

Language to RESPOND
So _____, what's your initial reaction?
My initial reaction is _____.
My initial reaction is related to _____'s.

🔍 ANALYZE SOURCES
Read a quote that either supports or opposes the debate question. Then paraphrase.

Quote	Paraphrase
Model: "It's also just genuinely hard to focus on the future when we're struggling under the weight of our day-to-day problems" (Samuel 137).	This quote makes it evident that focusing on our present _____ can be overwhelming and make it _____ to think about the future.
1. ". . . Snow might not fall in that area in the coming years. If snow doesn't fall, they can't have their ceremony. It takes away an entire aspect of their culture" (Twumasi 134).	In this quote, the interviewee explains a future _____ of climate change that will _____ affect her Indigenous culture.
2. "If our species lasts for as long as Earth remains a habitable planet, we're talking about at least 1 quadrillion people coming into existence—100,000 times the population of Earth today" (Samuel 141).	This quote makes it evident that there will be _____ more people in the _____ than there are in _____ day.
3. "Our lives may start to feel much more meaningful if we regularly pause to ask ourselves: How can I shape the larger story of humanity into something fruitful?" (Samuel 142).	In this quote, the author makes a case that thinking about our _____ on all of humanity, because doing so can give our lives _____.
4. "84 percent of teens believe that if we don't address climate change today, it will be too late for future generations" (National 4-H Council 143).	This quote makes it evident that we most teens think we need to _____ _____ on climate change now to _____ the future.

Debate Ideas

SYNTHESIZE IDEAS

Write a response to the debate question, including a paraphrase of a text quote and elaboration on the quote.

Claim: My position is that prioritizing the present (is/is not) _____ more important than making sacrifices for the future.

Transitional Statement: I have (one key reason/a compelling reason) _____ _____ for taking this stance.

Quote Paraphrase: (According to _____,/The author points out _____.)

_____
_____
_____

Quote Elaboration: (As a result, _____./Consequently, _____.)

_____
_____
_____

PRESENT EVIDENCE

Including Digital Media
When presenting ideas during class or in a meeting, include **digital media.** Consider including images, graphics, audio, or video to express information, strengthen claims and evidence, and add interest.

LISTEN AND TAKE NOTES

Listen attentively and take notes. Then indicate whether you agree (+) or disagree (–).

> **Language to AFFIRM AND CLARIFY**
>
> That's a thought-provoking point of view.
>
> Could you clarify what you mean by _____?

Classmate's Name	Idea	+/–

Future Focus 271

Academic Writing

ANALYZING TEXT ELEMENTS

Student Writing Model

Academic Writing Type

An **argument** states a claim and supports it with logical reasons and relevant evidence from sources.

A. The **thesis statement** clearly states the writer's claim and tells what the writer will explain about the topic.

B. **Supporting paragraphs** support the claim with reasons and evidence from sources. The writer also presents counterclaims and responds with evidence.

C. The **conclusion** restates the writer's claim about the issue.

ANALYZE TEXT
Read this student model to analyze elements of an argument research paper.

A After examining the issues surrounding the future, I am convinced that it is more important to prioritize the present than to make sacrifices for the future.

B One reason I maintain this position is that it is impossible to sustain a viable future without addressing our current needs. In "What We Owe to Future Generations," Sigal Samuel emphasizes that we consider the long-term effects of our actions, while also acknowledging the challenges. She points out that "It's also just genuinely hard to focus on the future when we're struggling under the weight of our day-to-day problems" (137). As a teen, I have firsthand experience with daily problems that affect my capacity to consider the long-term future. To illustrate, issues like poverty and inequality need to be prioritized to improve the lives of people today, which then can benefit those in the future. In contrast, proponents of long-term thinking argue that focusing on the future will benefit us today, and we owe it to future generations to put them first. However, I wholeheartedly believe that we owe it to ourselves and to those who are alive now to prioritize the present.

The true account of the "Brave Boys of Greensboro" has also strengthened my perspective that addressing our present circumstances must take priority before contemplating the future. In the retelling of their story, we learn that they faced threats of violence, abuse, and arrest for protesting segregation (152). Although it can be said that their sacrifices ensured a better future for subsequent generations, I don't find this reasoning compelling. Clearly, by endangering their lives, they risked diminishing their potential impact on the world, and their immediate safety should have been prioritized.

C The question of whether the present or future should command our focus is intriguing. My analysis of this issue has left me with little doubt that we cannot effectively shape the future until we take care of ourselves in the present.

Argument
ANALYZING TEXT ELEMENTS

💬 MARK AND DISCUSS ELEMENTS
Mark the argument elements and use the frames to discuss them with your partner.

1. **Circle the writer's claim within the thesis statement.** *The writer's claim is _____.*
2. **Underline and label two reasons that support the writer's claim with the letter *R*.** *One reason that supports the writer's claim is _____.*
3. **Underline and label four pieces of evidence that support the writer's claim with the letter *E*.** *One piece of evidence that supports the writer's claim is _____.*
4. **Draw boxes around two counterclaims.** *One counterclaim is _____.*
5. **Star four precise topic words and check four high-utility academic words.** *An example of a (precise topic word/high-utility academic word) is _____.*

Scoring Guide	
1	Insufficient
2	Developing
3	Sufficient
4	Exemplary

✍️ ASSESS A STUDENT SAMPLE
Read an additional student writing sample and rate it.

1. Does the thesis statement clearly state the claim?	1	2	3	4
2. Do supporting paragraphs begin with a topic sentence that specifies a reason?	1	2	3	4
3. Did the writer give evidence drawn primarily from sources to support the claim?	1	2	3	4
4. Did the writer explain why the evidence is relevant and significant?	1	2	3	4
5. Did the writer include complex sentences to present and respond to counterclaims?	1	2	3	4
6. Did the writer use strong verbs and verb phrases to express opinions?	1	2	3	4
7. Did the writer use transitions to introduce reasons and evidence?	1	2	3	4
8. Did the writer use precise adjectives to describe evidence?	1	2	3	4
9. Did the writer include citation information for text evidence?	1	2	3	4
10. Did the writer include precise topic words and high-utility words?	1	2	3	4
11. Does the conclusion strongly restate the claim using new wording?	1	2	3	4

👥 REFLECT AND REVISE
Record specific priorities and suggestions to help the writer.

I appreciated the student's (effort to/use of/skillful) _____

_____

One suggestion I have to revise this argument research paper is to _____

_____

Another suggestion I have to strengthen this argument research paper is to _____

_____

Academic Writing
FRONTLOADING LANGUAGE

Noun Phrases to Describe Evidence

Guidelines for Using Noun Phrases to Describe Evidence

Use **noun phrases** to describe the data, statistics, and other evidence you present to support your claim.

Everyday Words	Noun Phrases
a lot of	a/the high percentage of
many	a/the high number of
more	an/the increase in
little/few	a/the low percentage of, a/the limited number of
less	a/the decrease in

✏️ WRITE NOUN PHRASES
Complete the sentences with noun phrases.

1. I am in favor of making world-language study a requirement for graduation due to _____ colleges that only accept applicants who have studied an additional language.

2. Proponents of mandatory voting contend that it would remedy _____ _____ voter turnout that has been evident since the 1950s.

3. Clearly, there is substantial evidence that shows _____ _____ people in debt before the age of 25.

Use noun phrases to complete the sentences about the claim.
Claim: States should increase the minimum driving age.

1. **Evidence:** In "DN'T TXT N DRV," Nancy Mann Jackson emphasizes that _____ _____ vehicle crashes can be linked to teens, who are more likely to be distracted while driving.

2. **Evidence:** To illustrate, _____ teen drivers admitted to texting behind the wheel.

3. **Counterclaim:** Although a common argument against raising the driving age is _____ _____ vehicle crashes involving inexperienced 18-year-old drivers, I don't find the evidence compelling.

4. **Response to Counterclaim:** Clearly, there is striking evidence that shows _____ _____ teen car accidents in states that have raised the driving age.

5. **Restating Claim:** My analysis of this issue has left me with little doubt that raising the driving age would result in _____ of fatal car accidents due to teen drivers.

Complex Cause and Effect Sentences

Guidelines for Expressing Cause and Effect

A **cause** is the reason something happens. An **effect** is the result, or what happens.

> *Teens are sleep deprived. Teens may lose focus in class.*
> (cause) (effect)

After stating an effect, use **because** or **since** to signal that the cause follows.

> *Teens may lose focus in class **because** they are sleep deprived.*
> (effect) (cause)

Use **due to** or **as a result of** when you want to state the cause with a noun phrase.

> *Teens may suffer from serious health problems **due to** a lack of sleep.*
> (effect) (cause)
> *Memory loss is common among teens **as a result of** not getting enough sleep.*
> (effect) (cause)

State the cause first to emphasize it. Begin with **because**, **since**, **due to**, or **as a result of** and put a comma after the cause.

> ***Because** teens are sleep deprived, they may lose focus in class.*
> (cause) (effect)

✏ WRITE COMPLEX SENTENCES
Combine simple sentences to create complex cause-and-effect sentences.

1. Learning another language can improve grades. Bilingualism increases cognitive abilities.

   a) _____ because
   _____

   b) Because _____
   _____

2. Many young people cannot manage their money. Many young people are in debt.

   a) _____ due to
   _____

   b) Due to _____
   _____

3. Schools don't teach job skills. Many high school graduates are unemployed.

   a) _____ as a result of
   _____

   b) As a result of _____
   _____

4. Virtual reality is engaging. Many users spend free time in virtual worlds.

   a) _____ since
   _____

   b) Since _____
   _____

Academic Writing
PLANNING TO WRITE

Organize an Argument

Prompt Is it more important to prioritize the present or make sacrifices for the future? Write an argument that states your claim and supports it with text evidence.

Guidelines for Citing Text Evidence
Paraphrase text evidence when you want to summarize a longer section of text or multiple ideas. Use **direct quotes** when the author has used strong wording that is difficult to improve or simplify.

Quote	Cited Evidence
"... a judge ruled that Montana must consider the effects of climate change when deciding whether to begin or renew fossil-fuel projects" (Twumasi 131).	A court decision requires that the state of Montana must assess the environmental consequences of fossil-fuel projects before they begin or resume (Twumasi 139).
"... some creatures have managed to survive for 10,000 generations and beyond: by taking care of the place that will take care of their offspring" (Samuel 144).	By preserving the environment that will sustain their future offspring, some species "have managed to survive for 10,000 generations" (Samuel 137).

✏️ WRITE A THESIS STATEMENT
Describe your claim.

My claim: _____

Use academic language to restate your claim as a thesis statement.

_____ the future, I
(Thesis starter)

_____ that _____
(verb/verb phrase to express opinion)   (strongly state your claim)

_____

💡 CHOOSE SUPPORTING TOPICS
List each topic you will write about to support your claim.

Supporting Paragraph 1

Topic: _____

_____

Supporting Paragraph 2

Topic: _____

_____

Find text evidence that supports your claim and write a sentence that paraphrases it or incorporates a direct quote.

_____
_____
_____

Argument
PLANNING TO WRITE

📋 PLAN SUPPORTING PARAGRAPHS
List reasons and evidence that support your claim. You may draw from texts, your experience, or a classmate's experience.

Supporting Paragraph 1:

Reason 1: _____

_____

Evidence: _____

_____

Source/Page Number: _____

Author: _____

Counterclaim 1: _____

_____

Response to Counterclaim: _____

_____

Source/Page Number: _____

Author: _____

Supporting Paragraph 2:

Reason 2: _____

_____

Evidence: _____

_____

Source/Page Number: _____

Author: _____

Counterclaim 2: _____

_____

Response to Counterclaim: _____

_____

Source/Page Number: _____

Author: _____

✏️ WRITE A CONCLUSION
Plan a conclusion that restates your claim.

The question of whether or not to _____
                                        (restate the issue)

_____ is _____

My analysis of this issue has left me with little doubt that _____
                                                                (restate your claim)

_____

Future Focus **277**

Academic Writing
WRITING A DRAFT

Write an Argument

Prompt: Is it more important to prioritize the present or make sacrifices for the future? Write an argument that states your claim and supports it with text evidence.

✎ WRITE A RESEARCH PAPER
Use the frame to write your thesis statement, supporting paragraphs, and conclusion.

A

_____
(Thesis starter)

_____
(topic)

I _____
(verb/verb phrase to express opinion)

that _____
(strongly state your claim)

B1

One reason I maintain this position is that _____
(1st reason that supports your claim)

In _____
(Title of Source)

_____ emphasizes that _____
(Author's Full Name)   (evidence from source)

As a teen, I have firsthand experience with _____
(situation or issue)

_____ _____
(transition introducing evidence)   (evidence from your experience)

In contrast, _____
(group with an opposing claim)

_____ that _____
(verb/verb phrase to express opinion)   (counterclaim from source or your experience)

However, I _____ that _____
(verb/verb phrase to express opinion)   (your response to the counterclaim)

Argument
ASSESSING AND REVISING

B2

_____ analysis of _____
(Author's Full Name + 's)   (topic)

in _____
   (Title of a Different Source)

has strengthened my perspective that _____
                                       (2nd reason that supports your claim)

_____ _____
(Transition introducing evidence)   (evidence from source or your experience)

Although a common argument (in favor of/against) _____
_____
        (issue)
is _____
   (counterclaim from source or your experience)

I don't find the evidence (adjective: compelling, substantial) _____
_____ Clearly, there is (adjective: sufficient, adequate, striking)
_____ evidence that (shows/proves) _____
_____
(your response to the counterclaim)

C

The question of whether or not to _____
                                   (restate the issue)

_____ is _____
                       (precise adjective to respond)

My analysis of this issue has left me with little doubt that _____
                                                             (restate your claim)

Presenting Ideas

Two-Minute Speech

🔍 IDENTIFY TOPIC
Choose one of the questions below to address in a two-minute speech.
- ☐ Should our city require everyone to vote in local elections?
- ☐ Should our state invest in programs for current residents or in sustainability for the future?

💡 BRAINSTORM IDEAS
Write your position and two reasons that support it.

My Claim: _____

Reason 1: _____

Reason 2: _____

📄 SYNTHESIZE IDEAS
Take notes on supporting evidence and a counterclaim.

Evidence 1: _____

_____

Evidence 2: _____

_____

Counterclaim: _____

_____

Response: _____

_____

✏️ WRITE A SPEECH
Write a two-minute speech that states your claim and includes reasons, evidence, and a counterclaim.

From my point of view, _____

_____

One reason is that _____

_____

Secondly, _____

_____

For example, _____

_____

Critics might claim that _____

_____

However, _____

_____

For these reasons, I _____ that _____

_____

Present and Rate Your Speech

Including Digital Media
When presenting ideas during class or in a meeting, include **digital media**. Consider including images, graphics, audio, or video to express information, strengthen claims and evidence, and add interest.

PRESENT YOUR SPEECH
Present your speech to the small group. Make sure to include digital media.

LISTEN AND TAKE NOTES
Listen attentively and take notes. Then indicate whether you agree (+) or disagree (–).

Language to AFFIRM AND CLARIFY
That's a thought-provoking point of view.

Could you clarify what you mean by _____?

Classmate's Name	Idea	+/–

ASSESS YOUR SPEECH
Use the Scoring Guide to rate your speech.

Scoring Guide				
1	Insufficient		3	Sufficient
2	Developing		4	Exemplary

1. Did your topic sentence clearly state your claim?	1	2	3	4
2. Did you include strong reasons and evidence to support your speech?	1	2	3	4
3. Did you include precise topic words?	1	2	3	4
4. Were you easy to understand?	1	2	3	4
5. Did you include digital media?	1	2	3	4

REFLECT
Think of two ways you have improved on your speeches.

Praise 1: In my speeches, I was successful with _____

_____

_____

Praise 2: My greatest area of improvement was _____

_____

_____

Review and Assess

Completing the Daily Do Now

DAILY DO NOW ROUTINE
Follow these steps each day when you enter class:

1. **Open** the Daily Do Now on Ed or in your *Language & Writing Portfolio*.
2. **Read** the task, think carefully, and write an appropriate response.
3. **Listen** to classmates share their responses and share your response if asked.
4. **Score** your response using the Scoring Guide.
5. **Read** your response aloud to your partner.
6. **Switch** devices or *Language & Writing Portfolios* with your partner and their response.

DAILY DO NOW TYPES
There are two types of Daily Do Nows. Complete the Daily Do Now according to the type of task.

Show You Know
Example: (advantage) One _____ of living near school is being able to _____.

- Write the correct form of the word in one of the blanks. If it is a noun, you may need to make it plural (often by adding –s or –es). If it is a verb, you may need to change its tense (often by adding –ed or –s).
- Complete the rest of the sentence with content that shows you understand the word's meaning.

Date 9 / 23 / 25
One advantage of living near school is being able to sleep later in the mornings.

Academic Talk
Example: Students who are <u>not getting enough sleep</u> often feel <u>very tired</u> during _____.

- Replace the underlined words or phrases with academic words you would use to communicate in a formal setting, such as with the principal or an employer.
- Complete the rest of the sentence with content that shows you understand the words' meaning.

Date 10 / 21 / 25
Students who are sleep deprived often feel fatigued during morning classes.

Scoring the Daily Do Now

DETERMINING A SCORE

Use this rubric and the Scoring Guide to score your Daily Do Nows. Record two points for accurate use of vocabulary and one point for each of the other elements.

	Complete Do Now	Use Vocabulary	Add Content	Correct Grammar
Points	1	2	1	1
Show You Know	Copied the sentence if using the print *Portfolio* and completed the blank(s)	Used cues in the sentence to write the correct form of the word	Added relevant content that shows understanding of the word meaning	Completed the sentence using correct grammar
Academic Talk	Copied the sentence if using the print *Portfolio*, replaced the underlined words, and completed the blank	Used accurate, precise synonyms to replace the underlined everyday words	Added relevant content that shows understanding of the word meaning	Substituted words that are the same part of speech and agree with the sentence

CALCULATING A GRADING TOTAL

At the end of each Issue, calculate your Grading Total by dividing the Total Points by the Possible Points and then multiplying by 100.

	Total Points	Possible Points	Grading Total (Total Points/Possible Points x 100)
Getting Started			
Issue 1			
Issue 2			
Issue 3			
Issue 4			
Issue 5			
Issue 6			
Issue 7			
Issue 8			

Growing	Developing	Proficient	Exceptional
0–50%	51–70%	71–90%	91–100%

Review and Assess

Daily Do Now

Record the Daily Do Now at the beginning of each class. Complete the task using appropriate content, precise vocabulary, and correct grammar.

	Scores				
	Complete Do Now	Use Vocabulary	Add Content	Correct Grammar	Total

Date ____ / ____ / _____
_____
_____
_____ Self
_____
_____ Partner

Date ____ / ____ / _____
_____
_____
_____ Self
_____
_____ Partner

Date ____ / ____ / _____
_____
_____
_____ Self
_____
_____ Partner

Date ____ / ____ / _____
_____
_____
_____ Self
_____
_____ Partner

Date ____ / ____ / _____
_____
_____
_____ Self
_____
_____ Partner

Total Points

Scoring Guide	Self	Partner
Did you/your partner **complete** the Daily Do Now?	+1	+1
Did you/your partner **use vocabulary** accurately?	+2	+2
Did you/your partner **add content** that is relevant?	+1	+1
Did you/your partner **use correct grammar**?	+1	+1

Scores: Complete Do Now | Use Vocabulary | Add Content | Correct Grammar | Total

Date ____ / ____ / ____ — Self / Partner

Date ____ / ____ / ____ — Self / Partner

Date ____ / ____ / ____ — Self / Partner

Date ____ / ____ / ____ — Self / Partner

Date ____ / ____ / ____ — Self / Partner

Total Points

Review and Assess

Daily Do Now

Record the Daily Do Now at the beginning of each class. Complete the task using appropriate content, precise vocabulary, and correct grammar.

	Scores				
	Complete Do Now	Use Vocabulary	Add Content	Correct Grammar	Total

Date ____ / ____ / _____

_____
_____
_____
_____

Self / Partner

Date ____ / ____ / _____

_____
_____
_____
_____

Self / Partner

Date ____ / ____ / _____

_____
_____
_____
_____

Self / Partner

Date ____ / ____ / _____

_____
_____
_____
_____

Self / Partner

Date ____ / ____ / _____

_____
_____
_____
_____

Self / Partner

Total Points

Scoring Guide	Self	Partner
Did you/your partner **complete** the Daily Do Now?	+1	+1
Did you/your partner **use vocabulary** accurately?	+2	+2
Did you/your partner **add content** that is relevant?	+1	+1
Did you/your partner **use correct grammar**?	+1	+1

Scores: Complete Do Now | Use Vocabulary | Add Content | Correct Grammar | Total

Date ____ / ____ / _____ — Self / Partner

Date ____ / ____ / _____ — Self / Partner

Date ____ / ____ / _____ — Self / Partner

Date ____ / ____ / _____ — Self / Partner

Date ____ / ____ / _____ — Self / Partner

Total Points

Daily Do Now 287

Review and Assess

Daily Do Now

Record the Daily Do Now at the beginning of each class. Complete the task using appropriate content, precise vocabulary, and correct grammar.

	Scores				
	Complete Do Now	Use Vocabulary	Add Content	Correct Grammar	Total

Date _____ / _____ / _____

_____
_____
_____
_____
_____

Self / Partner

Date _____ / _____ / _____

_____
_____
_____
_____
_____

Self / Partner

Date _____ / _____ / _____

_____
_____
_____
_____
_____

Self / Partner

Date _____ / _____ / _____

_____
_____
_____
_____
_____

Self / Partner

Date _____ / _____ / _____

_____
_____
_____
_____
_____

Self / Partner

Total Points

Scoring Guide	Self	Partner
Did you/your partner **complete** the Daily Do Now?	+1	+1
Did you/your partner **use vocabulary** accurately?	+2	+2
Did you/your partner **add content** that is relevant?	+1	+1
Did you/your partner **use correct grammar**?	+1	+1

Scores: Complete Do Now | Use Vocabulary | Add Content | Correct Grammar | Total

Date ____ / ____ / _____

Date ____ / ____ / _____

Date ____ / ____ / _____

Date ____ / ____ / _____

Date ____ / ____ / _____

Total Points

Daily Do Now 289

Review and Assess

Daily Do Now

Record the Daily Do Now at the beginning of each class. Complete the task using appropriate content, precise vocabulary, and correct grammar.

	Scores				
	Complete Do Now	Use Vocabulary	Add Content	Correct Grammar	Total

Date _____ / _____ / _____

_____
_____
_____
_____

Self / Partner

Date _____ / _____ / _____

_____
_____
_____
_____

Self / Partner

Date _____ / _____ / _____

_____
_____
_____
_____

Self / Partner

Date _____ / _____ / _____

_____
_____
_____
_____

Self / Partner

Date _____ / _____ / _____

_____
_____
_____
_____

Self / Partner

Total Points

Scoring Guide	Self	Partner
Did you/your partner **complete** the Daily Do Now?	+1	+1
Did you/your partner **use vocabulary** accurately?	+2	+2
Did you/your partner **add content** that is relevant?	+1	+1
Did you/your partner **use correct grammar**?	+1	+1

Scores: Complete Do Now | Use Vocabulary | Add Content | Correct Grammar | Total

Date ____ / ____ / _____

(Self / Partner)

Date ____ / ____ / _____

(Self / Partner)

Date ____ / ____ / _____

(Self / Partner)

Date ____ / ____ / _____

(Self / Partner)

Date ____ / ____ / _____

(Self / Partner)

Total Points

Review and Assess

Daily Do Now

Record the Daily Do Now at the beginning of each class. Complete the task using appropriate content, precise vocabulary, and correct grammar.

Scores: Complete Do Now | Use Vocabulary | Add Content | Correct Grammar | Total

Date ____ / ____ / _____

_____
_____
_____
_____

Self / Partner

Date ____ / ____ / _____

_____
_____
_____
_____

Self / Partner

Date ____ / ____ / _____

_____
_____
_____
_____

Self / Partner

Date ____ / ____ / _____

_____
_____
_____
_____

Self / Partner

Date ____ / ____ / _____

_____
_____
_____
_____

Self / Partner

Total Points

Scoring Guide	Self	Partner
Did you/your partner **complete** the Daily Do Now?	+1	+1
Did you/your partner **use vocabulary** accurately?	+2	+2
Did you/your partner **add content** that is relevant?	+1	+1
Did you/your partner **use correct grammar**?	+1	+1

Scores: Complete Do Now | Use Vocabulary | Add Content | Correct Grammar | Total

Date ____ / ____ / _____

(Self / Partner)

Date ____ / ____ / _____

(Self / Partner)

Date ____ / ____ / _____

(Self / Partner)

Date ____ / ____ / _____

(Self / Partner)

Date ____ / ____ / _____

(Self / Partner)

Total Points

Review and Assess

Daily Do Now

Record the Daily Do Now at the beginning of each class. Complete the task using appropriate content, precise vocabulary, and correct grammar.

Scores: Complete Do Now | Use Vocabulary | Add Content | Correct Grammar | Total

Date ____ / ____ / _____

_____
_____
_____
_____
_____

Self / Partner

Date ____ / ____ / _____

_____
_____
_____
_____
_____

Self / Partner

Date ____ / ____ / _____

_____
_____
_____
_____
_____

Self / Partner

Date ____ / ____ / _____

_____
_____
_____
_____
_____

Self / Partner

Date ____ / ____ / _____

_____
_____
_____
_____
_____

Self / Partner

Total Points _____

Scoring Guide	Self	Partner
Did you/your partner **complete** the Daily Do Now?	+1	+1
Did you/your partner **use vocabulary** accurately?	+2	+2
Did you/your partner **add content** that is relevant?	+1	+1
Did you/your partner **use correct grammar**?	+1	+1

Scores
- Complete Do Now
- Use Vocabulary
- Add Content
- Correct Grammar
- Total

Date ____ / ____ / _____

(Self / Partner)

Date ____ / ____ / _____

(Self / Partner)

Date ____ / ____ / _____

(Self / Partner)

Date ____ / ____ / _____

(Self / Partner)

Date ____ / ____ / _____

(Self / Partner)

Total Points

Review and Assess

Daily Do Now

Record the Daily Do Now at the beginning of each class. Complete the task using appropriate content, precise vocabulary, and correct grammar.

	Scores				
	Complete Do Now	Use Vocabulary	Add Content	Correct Grammar	Total

Date _____ / _____ / _____

_____
_____
_____
_____

— Self
— Partner

Date _____ / _____ / _____

_____
_____
_____
_____

— Self
— Partner

Date _____ / _____ / _____

_____
_____
_____
_____

— Self
— Partner

Date _____ / _____ / _____

_____
_____
_____
_____

— Self
— Partner

Date _____ / _____ / _____

_____
_____
_____
_____

— Self
— Partner

Total Points

Scoring Guide	Self	Partner
Did you/your partner **complete** the Daily Do Now?	+1	+1
Did you/your partner **use vocabulary** accurately?	+2	+2
Did you/your partner **add content** that is relevant?	+1	+1
Did you/your partner **use correct grammar**?	+1	+1

Scores: Complete Do Now | Use Vocabulary | Add Content | Correct Grammar | Total

Date ____ / ____ / _____

Date ____ / ____ / _____

Date ____ / ____ / _____

Date ____ / ____ / _____

Date ____ / ____ / _____

Total Points

Review and Assess

Daily Do Now

Record the Daily Do Now at the beginning of each class. Complete the task using appropriate content, precise vocabulary, and correct grammar.

	Scores			
Complete Do Now	Use Vocabulary	Add Content	Correct Grammar	Total

Date _____ / _____ / _____
_____
_____
_____
_____

 — Self
 — Partner

Date _____ / _____ / _____
_____
_____
_____
_____

 — Self
 — Partner

Date _____ / _____ / _____
_____
_____
_____
_____

 — Self
 — Partner

Date _____ / _____ / _____
_____
_____
_____
_____

 — Self
 — Partner

Date _____ / _____ / _____
_____
_____
_____
_____

 — Self
 — Partner

Total Points

Scoring Guide	Self	Partner
Did you/your partner **complete** the Daily Do Now?	+1	+1
Did you/your partner **use vocabulary** accurately?	+2	+2
Did you/your partner **add content** that is relevant?	+1	+1
Did you/your partner **use correct grammar**?	+1	+1

Scores: Complete Do Now | Use Vocabulary | Add Content | Correct Grammar | Total

Date ____ / ____ / _____

(Self / Partner)

Date ____ / ____ / _____

(Self / Partner)

Date ____ / ____ / _____

(Self / Partner)

Date ____ / ____ / _____

(Self / Partner)

Date ____ / ____ / _____

(Self / Partner)

Total Points

Review and Assess

Daily Do Now

Record the Daily Do Now at the beginning of each class. Complete the task using appropriate content, precise vocabulary, and correct grammar.

	Scores				
	Complete Do Now	Use Vocabulary	Add Content	Correct Grammar	Total

Date ____ / ____ / _____

— Self
— Partner

Date ____ / ____ / _____

— Self
— Partner

Date ____ / ____ / _____

— Self
— Partner

Date ____ / ____ / _____

— Self
— Partner

Date ____ / ____ / _____

— Self
— Partner

Total Points

Scoring Guide	Self	Partner
Did you/your partner **complete** the Daily Do Now?	+1	+1
Did you/your partner **use vocabulary** accurately?	+2	+2
Did you/your partner **add content** that is relevant?	+1	+1
Did you/your partner **use correct grammar**?	+1	+1

Scores: Complete Do Now | Use Vocabulary | Add Content | Correct Grammar | Total

Date ____ / ____ / _____

Self

Partner

Date ____ / ____ / _____

Self

Partner

Date ____ / ____ / _____

Self

Partner

Date ____ / ____ / _____

Self

Partner

Date ____ / ____ / _____

Self

Partner

Total Points

Review and Assess

Daily Do Now

Record the Daily Do Now at the beginning of each class. Complete the task using appropriate content, precise vocabulary, and correct grammar.

	Scores				
Complete Do Now	Use Vocabulary	Add Content	Correct Grammar	Total	

Date ____ / ____ / _____

_____
_____
_____
_____

Self

Partner

Date ____ / ____ / _____

_____
_____
_____
_____

Self

Partner

Date ____ / ____ / _____

_____
_____
_____
_____

Self

Partner

Date ____ / ____ / _____

_____
_____
_____
_____

Self

Partner

Date ____ / ____ / _____

_____
_____
_____
_____

Self

Partner

Total Points

Scoring Guide

	Self	Partner
Did you/your partner **complete** the Daily Do Now?	+1	+1
Did you/your partner **use vocabulary** accurately?	+2	+2
Did you/your partner **add content** that is relevant?	+1	+1
Did you/your partner **use correct grammar**?	+1	+1

Scores

	Complete Do Now	Use Vocabulary	Add Content	Correct Grammar	Total	
Date ___ / ___ / _____						Self
						Partner
Date ___ / ___ / _____						Self
						Partner
Date ___ / ___ / _____						Self
						Partner
Date ___ / ___ / _____						Self
						Partner
Date ___ / ___ / _____						Self
						Partner
Total Points						

Review and Assess

Daily Do Now

Record the Daily Do Now at the beginning of each class. Complete the task using appropriate content, precise vocabulary, and correct grammar.

	Scores				
	Complete Do Now	Use Vocabulary	Add Content	Correct Grammar	Total

Date _____ / _____ / _____

_____
_____
_____

— Self
— Partner

Date _____ / _____ / _____

_____
_____
_____
_____

— Self
— Partner

Date _____ / _____ / _____

_____
_____
_____
_____

— Self
— Partner

Date _____ / _____ / _____

_____
_____
_____

— Self
— Partner

Date _____ / _____ / _____

_____
_____
_____

— Self
— Partner

Total Points

Scoring Guide	Self	Partner
Did you/your partner **complete** the Daily Do Now?	+1	+1
Did you/your partner **use vocabulary** accurately?	+2	+2
Did you/your partner **add content** that is relevant?	+1	+1
Did you/your partner **use correct grammar**?	+1	+1

Scores: Complete Do Now | Use Vocabulary | Add Content | Correct Grammar | Total

Date ____ / ____ / _____

(Self / Partner)

Date ____ / ____ / _____

(Self / Partner)

Date ____ / ____ / _____

(Self / Partner)

Date ____ / ____ / _____

(Self / Partner)

Date ____ / ____ / _____

(Self / Partner)

Total Points

Review and Assess

Daily Do Now

Record the Daily Do Now at the beginning of each class. Complete the task using appropriate content, precise vocabulary, and correct grammar.

	Scores				
Complete Do Now	Use Vocabulary	Add Content	Correct Grammar	Total	

Date ____ / ____ / _____

_____
_____
_____
_____

Self / Partner

Date ____ / ____ / _____

_____
_____
_____
_____

Self / Partner

Date ____ / ____ / _____

_____
_____
_____
_____

Self / Partner

Date ____ / ____ / _____

_____
_____
_____
_____

Self / Partner

Date ____ / ____ / _____

_____
_____
_____
_____

Self / Partner

Total Points

Scoring Guide	Self	Partner
Did you/your partner **complete** the Daily Do Now?	+1	+1
Did you/your partner **use vocabulary** accurately?	+2	+2
Did you/your partner **add content** that is relevant?	+1	+1
Did you/your partner **use correct grammar**?	+1	+1

Scores: Complete Do Now | Use Vocabulary | Add Content | Correct Grammar | Total

Date ___ / ___ / _____

Date ___ / ___ / _____

Date ___ / ___ / _____

Date ___ / ___ / _____

Date ___ / ___ / _____

Total Points

Daily Do Now 307

Review and Assess

Daily Do Now

Record the Daily Do Now at the beginning of each class. Complete the task using appropriate content, precise vocabulary, and correct grammar.

	Scores				
	Complete Do Now	Use Vocabulary	Add Content	Correct Grammar	Total

Date ____ / ____ / _____

_____
_____
_____
_____

Self / Partner

Date ____ / ____ / _____

_____
_____
_____
_____

Self / Partner

Date ____ / ____ / _____

_____
_____
_____
_____

Self / Partner

Date ____ / ____ / _____

_____
_____
_____
_____

Self / Partner

Date ____ / ____ / _____

_____
_____
_____

Self / Partner

Total Points

Scoring Guide

	Self	Partner
Did you/your partner **complete** the Daily Do Now?	+1	+1
Did you/your partner **use vocabulary** accurately?	+2	+2
Did you/your partner **add content** that is relevant?	+1	+1
Did you/your partner **use correct grammar**?	+1	+1

Scores: Complete Do Now | Use Vocabulary | Add Content | Correct Grammar | Total

Date ____ / ____ / ____

Date ____ / ____ / ____

Date ____ / ____ / ____

Date ____ / ____ / ____

Date ____ / ____ / ____

Self / Partner

Total Points

Review and Assess

Daily Do Now

Record the Daily Do Now at the beginning of each class. Complete the task using appropriate content, precise vocabulary, and correct grammar.

	Scores				
	Complete Do Now	Use Vocabulary	Add Content	Correct Grammar	Total

Date ____ / ____ / _____

_____
_____
_____
_____

Self / Partner

Date ____ / ____ / _____

_____
_____
_____
_____

Self / Partner

Date ____ / ____ / _____

_____
_____
_____
_____

Self / Partner

Date ____ / ____ / _____

_____
_____
_____
_____

Self / Partner

Date ____ / ____ / _____

_____
_____
_____
_____

Self / Partner

Total Points

Scoring Guide

	Self	Partner
Did you/your partner **complete** the Daily Do Now?	+1	+1
Did you/your partner **use vocabulary** accurately?	+2	+2
Did you/your partner **add content** that is relevant?	+1	+1
Did you/your partner **use correct grammar**?	+1	+1

Scores: Complete Do Now | Use Vocabulary | Add Content | Correct Grammar | Total

Date _____ / _____ / _____
_____
_____
_____
_____
(Self / Partner)

Date _____ / _____ / _____
_____
_____
_____
_____
(Self / Partner)

Date _____ / _____ / _____
_____
_____
_____
_____
(Self / Partner)

Date _____ / _____ / _____
_____
_____
_____
_____
(Self / Partner)

Date _____ / _____ / _____
_____
_____
_____
_____
(Self / Partner)

Total Points

Review and Assess

Daily Do Now

Record the Daily Do Now at the beginning of each class. Complete the task using appropriate content, precise vocabulary, and correct grammar.

	Scores					
	Complete Do Now	Use Vocabulary	Add Content	Correct Grammar	Total	

Date ____ / ____ / _____
_____
_____
_____
_____

— Self
— Partner

Date ____ / ____ / _____
_____
_____
_____
_____

— Self
— Partner

Date ____ / ____ / _____
_____
_____
_____
_____

— Self
— Partner

Date ____ / ____ / _____
_____
_____
_____
_____

— Self
— Partner

Date ____ / ____ / _____
_____
_____
_____
_____

— Self
— Partner

Total Points

Scoring Guide

	Self	Partner
Did you/your partner **complete** the Daily Do Now?	+1	+1
Did you/your partner **use vocabulary** accurately?	+2	+2
Did you/your partner **add content** that is relevant?	+1	+1
Did you/your partner **use correct grammar**?	+1	+1

Scores: Complete Do Now | Use Vocabulary | Add Content | Correct Grammar | Total

Date ____ / ____ / _____

Date ____ / ____ / _____

Date ____ / ____ / _____

Date ____ / ____ / _____

Date ____ / ____ / _____

(Self / Partner scoring columns for each date)

Total Points

Daily Do Now 313

Review and Assess

Daily Do Now

Record the Daily Do Now at the beginning of each class. Complete the task using appropriate content, precise vocabulary, and correct grammar.

	Scores				
	Complete Do Now	Use Vocabulary	Add Content	Correct Grammar	Total

Date _____ / _____ / _____

_____
_____
_____
_____
_____

Self / Partner

Date _____ / _____ / _____

_____
_____
_____
_____
_____

Self / Partner

Date _____ / _____ / _____

_____
_____
_____
_____
_____

Self / Partner

Date _____ / _____ / _____

_____
_____
_____
_____
_____

Self / Partner

Date _____ / _____ / _____

_____
_____
_____
_____
_____

Self / Partner

Total Points

Scoring Guide

	Self	Partner
Did you/your partner **complete** the Daily Do Now?	+1	+1
Did you/your partner **use vocabulary** accurately?	+2	+2
Did you/your partner **add content** that is relevant?	+1	+1
Did you/your partner **use correct grammar**?	+1	+1

Scores: Complete Do Now | Use Vocabulary | Add Content | Correct Grammar | Total

Date ____ / ____ / _____ — Self / Partner

Date ____ / ____ / _____ — Self / Partner

Date ____ / ____ / _____ — Self / Partner

Date ____ / ____ / _____ — Self / Partner

Date ____ / ____ / _____ — Self / Partner

Total Points

Review and Assess

Daily Do Now

Record the Daily Do Now at the beginning of each class. Complete the task using appropriate content, precise vocabulary, and correct grammar.

	Scores				
	Complete Do Now	Use Vocabulary	Add Content	Correct Grammar	Total

Date ____ / ____ / _____

_____
_____
_____
_____

Self / Partner

Date ____ / ____ / _____

_____
_____
_____
_____

Self / Partner

Date ____ / ____ / _____

_____
_____
_____
_____

Self / Partner

Date ____ / ____ / _____

_____
_____
_____
_____

Self / Partner

Date ____ / ____ / _____

_____
_____
_____
_____

Self / Partner

Total Points

Scoring Guide	Self	Partner
Did you/your partner **complete** the Daily Do Now?	+1	+1
Did you/your partner **use vocabulary** accurately?	+2	+2
Did you/your partner **add content** that is relevant?	+1	+1
Did you/your partner **use correct grammar**?	+1	+1

Scores: Complete Do Now | Use Vocabulary | Add Content | Correct Grammar | Total

Date ____ / ____ / _____ (Self / Partner)

Date ____ / ____ / _____ (Self / Partner)

Date ____ / ____ / _____ (Self / Partner)

Date ____ / ____ / _____ (Self / Partner)

Date ____ / ____ / _____ (Self / Partner)

Total Points

Daily Do Now 317

Review and Assess

Daily Do Now

Record the Daily Do Now at the beginning of each class. Complete the task using appropriate content, precise vocabulary, and correct grammar.

	Scores				
	Complete Do Now	Use Vocabulary	Add Content	Correct Grammar	Total

Date _____ / _____ / _____

_____
_____
_____ Self
_____
_____ Partner

Date _____ / _____ / _____

_____
_____
_____ Self
_____
_____ Partner

Date _____ / _____ / _____

_____
_____
_____ Self
_____
_____ Partner

Date _____ / _____ / _____

_____
_____
_____ Self
_____
_____ Partner

Date _____ / _____ / _____

_____
_____
_____ Self
_____
_____ Partner

Total Points

Scoring Guide

	Self	Partner
Did you/your partner **complete** the Daily Do Now?	+1	+1
Did you/your partner **use vocabulary** accurately?	+2	+2
Did you/your partner **add content** that is relevant?	+1	+1
Did you/your partner **use correct grammar**?	+1	+1

Scores: Complete Do Now | Use Vocabulary | Add Content | Correct Grammar | Total

Date ____ / ____ / _____ — Self / Partner

Date ____ / ____ / _____ — Self / Partner

Date ____ / ____ / _____ — Self / Partner

Date ____ / ____ / _____ — Self / Partner

Date ____ / ____ / _____ — Self / Partner

Total Points

CREDITS

Cover *brown paper* ©Piotr Zajc/Shutterstock; *white paper* ©Flavio Coelho/Moment/Getty Images; *floating island* ©iStock/Getty Images Plus/ronniechua/Getty Images; *sky* ©Shutterstock; *skyscrapers* ©iStock/Getty Images Plus/urfinguss/Getty Images; *road* ©iStock/Getty Images Plus/visualspace/Getty Images; *clouds* ©Vera NewSib/Adobe Stock*teens* ©HMH 2 (br) ©VK Studio/Adobe Stock; 2 (tr) ©E+/Sladic/Getty Images; 2 (bl) ©Laurence Mouton/Media Bakery; 2 (tl) ©Media Bakery; 2 (bg) ©Planetz/Adobe Stock; 3 (tr) ©RCWW, Inc./Corbis/Getty Images; 3 (br) ©Jacob Lund/Shutterstock; 3 (tl) ©Roman Chazov/Shutterstock; 3 (bl) ©E+/sturti/Getty Images; 4 (tl) ©Media Bakery; 4 (cr) ©Kim Hairston/Baltimore Sun/MCT/Getty Images; 4 (bl) ©Boris Shevchuk/Dreamstime; 4 (br) ©Tony Hopewell/Media Bakery; 4 (bg) ©Planetz/Adobe Stock; 5 (cl) ©RCWW, Inc./Corbis/Getty Images; 5 (br) ©Jacob Lund/Shutterstock; 5 (tr) ©Roman Chazov/Shutterstock; 5 (tr) ©E+/sturti/Getty Images; 5 (bg) ©Moment/Getty Images; 5 (bg) ©rangizzz/Adobe Stock; 5 (bg) Photodisc/Getty Images; 18 (t) ©Media Bakery; 18 (bg) ©Planetz/Adobe Stock; 50 (t) ©Laurence Mouton/Media Bakery; 50 (bg) ©RichVintage/E+/Getty Images; 84 (bg) ©Russell Shively/Dreamstime; 84 (t) ©ZargonDesign/iStock/Getty Images; 116 (bg) ©Oblachko/Dreamstime; 116 (t) ©Cla78/Dreamstime; 150 (t) ©Roman Chazov/Shutterstock; 182 (t) ©E+/sturti/Getty Images; 182 (bg) ©iStock/Getty Images Plus/hallojulie/Getty Images; 216 (t) ©RCWW, Inc./Corbis/Getty Images; 216 (tl) ©szsz/Thinkstock; 248 (t) ©Jacob Lund/Shutterstock; 248 (bg) Photodisc/Getty Images